ANGEL

THE CASEFILES VOLUME 2

By PAUL RUDITIS
and DIANA G. GALLAGHER

Based on the television series created by
JOSS WHEDON & DAVID GREENWALT

POCKET
BOOKS

London   New York   Toronto   Sydney

SPECIAL THANKS TO THE FOLLOWING PEOPLE:

Everyone at Mutant Enemy, Debbie Olshan, Allen Tuchman,
Alison Wallace, Crystal Yang, Jean Yuan, Katherine Devendorf, Jen Bergstrom,
Tricia Boczkowski, Lisa Clancy, Robin Corey, Lauren Forte, Russell Gordon,
Patrick Price, Elizabeth Shiflett, Wendy Wagner, and Sammy Yuen Jr.

POCKET
BOOKS

An imprint of Simon & Schuster
Africa House, 64–78 Kingsway, London WC2B 6AH
™ and © 2004 by Twentieth Century Fox Film Corporation

Designed by Lili Schwartz
Edited by Steven Brezenoff and Elizabeth Bracken
Cover Design by Sammy Yuen Jr.
Videograbs courtesy of Omnigraphics

Manufactured by WS Bookwell, Finland
First Edition
10 9 8 7 6 5 4 3 2 1
A CIP catalogue record for this book is available from the British Library
ISBN 0-7434-9233-1

DEDICATIONS

For Chris, the enabler for my TV addiction
—P. R.

With love and appreciation for
Chelsea A. Streb,
daughter, first reader,
and dedicated *Angel* fan!
—D. G.

ACKNOWLEDGMENTS

First and foremost, my gratitude to the entire cast and crew of *Angel* for five seasons of outstanding entertainment. Special thanks to Joss Whedon for his creative vision and to David Boreanaz, Charisma Carpenter, Alexis Denisof, J. August Richards, Amy Acker, and Andy Hallett for making the characters real. As with any literary project, people too numerous to name contributed to the process. I'm indebted to all, but most especially to my editors at Simon & Schuster, Tricia Boczkowski and Elizabeth Bracken, and to Micol Ostow for giving me the assignment. As always, my agent, Ricia Mainhardt, provided unwavering support and encouragement as did her partner, A. J. Janschewitz.   —D. G.

Thanks to the cast and crew of *Angel* for being so welcoming and taking time out of their crazy-busy schedules to be interviewed for this book. A special note of thanks goes out to the folks at Fox for pulling it all together, especially Debbie Olshan, Alison Wallace, and Crystal Yang. And of course this book would not be possible without the hardworking team at Simon & Schuster, with a special tip of the hat to Tricia Boczkowski, Patrick Price, Beth Bracken, and Micol Ostow, who started the ball rolling.   —P. R.

CONTENTS

FOREWORD

In *Angel,* the midseries spin-off of the phenomenally popular *Buffy the Vampire Slayer,* Joss Whedon successfully captured the character and story dynamics of his original creation and expanded the scope of both programs. Utilizing the events and personal histories Angel, Cordelia, and Wesley established in *Buffy* provided a sense of the continuity and evolution people experience in real life.

During the first two seasons of *Angel,* which are covered in the comprehensive companion book, *The Casefiles, Volume 1* by Nancy Holder, Jeff Mariotte, and Maryelizabeth Hart, Angel and his old friends from Sunnydale find new friends and purpose fighting evil in Los Angeles. An ongoing storyline weaves through these episodes, laying the groundwork for the double-season epic to come.

The Casefiles, Volume 2 encompasses the saga of Angel and his son, Connor, as told in Seasons Three and Four. Structured much like a novel, Connor's story has a beginning, a middle, and an end that prepares the characters and the viewer for the unexpected and fascinating promise of Season Five.

But that's another story. . . .

—DIANA G. GALLAGHER AND PAUL RUDITIS

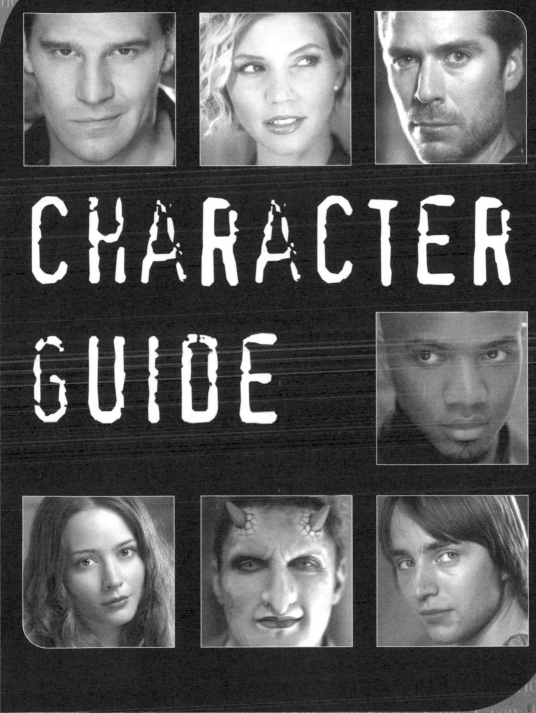

CHARACTER GUIDE

ne Jasmine Gavin Linwood The Groosalugg Skip The Beast Faith Gwen Willo
Angel Cordelia Wesley Gunn Fred The Host Connor Lilah Darla Captain Dan
Justine Jasmine Gavin Linwood The Groosalugg Skip The Beast Faith Gw
Knox Angel Cordelia Wesley Gunn Fred The Host Connor Lilah Da
in Daniel Holtz Justine Jasmine Gavin Linwood The Groosalugg Skip T
Faith Gwen Willow Knox Angel Cordelia Wesley Gunn Fred The Host Conn
Darla Captain Daniel Holtz Justine Jasmine Gavin Linwood The Groosalug
The Beast Faith Gwen Willow Knox Angel Cordelia Wesley Gunn Fred T
Connor Lilah Darla Captain Daniel Holtz Justine Jasmine Gavin Linwood T
alugg Skip The Beast Faith Gwen Willow Knox Angel Cordelia Wesley Gu
The Host Connor Lilah Darla Captain Daniel Holtz Justine Jasmine Gav
od The Groosalugg Skip The Beast Faith Gwen Willow Knox Angel Corde
y Gunn Fred The Host Connor Lilah Darla Captain Daniel Holtz Justi
ne Gavin Linwood The Groosalugg Skip The Beast Faith Gwen Willow Kn
Cordelia Wesley Gunn Fred The Host Connor Lilah Darla Captain Daniel Ho
e Jasmine Gavin Linwood The Groosalugg Skip The Beast Faith Gwen Willo
Angel Cordelia Wesley Gunn Fred The Host Connor Lilah Darla Capta
l Holtz Justine Jasmine Gavin Linwood The Groosalugg Skip The Beast Fai
Willow Knox Angel Cordelia Wesley Gunn Fred The Host Connor Lilah Dar
in Daniel Holtz Justine Jasmine Gavin Linwood The Groosalugg Skip T
Faith Gwen Willow Knox Angel Cordelia Wesley Gunn Fred The Host Conn
Darla Captain Daniel Holtz Justine Jasmine Gavin Linwood The Groosalug
The Beast Faith Gwen Willow Knox Angel Cordelia Wesley Gunn Fred T
Connor Lilah Darla Captain Daniel Holtz Justine Jasmine Gavin Linwood T
alugg Skip The Beast Faith Gwen Willow Knox Angel Cordelia Wesley Gu
The Host Connor Lilah Darla Captain Daniel Holtz Justine Jasmine Gav
od The Groosalugg Skip The Beast Faith Gwen Willow Knox Angel Corde
y Gunn Fred The Host Connor Lilah Darla Captain Daniel Holtz Justi
ne Gavin Linwood The Groosalugg Skip The Beast Faith Gwen Willow Kn
Cordelia Wesley Gunn Fred The Host Connor Lilah Darla Captain Daniel Ho
e Jasmine Gavin Linwood The Groosalugg Skip The Beast Faith Gwen Willo

ANGEL (Liam, Angelus)

"Nothing in the world is as it oughta be. It's harsh and cruel,
but that's why there's us. Champions. Doesn't matter where we came from,
what we've done or suffered, or even if we make a difference. We live as though
the world was as it should be, to show it what it *can* be."

Once the scourge of Europe, then Champion of The Powers That Be, Angel exists to defend good against evil. For the vampire with a soul, the battle never ends, the enemy never rests, and the most dangerous demon attacks from within. Still, he never abandons the fight to rise above what he is and was. . . .

As a young wastrel known as Liam in eighteenth-century Galway, Angelus was sired by Darla in 1753 and promptly slaughtered his family. With Darla at his side he swept across Europe, leaving a legacy of brutality unequaled before or since.

The couple was relentlessly pursued by Captain Daniel Holtz, a vampire hunter sworn to exterminate all soulless creatures of darkness. Angelus and Darla, however, killed his wife and infant son, and changed his young daughter in 1764. After burning his vampire child in the sun, Holtz vowed to get revenge. Although Holtz captured Angelus in Marseilles and Rome, the vampire escaped destruction.

In 1860 Angelus took perverse interest in a fragile young Englishwoman, Drusilla. He murdered her family and drove her mad before finally changing her. Twenty years later Drusilla created Spike as a companion of her own. Spike, Drusilla, Darla, and Angelus terrorized the Old World until the end of the nine-teenth century, when Darla captured a Romanian Gypsy girl as a birthday gift for Angelus. He killed the girl, and her Gypsy clan cursed him with the return of his soul.

Rejected by Darla, who was repulsed by his soul, Angel fled to America in 1902, but he could not escape his past or himself. Denying his hunger for human blood was a constant struggle made harder by constant temptation. He saved a puppy on the streets of Chicago in 1924 yet longed to bite into its owner's

3

savory neck. In San Francisco in 1978 he drank the blood of a donut shop clerk who had died in his arms of a gunshot wound. After that, the self-loathing was more than he could bear. Angel skulked about alleys feeding on rats for almost twenty years, becoming the ultimate lost soul until Whistler took him to Buffy Summers, the Vampire Slayer, in 1997.

Protecting the Slayer gave Angel purpose, but loving her gave him a moment of perfect bliss, which reversed the Romani curse and turned him back into Angelus. Willow Rosenberg, then a fledgling witch, restored his soul, just before Buffy sent him to Hell. Soon after The Powers brought him back, Angel realized that Buffy deserved more than he could ever give. He left her and Sunnydale.

At first Angel fought the forces of darkness in L.A. aided only by Doyle, a demon who had prescient visions. Following a chance encounter at a Hollywood party, Cordelia Chase hired herself as Angel's office temp and created Angel Investigations. The agency soon expanded to include ex-Watcher Wesley Wyndam-Pryce and vampire fighter Charles Gunn. The law firm of Wolfram & Hart became a major adversary with a disturbing interest in Angel, who would play a pivotal role—good or evil—in the apocalypse.

After moving into the Hyperion Hotel, the bonds connecting Angel's business family became strained. Obsessed with Darla, who was revived by Wolfram & Hart to distract him, Angel seemed to succumb to his dark side. He fired everyone and made love to Darla, an act of despair that became an enlightening turning point. Angel realized he had to champion good, not for redemption, but because fighting back against evil was the world's only hope.

Cordelia, Wesley, and Gunn took Angel back as an Angel Investigations employee—with reservations. Their concerns were dispelled when everyone risked everything to rescue Cordy and Winifred Burkle from their demon friend Lorne's home dimension, Pylea. Angel and company return as a team—back on track with a renewed commitment to help those in trouble because it was the right thing to do.

"In all those years, no one ever mattered, not like [Buffy] did. And now she's gone, forever."

Devastated when Buffy died, Angel spent three months grieving at a monastery in Sri Lanka. Shortly after his return to the Hyperion Hotel, he killed Elisabeth, the vampiric true love of James, both of them acquaintances he had last seen in eighteenth-century France. Confronted by James's unwillingness to exist without the woman he loved, Angel confessed to Cordy that the hardest thing about losing Buffy was realizing he *could* deal with the loss and go on.

During the next few weeks Angel focused on his friends' issues: Fred's adjustment to life on the demon side of L.A., Cordy's debilitating visions, and Gunn's loyalty. He didn't take offense when Gunn announced that he could never call a vampire friend. It was more important to know that Gunn would kill him if it ever became necessary.

"Certain friends and coworkers have been known to accuse me of being the quiet, stay-at-home, sulky one. I guess some people just don't know how to have fun anymore."

With the resolution of several unconnected cases, Angel's existence settled back into what passes for normal at the Hyperion. Being the victim of an old man's body-switching spell was humiliating and almost fatal—of the never-to-return variety—but shattering Fred's infatuated hope that they could be more than friends was more difficult. Recognizing he had suppressed feelings for Cordelia was a shock, but not as shocking as Darla's sudden appearance in the lobby to announce that she was pregnant and that Angel was the father.

Wesley's recent translation of the Nyazian Scroll predicted the imminent coming of an undefined Tro-Clon. Since a vampire pregnancy should not be possible, Angel couldn't dismiss the likelihood that a child born of two vampires was the monstrous being the ancient prophecy foretold. The fact that Darla couldn't terminate the pregnancy added weight to the cataclysmic-evil-about-to-be-born theory. To find out, Angel used the magical talent of the Host and the modern medical technique of ultrasound. He was stunned and thrilled to learn that Darla's baby was human and a boy, with a heartbeat and a soul, and of great interest to L.A.'s unsavory elements.

> ANGEL: "Someone's always uncovering some ancient scroll and they always say the same thing. Something terrible's coming. Do you have any idea how many of these things I've seen in my very long life?"
>
> CORDY: "Four?"
>
> ANGEL: "Three, but there's nothing to worry about."

From the moment Darla sacrificed herself to save her baby's life, the infant, Connor, became the center of Angel's universe. In addition to the usual care, feeding, and financial concerns of a new parent, he had to worry about numerous evil entities that wanted the child for nefarious purposes. Linwood Murrow, a prominent executive with Wolfram & Hart, was strongly advised—with Angel's firm grip on his throat—that he would be held personally responsible for any harm that came to his son.

Connor, however, was not the only one being hunted. Daniel Holtz, whose life and vengeance quest had been put on hold for two hundred years, returned to bring Angelus to justice. Nothing, not Angel's soul, good deeds, or innocent child, would divert Holtz from having his revenge. Being stalked by the vampire hunter was a troubling danger, but not as annoyingly gut-wrenching as Cordelia's fairytale romance with the heroic Groosalugg, newly emigrated from Pylea.

Angel's true measure as a Champion overcame his petulant jealousy: Cordy's happiness mattered more than his own desires.

"Helping the helpless, finding Holtz, and making money are our three number one priorities right now."

"I thought love was something that ripped you up inside, that swallowed you whole. But what I feel for Connor—even that fear—it's not terrible, Wes. It's beautiful."

However, Angel could not dismiss anything that imperiled his son. Wesley's misguided attempt to save Connor from Angel doomed the boy to life in the hell dimension Quor-toth with Holtz. The betrayal was unforgivable. Prevented from killing Wesley, Angel banished him.

Refusing to accept that his son was gone forever, Angel resorted to black magic to call Sahjhan, the demon who had spent centuries plotting Connor's death. Stronger than the vampire, the corporeal Sahjhan taunted Angel with the fact that the hell dimension Quor-toth could only be accessed once. Angel found no consolation when the demon's essence was trapped in a Resikhian urn. Connor was gone, but the rift in reality that Angel's spell had opened remained.

"My track record with the whole man/woman thing, it's, you know, I don't want to use the words 'tragic farce . . .'"

"That spell I did was for nothing. I didn't find my son. Now he's gone forever. So you ask me was it worth it? Would I do it again? In a heartbeat. Because he was my son."

Several days later the hotel was infested with thirsty, translucent "sluks" that foretold the coming of The Destroyer. The fearsome creature that dropped through the cosmic crack to challenge Angel was a human boy: Connor.

His son had survived eighteen years in Hell with Holtz.

Reeking of hatred for his vampire father, the teenager attacked, then ran. Convinced that patience and love could undo Holtz's lies and influence, Angel tried to win Connor's trust. His mistake was underestimating how thoroughly the vampire hunter had poisoned the boy against him and how much Holtz still wanted vengeance for the family Angelus had slain. Holtz wanted nothing more than to take from Angel what the vampire had taken from him: Justice would be served if Angel lost his son. To this end, Holtz arranged his own death so Connor would blame and despise Angel.

Sealed in a metal box by the grieving Connor and Holtz's soldier Justine, Angel sank into the fathomless depths of the ocean declaring his love for the boy who condemned him to eternal isolation.

When Wesley pulled him out of the sea, Angel had passed three months in reflection and hallucination. He had come to terms with Wesley's reasons for taking Connor, but not with Connor's refusal to believe he had not killed Holtz. His first act after returning to the hotel was to confront the boy with the truth, declare his love again, and kick the kid out of his house.

In addition to keeping an eye on Connor, Angel's next order of business was to find Cordelia, who had been missing since the night he vanished. Using a mystical artifact, he found her in a heavenly dimension of peace and happiness—out of reach. He opted to move on rather than wallow, but The-Powers-That-Won't-Let-Angel-Catch-A-Break had another cruel jolt in store. Cordelia was returned with no explanation and with no memory of him, her friends, or herself. Because Angel lied to protect her, she rejected him and chose to stay with Connor. After she regained her memory and knew she loved Angel, she rejected him because she couldn't deal with his past. As a higher being, Cordelia had seen every atrocity Angel had committed as the despicable Angelus and how much he had enjoyed making his victims suffer.

"Life should be beautiful and bright, but . . . no matter how hard I try, everything I touch turns to ashes."

Angel couldn't fault Cordelia's decision based on his past sins, but nothing could justify her taking comfort in his son's bed when fire rained from the sky. He couldn't erase the hurt, but he had to rise above it when the Beast darkened the sun and the apocalypse began. The Beast had known Angelus, and Angelus was the key to saving the world.

To bring Angelus back, Angel had to lose his soul in a moment of perfect happiness, an event that was highly unlikely given his circumstances. Wesley found a shaman who used illusion to simulate a scenario in which Angel put everything right in his world: He forgave Wesley, Connor forgave him, and then he and Cordelia made love. The effect of the illusion was the same as though it had all really happened. Angelus returned.

"Is there no fast food left in Los Angeles?"

"I don't like having my string yanked. And I don't like being kept in the dark."

"Hey, preaching to the guy who ate the choir."

Patient and cunning, Angelus focused on escape from the cage Wesley and Gunn had built to contain him. He taunted his captors with their shortcomings and secrets, but no one cracked to give him an opening. Then Cordelia offered herself in exchange for information about the Beast. Angelus told Wesley what he knew and was angry, but not surprised, when Cordelia reneged on their deal. The surprise came when Cordelia, believing she had restored his soul with some black magic mumbo-jumbo, set him free. Fortified with the blood of Wolfram & Hart lawyer Lilah, Angelus skewered the Beast and focused on another, better prize—the Slayer Faith.

But Angelus underestimated Faith's determination to save Angel. She injected herself with a vampire narcotic, felling Angelus when he ingested her blood. Under the influence of the Orpheus drug, he fought a mental battle with Angel for supremacy and lost when Willow restored his soul again.

Angel was as disturbed by Cordelia and Connor's impending parenthood as he was relieved to be back, but it wasn't jealousy. He knew everything Angelus had experienced, said, and done. Angelus had not killed Lilah, and Cordelia was the Master that had spoken in Angelus's head. When he confirmed that a horrendous demonic "bad" was using Cordy to birth itself into the world, he could not neglect his duty as a Champion of good. He found Cordelia, fought off Connor, and prepared to cut off the head of the woman he loved. But before he could strike, Connor and Cordy's offspring emerged in a burst of blazing light.

"We're not going to kill her. We just want to find her so we can worship her."

Mesmerized by the glorious aura of the beautiful woman, Angel became a devoted, unquestioning ally. Jasmine's calming influence healed the breach between him and Connor, the son whose existence he had earned undergoing the trials to save Darla's life. All his friends were drawn together in a common cause: to rid the world of evil for Jasmine. The vampire carried out the mission with the unwavering conviction and fury of the righteous. Then Fred rejected Jasmine's love and tried to kill her. Angel took the arrow instead. He did not see the evil hidden behind Jasmine's benevolent mask until Fred shot her and he was hit by the blood-soaked bullet that had passed through the demon's flesh.

With the spell broken and Jasmine's hideous face revealed, Angel was again poised to save the world. Using Cordy's blood, he and Fred freed Wesley, Gunn, and Lorne from the demon's hypnotic spell. The cure had no effect on Connor, who continued to protect and fight for the monster he had spawned. With information Wesley gained from a giant insect being, Angel journeyed to the last world Jasmine had enslaved. When he returned, he brought the severed head that spoke her true name and destroyed most of her powers. Everyone everywhere regained free will, and chaos returned to the streets of Los Angeles. That, Angel knew, was the price sentient beings had to pay for the right to choose between good and evil.

More disheartening than human nature run amok was the warning from the priest Angel had encountered in the insect world: He had lost Cordelia, and he would lose his son. Angel had never had Connor's trust or love, but that was Holtz's fault, as was the tragedy of a life, forged in Quor-toth and built on lies, Connor no longer wanted to live. Angel had no words to make things right for the boy, but then Lilah gave him a once-only, take-it-or-leave-it opportunity to rectify the wrongs Connor had endured. Angel took it.

The boy was placed in a loving human family, with good grades, a bright future, and no memory of his previous reality. No one who had known Connor, except his father, remembered him. In exchange for his son's new life, Angel assumed control of the Los Angeles branch of Wolfram & Hart, gambling that he could use the vast resources of the evil firm to fight for good.

**"People like you, this place . . . that's what's wrong with the world, Lilah.
It turns my stomach just being here. I'll never be a part of this. Not the way
you're hoping, at least. Now let me tell *you* what the deal's gonna be. . . ."**

Angel is played by David Boreanaz. He appears in every episode of Seasons Three and Four.

CORDELIA CHASE (Cordy, Cor; Beast Master)

"I was the ditsiest (bitch) in Sunnydale, coulda had any man I wanted;
now I'm all superhero-y and the best action I can get is an invisible ghost with a loofah."

Rich and popular in high school, Cordelia Chase was reluctantly and constantly drawn into the creepy affairs of the Slayer, Buffy Summers. Cordy fully intended to leave the whole demon-fighting scene behind for college, but settled for L.A. when her bankrupt father went to prison for tax evasion. Armed with a cutting tongue and the undaunted determination of a Sunnydale High graduation survivor, she insisted on working for Angel while she waited for her big break in show biz.

Cordelia turned the one-vampire vigilante operation into Angel Investigations, which eventually acquired the services of Wesley Wyndam-Pryce, Charles Gunn, and a demonic empath, Lorne. Cordy inherited Doyle's visions—planted with a kiss just before he died. The visions, Angel's link to the Powers That Be and those needing his help, gave Cordy a deeper sense of purpose—and progressively worsening pain.

When Angel abandoned his friends and the agency for Darla, Cordy convinced Wes and Gunn to keep the business going. When Angel returned, having realized that doing good was all that matters, she was hesitant to renew their close bond until he surprised her with a new wardrobe.

Dedicated to her work and her friends, Cordy gave up her ambitions and any chance at a normal life. Still, she didn't understand how much a part of her the visions had become until the Groosalugg, her handsome intended in Pylea, offered to take the burden from her. Cordelia refused and returned to L.A. with the visions and their increasingly dangerous effects.

"Minion of darkness, Satan's toady, but that's a nice suit."

While Angel was off getting over Buffy's death, Cordy withstood the excruciating visions without complaint. However, she couldn't hide the

9

claw marks, boils, and burns that ravaged her soon after Angel came back. Lilah used a demon to inflict the physical manifestations on Cordy in order to blackmail Angel. Angel freed a Wolfram & Hart client, Billy Blim, from a demon dimension to save Cordelia.

When Billy Blim's mind-manipulation of men caused the battering and murder of several women, Cordelia blamed herself. Trained by Angel in offensive combat and armed with his weapons, she would have gladly sent Billy back to Hell if Lilah had not shot him first. As Cordy had reminded the lawyer, no woman should have to put up with Billy's kind of brutality.

To Angel's surprise, Cordy turned on him when Darla became pregnant. Cordelia's outrage and protective feelings for another wronged female were quickly dispelled, though, when Darla bit her to satisfy an insatiable vampire-mommy-to-be hunger. Cordy did not mourn Darla's demise, and as soon as she convinced Angel he needed help taking care of Connor, she became the baby's substitute mom.

"It's not the pain. It's the helplessness. It's the certainty that there's nothing that you can do to stop it, that your life can be thrown away in an instant by someone else."

"It's weird. I'm starting to get used to being creeped out and comforted at the same time."

Birthdays were lavish affairs when Cordelia was growing up as the darling daughter of rich parents. However, no present she had ever gotten could match the gifts from The Powers. After a year of CAT scans, MRIs, and migraine medications, Cordy collapsed during a vision in the Hyperion lobby. The demon called Skip explained that a human could not survive having a demonic power and gave her two choices—dying, or living the life she had forfeited when she cast her lot with Angel. She could have been a star with a TV show and had wealth and adoring fans. It was fabulous, but not her life or who she was, so Cordy chose to keep the visions, and The Powers infused her with a bit of demon to eliminate the pain and avert imminent death.

Life in the handsome hunk department also improved for Cordelia. Angel's flirtations after her near-death experience were amusing, but she didn't realize he was flirting—or how serious he was about her. Then the Groosalugg jumped dimensions to find his princess. With a fistful of money and a potion to prevent the transfer of her visions, Cordy took a vacation with Groo—compliments of Angel.

The instant she came back Cordelia knew that something terrible had happened. Dropping everything, including Groo, she devoted herself to helping Angel adjust to the unbearable pain of losing the only child he would ever have.

"Life'll just keep happening. There'll be people who need us— and so we'll help them. 'Cause that's what we do."

Focused on Angel's grief, Cordelia wasn't aware that her sympathy masked her real feelings for the vampire—until the neglected Groosalugg and her own mirrored-reflection told her. She had just discovered that she possessed a mystical light power that could obliterate deadly creepy crawlies and purge the poisons of Quor-toth from a troubled boy. Once the truth was known—that she loved Angel—Cordelia confronted it with the same forthright honesty and fervor she had everything else in her extraordinary life. She went for it.

"I'm just a somewhat normal girl who has visions and glows and occasionally blows things up with her crazy new power. I'm a higher being."

But the all-encompassing happiness of being deliciously in love with someone who felt the same way was not her destiny. Endowed with enormous powers, she had used them with no motive other than doing good. Despite an ache in her heart for Angel, Cordelia Chase could not refuse the calling to a higher plane and purpose.

"God, I am so bored."

From her vantage point on high, Cordelia worried and watched. She was relieved when Wesley rescued Angel from his watery tomb, but she had no hope of rescue from her tedious existence because she didn't register on anyone's radar. Hopeless, but not helpless, she couldn't stay adrift doing nothing when Angel became fixated on a Las Vegas slot machine. She arranged for him to win, setting off a series of events that restored his destiny.

That was the last thing she knew as Cordelia Chase.

When Cordelia landed in the lobby of the Hyperion Hotel, her personal memory was blank. She had no idea if the people who called her "friend" truly cared. They hid the truth about themselves and the horrors that inhabited the hotel, forcing her to trust the only person who had been honest—Angel's son, Connor.

"I have this horrible feeling that something bad is going to happen or maybe has happened and I can't remember it and I don't know what to do or who to trust."

Cordelia became a captive within her own mind. The sudden restoration of her memory, complete with all she had witnessed as a higher being, was an enormous shock. The Beast rising on the spot of Connor's birth, the fire storm, and the boy's guilt converged to drive her into Connor's arms and out of Angel's heart. From then on, Cordelia Chase was removed from every deceitful word and act committed in her name and body.

No one close to Cordelia realized she was not herself. Nor did anyone connect her to several things that went wrong: the mysterious death in Gwen's vault of the last Ra-Tet, the murder of the family with the power to banish the Beast, the disappearance of Angel's soul from the safe, and the casting of a soul restoration spell that didn't work. The entity within Cordelia killed Lilah. Angelus was caught drinking Lilah's blood and was blamed, which left the evil entity within Cordelia free to seduce Connor as an unknowing co-conspirator.

Unknown to all, the plan to use Cordelia as the vessel for Jasmine's entry into the world had been set in motion before Doyle transferred his visions. The evil that would become Jasmine had been embedded when Cordy was sent back from the higher plane, and was awakened by Lorne's memory restoration spell. Completely subverted when the entity growing within her emerged, Cordelia Chase fell into a deep coma.

Cordelia Chase is played by Charisma Carpenter. She appears in every episode of Season Three except # 15, 16, and 17 (although she's listed in the scripts) and every episode in Season Four.

WESLEY WYNDAM-PRYCE (Wes)

"We all get what we deserve."

Sent to Sunnydale to replace Rupert Giles as Buffy Summers's Watcher, Wesley Wyndam-Pryce's arrival launched him on a journey of inner struggle and self-discovery.

A stickler for the rules, Wesley's presence at Sunnydale High was of no consequence to anyone except the infatuated Cordelia Chase. Although Buffy and Faith dismissed him and his advice, he refused to quit. Eventually his exposure to Giles, the Slayers, and other free-thinkers cracked his unquestioning acceptance of established dictates, precepts, and authority.

Fired as a Watcher after the demon Mayor almost ate Buffy's graduating class, Wesley stayed in America to fight evil on his own. Tracking a demon led him to L.A. and through the doors of Angel Investigations, where his talents as a researcher and occult problem solver were welcome assets.

As part of Angel's team, Wesley improved his combat prowess. Angel's faith in him helped Wes resolve his issues with his father's lack of respect, a psychological obstacle that had kept him from real-

izing his potential as a man and warrior. Empowered, Wes ran the agency when Angel left to be with Darla and did not relinquish command when Angel returned.

On the rescue mission to Pylea, Wesley's abilities as a natural leader were cemented. After joining a ragtag band of revolutionaries, he devised strategies to defeat a superior foe, bore the burden of watching others die at his command, and led the rebel force to victory. He was no longer a pawn of outside influences or circumstance when he returned to L.A., but the self-assured master of his own mind and destiny.

"Things are not always so simple as going out and slaying the big, bad ugly."

As head honcho of Angel Investigations, Wesley did not feel guilty about relentlessly driving Cordy and Gunn while Angel was absent, grieving for Buffy. The agency's demon control services were more important than anyone's social concerns. Despite his soft-spoken manner, experience hardened his resolve and sense of self. If Gunn ever crossed him again, as he did by not revealing the identity of the demon Merl's human killers, Wes would not hesitate to fire him.

Although Wes wore his heart on his sleeve regarding Fred, only Cordelia was perceptive enough to notice. However, Wesley's newly established self-confidence did not extend to his relationships with women.

CORDY: "Wesley, if you want to get to know Fred better, maybe the next time you have her over for an intimate dinner for two—you won't ask the rest of us to come along."

Wesley did not abandon hope of winning Fred after he was infected by Billy Blim's blood and tried to kill her. She forgave him, then gave her heart to Gunn. A gentleman always, Wes respected Fred's decision and concentrated on translating the Nyazian Scroll. He and Fred had recently determined that the prophesied Tro-Clon was not a being, but a confluence of events that encompassed Angel and his offspring. Connor had been in grave danger from various demonic factions since birth. However, Wes was not prepared for the prophecy in the Nyazian Scroll that he tried to but could not disprove: The father will kill the son.

"It's never easy, the pull of divided loyalties. Any choice we do end up making, we feel as though we've betrayed someone."

Spurred to action by earthquake, fire, and blood—portents described by a giant plastic hamburger—Wesley kidnapped Connor to spare Angel the anguish of killing the boy. He meant to leave, never to return. Instead, Justine slit Wesley's throat and stole the baby for Holtz. Wesley didn't die, but that may have been preferable to a wretched life as Angel's enemy, knowing it was his fault Holtz had fled with Connor into the darkest of dark worlds—forever beyond reach.

"I needed to live to see my friends again, to explain to the people I trusted and loved my side of what happened."

Deserted and despised by Angel and everyone else at the Hyperion, Wesley became a bitter, cynical man. He withdrew completely, locking himself in a dingy, cluttered apartment behind impenetrable emotional walls. When Gunn needed a cure for Fred, Wesley gave it, but only on the condition that none of them ever bother him again.

Lilah Morgan's self-serving interest in him was a strange balm for Wesley's tortured existence, salt rubbed into the psychological wounds, a constant reminder that nothing mattered to him anymore. Not even Connor's return could touch him: He was responsible for the boy's suffering and stolen childhood. Lilah was the ideal companion for a man with nothing left to lose except a tattered soul. Resisting the temptations she dangled before him—a prominent position at Wolfram & Hart, revenge on Justine and Angel—was the only thing that kept him going until the son turned on the father.

When Angel went missing, Wesley went looking. He found Justine and conducted a systematic, nightly search of the ocean floor because Angel was "necessary." He revived the vampire with his own blood, delivered him to the hotel, and left. When Angel showed up to forgive him for taking Connor, he gave Angel his research file on Cordelia's disappearance as a final act of penance. He had his own demon-hunting operation and Lilah, inadequate substitutes for the life he had lost, but more than he thought he deserved. Then he foolishly allowed Lilah to play him, falling into her perfectly planned trap to distract Angel while Wolfram & Hart attacked the Host. It was time to choose sides, and he did not choose hers.

"No one likes to lose, whatever the circumstances."

Committing all his resources to the fight, he stood with Angel against the Beast, guns blazing, and wouldn't abandon Gunn when forced to retreat from the demon's fire storm. Alerted by his inside man at Wolfram & Hart, he helped Lilah escape the Beast's massacre of the firm's personnel and joined Angel to rescue Connor. He identified the ritually murdered members of the Order of Ra-Tet and helped Fred devise a portal to imprison the Beast. Their efforts to prevent the Beast from blotting out the sun failed, but Wesley was back where he belonged.

Since they needed Angelus to defeat the beast, Wesley brought the shaman Wo-Pang to remove Angel's soul. He knew that Angelus would focus on getting free to kill. Angelus knew Wesley felt like a failure, loved Fred, and had been with Lilah. The vampire made certain Fred knew of the Lilah affair too, ending Wes's hope of being with her. Still, Wesley found the strength to do what was needed, as he always did, despite his inner turmoil. He had foolishly thought he could save Lilah from herself. He couldn't, but he could and did behead her so she couldn't rise. Then he decided to save Angel.

Wesley enlisted Faith's help, knowing the Slayer would do everything possible to save Angel. He was correct in that assessment, feeling regret but not guilt when Faith drugged herself, risking her own life to sedate and capture Angelus. That she survived and saved the newly restored Angel from Connor made him immensely proud. He *had* been her Watcher.

"Angelus is an animal. The only way to defeat him is to be just as vicious as he is."

"I think my sense of humor is trapped in a jar somewhere as well."

The discovery that Angelus had not killed Lilah, and that Angel regretted her death because he cared, began healing Wesley's emotional wounds. When Angel left to kill Cordelia, hoping to stop a horrendous evil from being born, Wesley could do nothing but wait. He was as susceptible to Jasmine's hypnotic presence as everyone else, but when the spell was broken he sought the goddess demon's destruction with steeled courage. Captured by a member of the insect race Jasmine had enslaved centuries before, Wesley stayed calm, listened, and probed. With mere fragments of information, he produced a plausible theory for her destruction. Angel jumped through the portal he opened, and brought back the word that ended Jasmine's dominion over the world.

Wesley couldn't say that he had loved Lilah, but he couldn't say he hadn't, either. Still, seeing her in the hotel with her head neatly reattached was mildly shocking. After mocking them for ending world peace, Lilah calmly offered Angel control of Wolfram & Hart's Los Angeles branch. Wesley was unable to release Lilah from the firm's standard "in perpetuity" clause, but he decided to stay when Angel accepted the deal.

"As much as it pains me to admit it, there's probably a great deal we can accomplish with the resources here."

Wesley Wyndam-Pryce is played by Alexis Denisof. He appears in every episode of Seasons Three and Four.

CHARLES GUNN

"I was supposed to protect you. You were my sister."

After Gunn was forced to stake his vampire sister, the streetwise young hunter agreed to help Angel. Disciplined and aloof, he was not a perfect fit with the gang at Angel Investigations at first. Gunn had to learn that individual abilities are vital to the whole, that the weaknesses of one are offset by the strengths of another, that his friends, old and new, could make their own decisions, good and bad.

Fearless but not foolhardy, Gunn questioned the chances of successfully rescuing Cordy from Pylea, then went along for the ride—in Angel's convertible—as usual. The adventure through the portal was far more fulfilling than simply saving Cordy and coming back alive. Gunn gained new admiration and respect for Wesley and a sense of belonging that finally began to fill in the empty space created by his sister's death.

"So you think some fancy flippin' and a little hollerin' can intimidate guys like us?"

A few months later Gunn finally had to confront some disturbing truths: His friend Rondell and the old gang had betrayed their original mission to protect good from evil. Angel had the mission and Gunn's

loyalty, but even with all they had been through together, no vampire would ever be Gunn's friend. Discipline and trust were essential to their survival.

To make up for his loyalty lapse, Gunn worked with Wesley to secure missing pieces of the Nyazian Scroll. Protecting Angel's kid became a priority, but not knowing if Connor existed for good or evil was profoundly disturbing.

Although Wes and Gunn often disagreed about how to proceed, they never mentioned their mutual Billy Blim-blood-induced drive to kill Fred. They could not, however, avoid the conflict of their mutual romantic interest in her. Gunn was even more stunned when Fred chose him than he had been to discover he looked great in a tux and *liked* ballet!

Wesley's gracious acceptance of defeat was just as surprising. He asked only that Gunn make certain Fred was never hurt, a promise Gunn

15

almost couldn't keep when a casino repo man showed up to claim his soul. He had sold his future for a truck years before, never dreaming he'd have so much to lose. Rescuing him from his youthful folly drew Angel out of his room, where the vampire had been holed up mourning his son Connor's one-way trip to oblivion.

For months, no matter what went down, Gunn was the steadfast soldier who got the job done without question because of the mission. But when Fred was infected with a dehydrating transparent water beast, the mission got personal. He went to Wesley, who had become the traitor he had warned Gunn not to be. Fred was saved and stayed with him when everyone else disappeared.

"No Angel, no Cordy, we can't find Holtz, his psycho girlfriend's gone—we got nothin'."

Once Connor had returned, Gunn and Fred struggled to keep the agency operational while they followed cold leads regarding Angel and Cordelia's whereabouts. Keeping the headstrong Connor under control without decking him on a daily basis was hard. So when Angel came back and kicked Connor out, Gunn had two reasons to be glad. Connor would pay for dumping his dad in the drink, and Gunn didn't have to put up with the teenager's dangerous stunts anymore.

With the exception of being electrocuted and recharged by a cat burglar, Gunn couldn't complain. Loving Fred, killing demons, and a quick trip to Vegas was as good as he ever expected life to get.

"That's right, Sparky. Daddy's coming home.
And I'm thinkin' there's gonna be a spanking."

Gunn should have known that nothing lasted or came without a price. When he killed the professor who sent Fred to Pylea, so she wouldn't do the dirty deed herself, he doomed their relationship. After that, every time Fred looked at him she saw the sacrifice he had made to save her. Their love died a slow death of discomfort and guilt, a fact Gunn was forced to confront when he caught Fred and Wesley in an awkward moment. Fred wanted to be anywhere Gunn wasn't, with anyone but Gunn, but especially Wesley. They parted with a last, lingering kiss; it was over, but okay.

"Fred, if you do this, the demons you'll be living with won't be the horned, fangy kind.
They'll be the kind you can't get rid of."

Electric girl Gwen Raiden gave Gunn back a sense of purpose and self-esteem. He foiled her plan to use him as a patsy in a theft and shared in her first-ever moments of intimate human contact. Then he became one of Jasmine's mesmerized minions. He would have died under Connor's sword, happy to be his own man again fighting the good fight, but the Powers hadn't run out of cosmic punch lines, and Gunn was spared. He thought the offer to give Angel control of Wolfram & Hart in L.A. was a joke. After he met the jaguar in the White Room, he wasn't laughing. He signed on.

"I'm doin' this. Hope it's not just me, but if it is . . . that's all right, too."

Charles Gunn is played by J. August Richards. He appears in every episode of Seasons Three and Four.

FRED (Winifred Burkle)

"I used to dream I'd discover some revolutionary concept."

Winifred Burkle, a physics student known as Fred, disappeared from the Los Angeles Library. While investigating a vision of Fred's plight, Cordy was swept through the same portal into Pylea. During Fred's five years in the alternate dimension, she escaped captivity, eluded subsequent capture, and hid in caves composing complex equations she no longer understood. Although disoriented and unhinged, Fred endangered herself to assist Cordelia, who had been enslaved as a "cow."

After Angel refused to behead her, Fred calmed his inner beast, which physically manifested itself in the demonic realm. Fred's calculations pinpointed the portal that transported everyone home, and they did not leave her behind.

"If Cordelia's receiving visions from the Powers That Be, they're being transmitted somehow. Maybe we could figure out the frequency and trace the call."

Fred spent her first months back in L.A. in her room at the Hyperion, writing on the walls. She didn't begin to emerge from her room and her fears until Angel returned from Sri Lanka. Her emotional progress was gradual, but her scientific worldview and the quick thinking that saved her in Pylea became an invaluable addition to the agency. Fred tracked Cordelia's disfiguring visions to Wolfram & Hart and tricked Gio, a trigger-happy killer in Gunn's old gang, into giving her his weapon at Caritas.

Once Fred began to socially reintegrate, the process continued even after Angel admitted he was fond of her—as a friend. However, she didn't put the trauma of Pylea behind her until confronting her parents forced her to accept that the five-year sojourn in another dimension had really happened. The nightmare was finally over when Fred chose to live her new life at the Hyperion rather than retreat and withdraw.

17

"I didn't mean to get so lost."

Although small in stature with a tendency to speak in run-on sentences, Fred's gigantic intellect and ability to build demon-destructing or life-saving devices was indispensable. She saved herself from Wesley and Gunn's murderous intentions, saved Wesley from wallowing in self-loathing following the incident, reunited a bug-demon with its hatchlings, and used math to help Wesley translate the Nyazian Scroll. Quick to adapt, she was also quick to admit a miscalculation and never hesitated to voice her observations, such as the chemistry brewing between Angel and Cordelia.

"Moira's the gut physical attraction between two larger-than-life souls."

Fred's frightening encounter with Wesley and Gunn as Billy Blim's lethal surrogates may have subconsciously affected her perceptions of the two men. Wesley's infection manifested itself as cold, condescending calculation, while Gunn worried then warned her before he attacked. They both rushed to rescue her from the Nahdrah demons preparing to cut off her head, but her true feelings didn't surface until Gunn was wounded in the mystical backstage labyrinth of the ballet. A stakeout, a kiss, and a botched surveillance did not tarnish Fred's joy at finding someone to love who loved her back.

"The prophecy was false. Angel was never going to hurt Connor. It was all for nothing."

Fred was acutely affected by the loss of Angel's son. An interdimension survivor, she knew that the boy's life on the far side of a portal would be an unimaginable hell. Almost as bad, Wesley had acted on a false prophecy that had been rigged by the demon Sahjhan. If Wes had trusted his friends and taken them into his confidence, then his life, Connor's life, and all the lives the two of them touched would not have been changed in terrible ways that could never be fixed. As a friend betrayed, she had to tell Wesley that irrefutable truth, as well as that Angel would kill him, and that he could not come back to the hotel—ever. Still, when her life was threatened by the see-through "sluk" creature from Quor-toth, Wesley didn't hesitate to give Gunn the cure.

But the sluk's warning that The Destroyer was coming for Angel stuck in Fred's mind after Connor returned and Angel vanished without a trace.

"I know you're still hurting, but I promise . . .
it's not nearly as much as you're going to hurt for what you did to your father."

For the next several weeks Fred found the strength to keep looking for Angel and Cordy, keep an uneasy peace between Connor and Gunn, keep the agency running and the books up to date, and keep her chin up without falling apart. When Gunn died for a moment and left Fred alone, the absolute worst thing that anyone could do to her, she finally gave in to the pressure and lost it. Playing a major role in Lorne's rescue from Las Vegas got her back on track—just in time to deal with the unknown but totally terrible whatever that Lorne had heard in Cordelia's song and that Wolfram & Hart stole from his head.

"If I hadn't been sucked through that portal I never would
have figured out my string compactification theory."

Fred played with physics theory to distract herself from their paranormal problems. She was invited to speak at the Physics Institute when her article, "Supersymmetry and P-Dimensional Subspace," was published in *Modern Physics Review.* She was thrilled to see Professor Oliver Seidel again and appalled to learn that he used interdimensional portals to eliminate the competition in his field. Of the five students he had "disappeared," she was the only one to return. However, before she could send the professor to his doom in a portal she opened, Gunn broke the man's neck. Knowing that Gunn may have sacrificed his soul to save hers became a wedge that drove them farther and farther apart.

Fred and Gunn fought side by side trying to stop the Beast, putting off the inevitable finality of their broken relationship until Angelus forced her to face the truth. It hurt to lose Gunn and to know that Wesley cared, but Wesley had slept with Lilah, and Fred wasn't ready for another emotional investment. She concentrated on saving the world and Angel.

Fred was giddy with the chance to help Willow work the magic that restored Angel's soul. She was almost, but not quite, sorry that the demon Skip told Angel what he wanted to know about Cordelia's condition and pregnancy. She had been looking forward to whipping up the Sphere of Infinite Agonies Skip wanted to avoid.

Fred had thought nothing could be worse than being alone in a demon dimension. She was wrong. Even worse was being hunted by her friends because she alone knew that Jasmine was a disgusting abomination and not a loving goddess. On the run with nowhere to turn, she had to kill a demon before he killed her. However, the demon's death provided the vital clue she needed to solve the Jasmine problem: Jasmine's blood broke the hypnotic spell. Armed with that knowledge and her own inner grit, Fred freed Angel and her friends. She fought with them, never losing her nerve or sight of the mission, until the ancient evil was destroyed.

Fred wasn't sure what compelled her to get into the Wolfram & Hart limo at dawn the next day, but she didn't regret her decision. After touring the law firm's state-of-the-art science wing, she was on board when Angel announced that he was taking the deal and they were all moving in.

"Who's Connor?"

Fred Burkle is played by Amy Acker. She appears in every episode of Seasons Three and Four.

Jasmine Gavin Linwood The Groosalugg Skip The Beast Faith Gwen
Angel Cordelia Wesley Gunn Fred The Host Connor Lilah Darla Captain Dan
Just
Kn
Da
Faith
Con
Darla
osalu
The
red
Conn
ood
osalugg
G
The K
G
ood T
Cord
ey G
Just
me G
K
el Cord
el H
ne Jas
Wil
Ang
Cap
el Holt
st Fa
Wille
h Da
ain Da
kip
Faith
Con
Darla
osal
The
red
Conn
ood
salugg
G
The K
G
ood T
Cord
ey G
Just
me Gavin Linwood The Groosalugg Skip The Beast Faith Gwen Who
el Cordelia Wesley Gunn Fred The Host Connor Lilah Darla Captain Daniel
ne Jasmine Gavin Linwood The Groosalugg Skip The Beast Faith Gwen

THE HOST (Lorne/Krevlornswath of the Deathwok Clan)

"Did I mention the only shots I'm good at involve tequila?"

Tall and green with horns, the Host is an anagogic demon who can read auras and foresee the future of anyone he hears sing. His karaoke bar, Caritas, was built on the site in L.A. where the portal from Pylea spit him out, and it served as a haven for demons. When Lorne first met Angel, he was captivated by the vampire's defender-of-good essence.

Lorne's unerring understanding of personal conflict and problems quickly ensconced him as a trusted advisor at Angel Investigations. His counsel helped Angel recover from his dark sojourn with Darla. The Host's own moment of truth came when he returned to Pylea to help rescue Cordy. Disgraced in his home dimension, he returned to L.A. knowing that his mother did not completely despise him: She had not fed his decapitated body to maggots.

"Way outside my area of expertise. But, hey! Who knew William Shatner could sing?"

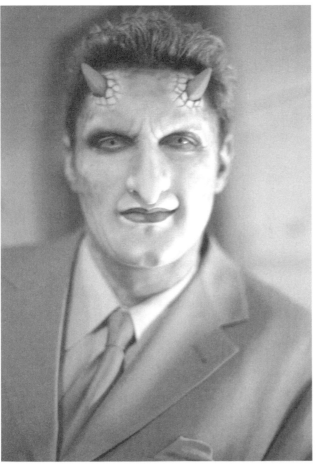

Angel's convertible caused extensive damage to Caritas on the return trip from Pylea. The Host repaired the bar and opened it again, but the Transuding Furies' monthly sanctorium spell to prevent demonic violence had no effect when Gunn's old, human gang opened fire on the demon patrons. The Host survived intact. The bar did not.

GUNN: "Don't go readin' me."

HOST: "I wouldn't, but, sweetie, you're a billboard."

"I'm not some mystical vending machine, here to spit out answers every time you waltz in here with a problem."

When Fred ran from her parents to Lorne in a panic, the Host quickly deduced that she still hadn't come to grips with her experience in Pylea. In the midst of rebuilding Caritas again, complete with a sanctuary spell for humans and demons, he was not empathically equipped to deal with Darla's pregnancy problem.

However, he couldn't turn her away when the imminent birth of Angel's child was threatened by the demon dregs of L.A. and one tenacious human. Caritas was destroyed one last time by a bomb, but the baby lived. And Lorne moved into the Hyperion.

"This is way beyond my ken—and my Barbie and all my action figures."

The Host's value as an associate encompassed more than reading the nature and intent of potential enemies in their song. He was a capable baby-sitter, and although his eavesdropping on casual hums was often disquieting, as when he learned Angel loves Cordy, Lorne's acute hearing detected the surveillance system Wolfram & Hart had installed in the hotel. He also discovered Wesley's plan to take Connor away, but not soon enough to stop him. Angel's emotional pain was difficult to bear, but being around teen-Connor's undiluted loathing for demons took the difficulty of being green to whole new levels of unbearable. When an old friend offered him a job in Las Vegas, Lorne didn't have to think about it.

"I've been booked out the wah and past the zoo.
If I get any hotter, they'll have to stamp me out."

The job didn't pan out as Lorne had hoped. He was imprisoned and blackmailed into mining his audience for valuable destinies his new boss offered for sale on the black market. Rescue, however, had to wait until Angel decided to take a vacation. When Angel became a victim, Lorne destroyed the mystic globe that held the vampire's future, saving him from an addiction to slot machines. They all got out of Vegas alive and walked right back into chaos central—L.A.

Cordelia's unexplained presence and amnesia were unsettling, but her karaoke reading was off the dark end of the charts. Though Lorne could only tell Angel a bit of what he saw, Wolfram & Hart successfully removed his horns and every trace of Cordelia from his mind. That turned out to be a blessing. The mysterious knowledge was causing Wolfram & Hart psychics to self-destruct, and it would have killed Lorne. Then Lorne would have missed the massive outbreak of paranormal strangeness that kept the agency's phones ringing off the hook, a prelude to the impromptu people-barbeque the Beast held before he made it rain fire. The emotional turmoil affecting all the primary players seemed trivial, except that they couldn't avert the apocalypse if they all became certified basket cases.

"Welcome to the big leagues, Angel—you're a Champion. You don't get personal days."

With everyone around him going through emotional meltdown, compliments of Angelus, Lorne tried to boost morale with his snappy patter and Pollyanna outlook. He was blindsided when he misread Angelus as Angel after Cordelia cast a spell to restore Angel's missing soul. He soldiered on, contributing a quickie version of the Furies' nonviolence spell to protect mortals in the hotel. Soon, however, it became apparent that his empathic ability had been short-circuited on purpose. Whatever was posing as Cordelia had worked a mojo on him while pretending to restore Angel's soul. He staged another ritual, pretending to restore his empathic power, which forced the thing inside Cordy to reveal itself.

"I'm guessing it wasn't a chubby little cherub."

Lorne's exposure to Jasmine and then Cordy's blood cure evoked the same reactions his friends experienced; he was hooked then released from the spell. The letdown after days of uninterrupted carefree vibes was particularly difficult for the musical empath. Still, the confusion and fear of L.A. normal was a plus compared to mindless thrall.

Despite his misgivings, Lorne couldn't resist checking out Wolfram & Hart via limo with built-in bar. His resolve to reject any temptation was firmly in place until he saw the entertainment department's client list. He was pretty sure using evil to champion good wasn't a mystical no-no, so why not? Besides, the acoustics in the lobby were great.

Lorne is played by Andy Hallett. He appears in every episode of Season Three except # 4, 8, and 15, and every episode of Season Four except # 2.

CONNOR (Steven Franklin Thomas, The Destroyer)

Connor's impossible conception came about through the passion of two vampires who were, apparently, destined to produce their impossible child. Protected by an unknown force, the unborn infant defied all Darla's attempts to terminate him. No shaman could explain him. Driven by desperation and an insatiable hunger for the pure blood of innocence, his mother went back to Los Angeles to find his father, Angel. Although Connor's existence was entwined with a mysterious confluence of events foretold in the ancient Nyazian Scroll, he entered the world in the dust of his mother's self-inflicted death.

> "... for surely in that time when the sky opens and the city weeps, there will be no birth. Only death."
> —*The Nyazian Scroll*

A human boy with a soul, Connor was also a mystical prize sought by many, not the least of which was Wolfram & Hart.

While Lilah plotted with Sahjhan to kill him and Wesley sought to save him, Holtz implemented his own insidious plan. Connor, innocent of anything except being Angel's child, was kidnapped and ulti-

mately condemned to live in the hellish world of Quor-toth, where Angel could not go. The loss of his son was Angel's punishment for killing Holtz's infant boy in 1764.

Connor, who was called Steven by Holtz, grew up learning to survive the horrors of Quor-toth and became its master, The Destroyer. Inter-dimensional creatures fled from the boy's wrath, widening the cosmic cracks he used to enter the old reality Holtz had fled to save him. For eighteen years Connor had trained to be Holtz's instrument of justice against the hated Angelus, his demon father.

"Hi. Dad."

The vampire was known as Angel now, but the boy was not fooled by a few good deeds or human friends. The demon's true face revealed the hideous monster Connor had sworn to kill. Then Holtz announced that the boy had to be with the vampire, for answers and purpose he couldn't find anywhere else. He went back, but the vampire wanted his own revenge and killed Holtz rather than let the old man leave, or so Connor was led to believe.

He found a natural ally in Justine, a woman who had loved Holtz as much as she hated vampires. Together, they waited for an opportune moment and ambushed Angel. The vampire declared his innocence and his love, but Connor was too blinded by grief and hatred to see that he was just another pawn in Holtz's scheme. Connor helped Justine seal his vampire father into a metal box. They dropped him into the sea and the anguish of an eternal loneliness that would surely drive Angel mad.

"You don't get to die, you get to live. Forever."

Certain that his father would never be found, Connor stayed at the hotel with Gunn and Fred. He tolerated Fred's motherly concern and Gunn's attempts to tame him because it played into their perceptions of him as the grieving son. He had to stay in the loop to make sure they didn't get a real lead on Angel's fate. Killing demons and vampires along the way was a bonus.

When his father returned, Connor ran a gauntlet of emotion—panic at being caught, surprise that Justine had killed Holtz, and a stubborn, adolescent refusal to admit he might be wrong. Angel as Angelus was a monster. Connor left without looking back, confident he could take care of himself, anxious to hunt the demons of L.A. on his own terms.

"Fathers. Don't they suck."

No one but Cordelia could breach the hardened walls around his heart. She needed and trusted him, and Connor loved her. She treated him like a man, trusted and confided in him. When the Beast broke into the world on the exact spot where Connor had been born, Cordelia almost convinced him it wasn't his fault. He spent the night it rained fire in her arms, a one-time-only happiness he treasured when he left to kill or be killed by the Beast that knew his name. Neither happened. He survived the destruction of Wolfram & Hart, but then the Beast came to his place to turn off the sun.

"The truth is, Angel's just something you're forced to wear. You're my *real* father."

"I don't give a flying sluk what Wesley says. He's not my boss."

Moving back into the hotel put Connor close to the action, which suited his agenda: being near Cordy, stopping the Beast, and, if necessary, keeping a promise to Angel to kill Angelus. That proved harder than he thought. Angelus outsmarted and outmaneuvered them, until Wesley brought in the Slayer. Like Quor-toth, Faith did not forgive incompetence, and she quelled insurrection with threats she was ready to carry out. He respected her, but his heart belonged to Cordelia and their unborn child.

"I don't even know what I am!"

When Lorne's no-demon-violence spell prevented Connor from attacking Angelus, he knew he had a demonic nature. That, combined with his naïveté and a measure of typical teenage angst, made him even more susceptible to Cordelia's manipulative lies. He didn't have a clue he was being used. Not even his dead mother's pleading could convince him that the woman he loved no longer existed. Stubborn and defiant, he became an accomplice to murder for the sake of his demon spawn.

No one ever understood the depth of Connor's torment, not Angel or Angel's friends. His whole life was a misery of pain and lies because the one man he had loved had exiled him to a hell dimension and taught him to hate. His very existence was a defiance of mystical truth: Two vampires could not conceive, but they had—so that Jasmine could be born.

> **JASMINE:** "I needed a unique soul to help create me, Connor. Yours. Even before you were born, I chose you to be my father."

When Connor destroyed Jasmine, he destroyed the reason he had been born. His vampire parents were killers. His human father loved him but hated Angel more. Cordelia was lost in sleep, and there was nothing left but wounds that couldn't be healed. He just wanted to die.

> **"There's only one thing that ever changes anything. And that's death. Everything else is just a lie. You can't be saved by a lie. You can't be saved at all."**

Connor didn't know that Angel made a deal with evil to save him. The impossible son of a vampire didn't remember anything but growing up as the smart, well-adjusted eldest son in an ordinary human family.

Connor is played by Vincent Kartheiser. He appears in episodes # 19, 20, 21, and 22 in Season Three and every episode in Season Four.

LILAH MORGAN

"We both knew, sooner or later, it would come to a messy end. For one of us, anyway."

An ambitious attorney at Wolfram & Hart, Lilah Morgan spared no atrocity trying to impress the Senior Partners after Darla and Dru killed Holland Manners. Competing with Lindsey McDonald to run Special Projects, she performs miserably, very often because of Angel's interference. Lilah is held responsible for a failed fundraiser and the loss of occult talent, while Lindsey, her partner, managed to escape blame for situations gone awry. Consequently, Lindsey was rewarded with the promotion, and Lilah was headed for the graveyard shift—literally. Reprieved when Lindsey quit and skipped town, Lilah took control of Special Projects.

Determined to keep moving up at Wolfram & Hart, Lilah curried favor with her superiors by any means necessary, including procuring Angel's services by targeting Cordelia. Chalking the whole affair up to nothing more than business, Lilah was only slightly perturbed when Angel killed the demon with the pulsing brain. Another attorney at the firm was of more immediate concern. While Gavin Park's methods seemed laughable, Lilah couldn't dismiss his ambitions. To counter his assault on the Hyperion, she secured all the necessary permits and inspection notices to put Angel's hotel beyond official bureaucratic harassment. When she hand delivered the paperwork, she did not resist Angel's assault on his desk. She was unaware that the elderly Marcus Roscoe was inhabiting the vampire's body, even when he tried to bite her.

Although Lilah knew that working at Wolfram & Hart could be dangerous, she was caught off guard when Gavin Park savagely beat her. Billy Blim, the congressman's nephew Angel rescued from a hell dimension, planted the impulse in his mind. Confronted by Cordelia Chase, Lilah put her own needs before

Wolfram & Hart and the client for a change. She saved Cordelia and Angel the trouble of sending Billy back to Hell by shooting him herself. The annoying Gavin, however, was not so easily removed as a threat.

When Lilah discovered Gavin's electronic surveillance of the Hyperion, she realized she had the edge because she was familiar with the players. She discovered Darla's pregnancy, an anomaly no one at the firm had anticipated. Then, while everyone else focused on Darla's unborn child, Lilah identified Holtz and interfered with his plan to kill Angel.

"Wolfram and Hart's official policy is to let Angel live until he becomes useful. I'm sworn to obey that policy."

Lilah existed in a dangerous mix of her own ambitions and self-preservation, the Senior Partners' dictates, and her rivals' machinations at Wolfram & Hart. Taking an occasional risk was a key factor in her rise within the company. Consequently, she could not pass up a chance to secure the prize of the century, if not the millennium, when Sahjhan offered her a deal for Angel's baby—dead. She agreed with no intention of honoring the deal. However, when circumstances brought all the players together, Holtz had the boy in his arms when he fled into the burning inferno of a hell world.

"The worst spot in hell is reserved for those who betray."

Losing points with Linwood after losing Angel's baby to a hell dimension, Lilah sought solace and an edge in the arms of Angel's ex-friend, Wesley Wyndam-Pryce. An outcast full of self-loathing, he should have been easy to tempt to the dark side. He wasn't, which intrigued her. His resistance to the perks evil had to offer was frustrating, but not without perks of its own. There was something immensely satisfying about being with a man who despised but couldn't resist her.

Lilah's preoccupation with Wesley did not go unnoticed by Linwood, nor did it dull her edge. Fed up with Gavin's schemes to destroy her career, and with Linwood's condescending attitude, she executed a power grab of her own. No one, including Gavin, challenged her new authority when Linwood literally lost his head sitting in his own chair. However, her plans to capture Connor were shelved as a result of Angel's threats. Cordelia, however, was another potentially useful target.

With an arrogance born of success, Lilah set Wesley up to distract Angel while a Wolfram & Hart team removed the most recent reading on Cordelia from the Host's brain. Lilah let the demon live because he had once been Wesley's friend, but the gesture wasn't enough to counter Wesley's outrage at being used. She dismissed his interest in Fred, but Lilah couldn't change his mind when he finally decided it was over.

LILAH: "And you just 'reckon' you'll toss in with the good guys?"

WESLEY: "There is a line, Lilah. Black and white. Good and evil."

A dramatic increase in paranormal activity gave Lilah cause for concern, especially since the coded information taken from the singing demon was blowing the brains out of the company psychics. Angel's offer to unite against a common foe gave her pause, but she didn't appreciate the power of the latest threat until it rained fire. When the Beast turned Wolfram & Hart into a high-rise killing field, she ran. She would not have escaped without Wesley's help, a favor she repaid by telling him that Connor was trapped inside. That was, perhaps, the only decent thing she had ever done outside of loving Wesley.

"I can't believe we didn't crush you people years ago."

Lilah learned that the Beast killed everyone employed at Wolfram & Hart, and she wanted revenge for what he'd done, forcing her to live in a sewer and on the run. She wanted her life back. Angelus was the only being that could make that happen. With no other options, she took refuge in the hotel and reluctantly cooperated with Wesley. When Angelus came back looking for munchies, she ran. Cordelia wielded the dagger that killed her.

"End world peace? You already took care of that. Congratulations."

Lilah returned—category of walking dead person unknown—to offer Angel and his associates a unique opportunity. Since the Senior Partners couldn't beat them, they had decided to reward them with the Los Angeles branch of Wolfram & Hart, and all its resources, to do with as they wished. She understood Angel's reservations and was touched by Wesley's futile attempt to release her from the "in perpetuity" clause in her contract. She also knew Angel would not turn down the offer when The Powers played their trump card: Connor. He didn't. In exchange for giving his son a normal life, the vampire took possession of the firm. Lilah's only regret was that she wouldn't be around to see what happened next.

"No game. In fact, game over. And guess what? You win."

Lilah Morgan is played by Stephanie Romanov. She appears in episodes # 3, 4, # 6, 8, 9, 10, 15, 16, 17, 20, 21, and 22 in Season Three and episodes # 1, 2, 4, 5, 7, 8, 12, 13, 21, and 22 in Season Four.

DARLA

"Life's full of surprises."

From the moment Darla changed Liam in 1753, until Angelus was cursed with the return of his soul in 1898, the vampire couple shared a bond of lust and malevolence. Their rampages were legendary, but no history could overcome the revulsion Darla felt when the corrupt Angelus was subverted by Angel, the vampire with a soul. Banished from her presence, Angel was relegated to memory until the Master brought Darla to Sunnydale in 1997. When she tried to seduce Angel back to the dark side, he killed her.

The finality of dust to dust did not apply when the Senior Partners at Wolfram & Hart revived Darla to distract Angel, who was a major impediment to their evil schemes. Human again and hating it, she begged Angel to change her back into a vampire. He refused, even though she was dying from incurable syphilis. Wolfram & Hart brought Drusilla in to change Darla. Then Darla and Drusilla slaughtered fifteen members of Wolfram & Hart.

The only thing Darla did not have was Angel. Seduced when despair had weakened his resolve, Angel did not experience bliss because he did not love the vampire who had sired him. Faced with this truth, Darla left unaware of the impossible seed they had spawned.

"Men are such babies."

"It's time to go see Daddy."

Pregnant and desperate, Darla tracked a shaman from Puerto Cabezas, Nicaragua to the Yoro Mountains in Honduras. The native medicine man had nothing to add that Darla didn't already know about her pregnancy. Since she couldn't get rid of the problem, she took the problem to the source: Angel.

After feeding on the blood of several bus passengers, Darla walked into the lobby of the Hyperion Hotel and announced that Angel was the father of her child. Watching him squirm under the glare of Cordelia's scorn amused Darla for a few seconds before she demanded help. After two bars of "Danny Boy" at Caritas, the Host was as clueless as the shamans. When Angel interrupted a Cordelia appetizer, Darla fled to a nearby arcade for a child chaser. Angel followed, rescued her meal, and almost put her out of her misery along with the baby—until he felt the heartbeat of a being with a soul.

Out of options, Darla returned to the hotel with Angel, then allowed herself to be dragged to a hospital. Magical methods hadn't revealed anything about the baby, but medical science confirmed that Darla was carrying a human male—who too many others knew too much about. She went into labor in an alley, waiting for Angel to return with the Nyazian Scroll, which Wesley needed to protect the child.

"This child, Angel. It's the one good thing we ever did together. The only good thing."

Devastated because she wouldn't love her baby or remember loving him when his human soul left her body, Darla wept. Knowing he would die in her lifeless womb, she drove a stake through her heart to save him.

The Powers—or the power of Connor's conscience—sent Darla back to plead with Connor not to murder an innocent, but she could not break through the lies and false love that bound her son to the Master of the Beast masquerading as Cordelia.

"Don't let this happen, Connor. Don't let my death mean nothing."

Darla is played by Julie Benz. She appears in episodes # 1, 3, 7, 8, and 9 of Season Three and episode # 17 of Season Four.

CAPTAIN DANIEL HOLTZ

"Just tell me where [Angelus] is."

Daniel Holtz hunted vampires in eighteenth-century England, determined to rid the world of the demon beasts. In 1764, believing he had run Angelus and Darla to ground, he found a note and knew—the vampire couple had attacked his family. His wife, Caroline, and infant son, Daniel, were killed; his young daughter, Sarah, was changed, then turned to dust when he heaved her into the morning sun.

Vowing to avenge them, Holtz chased Angelus and Darla across the continent. Three hundred and seventy-eight vampires were turned to dust over the years, but his primary prey eluded him. His last chance to kill Angelus was snatched away in 1771, when Darla rescued her vile companion from the torture chambers of the Order of Inquisitore in Rome. Two years later, back in York, a demon entered Holtz's home to propose an incredible bargain.

A demon who could travel between dimensions, Sahjhan knew that Holtz would not bring Angelus and Darla to justice. He would die an embittered, lonely old man—unless Holtz put his fate in Sahjhan's hands. All the demon asked in return for transporting Holtz to the future, where Angelus could be killed, was that Holtz show no mercy.

More than two hundred years later, the sarcophagus containing Holtz crumbled to release him. With the noncorporeal Sahjhan as a guide, Holtz played historical catch-up with television. He acquainted himself with the city and a gang of demonic minions Sahjhan had recruited before he moved on the Hyperion Hotel. After his new horde dispatched the Wolfram & Hart operatives waiting to capture Darla, he waited for the enemy he had stalked across time.

"Angelus, I've been looking for you."

Holtz quickly adjusted to the modern world and to hunting a vampire with a soul. Angel walked into his trap but had not lost his edge in a fight. The vampire escaped, and to Sahjhan's dismay, Holtz allowed him to walk away with his newborn son. Holtz had his own brand of "no mercy" to dispense in his own way and time. After he poisoned Sahjhan's demonic minions, he began to gather a group of warriors who would die for his cause, people like Justine Cooper whose loved ones had been victims of vampires.

Defying his deal with Sahjhan, Holtz devised a more appropriate punishment for Angel than death. A stake would end the vampire's misery too quickly. The torment and self-loathing he endured because of his soul could be made far more painful—for eternity. Holtz dispatched Justine to kidnap Angel's son from Wesley. He planned to raise the baby as his own, with Justine as his wife, in the remote mountains of Utah. If Angel lost a son he had no hope of finding, the vampire would suffer as Holtz had when *his* infant son died. But fate, Lilah Morgan, and Sahjhan were as tenacious as he.

"A child's coffin, Mr. Wyndam-Pryce . . . it weighs nothing."

Cornered under the Sixth Street Bridge, Holtz gambled that unlike the demon, neither Angel nor Lilah wanted the baby dead. He was trapped until Sahjhan opened a doorway into another world, demanding that Holtz kill the boy or be swallowed by Hell. Justice for his slaughtered family left Holtz no other option. He leaped into the hell world known as Quor-toth with Connor, and Sahjhan sealed the rift, keeping Angel out forever.

"I kept your son alive. You murdered mine."

Holtz was an old man when he followed Connor back through the rift eighteen years later, but the cunning and purpose that sustained him over two centuries and a lifetime in Hell had not waned. He had deprived Angel of his son—only days ago in this reality—but as he watched the vampire and the boy spar in an alley, Holtz knew the broken bond might be healed. There was, however, one way to make certain that did not happen.

"Hate's not enough, Justine. I have found that my love is far more powerful. And now there's just one thing I need you to do for me, and then I can finally be done with vengeance."

Holtz knew he had chosen well when Justine drove the ice pick into his neck once, and then a second time to simulate a vampire's bite. He died knowing the boy would blame Angelus for his death, ending any chance the vampire would ever know a son's love. It was enough.

Daniel Holtz is played by Keith Szarabajka. He appears in episodes # 1, 7, 8, 9, 10, 12, 15, 16, 20, 21, and 22 of Season Three.

JUSTINE COOPER

Justine's twin sister, Julia, was killed by a vampire, a loss she would never get over but could only try to avenge. Daniel Holtz found her hunting vampires in a cemetery. Tough and mean, she had the talent and hatred to become a dedicated instrument of vengeance, but she also had a stubborn streak and a mind of her own. She defiantly refused to show any weakness when Holtz drove an ice pick through her hand because she disobeyed an order. She could have left him then, but she knew she would be far more dangerous and destructive working with Holtz than she would working alone.

"I'd follow you to the gates of Hell to kill vampires, Daniel, you know that."

Before long, Justine's whole world revolved around Holtz. He punished her faults, praised her ferocity, and was a partner worthy of her passion. She did not hesitate to slit Wesley Wyndam-Pryce's throat when she took Angel's baby for Holtz, so no one would know who had the child. But they didn't go to the ranch in Utah as Holtz promised. When Sahjhan threatened to kill the child and everyone who wanted it to live, Holtz fled through a rift into a hell world with the baby and was gone.

Alone without the one person she loved again, Justine needed someone to blame: Angel. After her first attack was repelled, she retreated to Holtz's house to regroup. Confronted by Gunn and Fred, guilt drove her to confess that Wesley had not been working with Holtz and that she had tried to silence him. Her anger shifted to Sahjhan when he confirmed that Holtz and the child were sealed in a hell world that could not be reached a second time. Driven by vengeance, Justine captured Sahjhan's essence in Holtz's Resikhian urn.

"Hate gets a bad rap. It can keep you going sometimes when nothing else will."

In the ensuing weeks Justine vented her anger on every vampire that crossed her path, gaining a street rep as a deadly problem. She didn't realize she wanted to live until she was surrounded in a bar by demons with a grudge. She was saved by Connor and Angel, proof that fate has a sadistic and cruel sense of humor.

Heeding the word on the street, Justine tracked Holtz to a seedy motel. He was not as she remembered, strong and virile with the force of his conviction and intent. He had grown old, broken in body but not in spirit. She had hated him for leaving her, yet still loved him for giving her a reason to be. When Holtz asked her to end his life, she couldn't say no.

Holtz died in her arms without knowing that his last act of vengeance would work as planned. Connor swore to make Angelus pay, and Justine swore to help him. Together, they sealed Angel into a metal box and committed him to the deep, never, ever to be found.

She hadn't counted on Wesley Wyndam-Pryce solving the mystery of Angel's disappearance or caring enough to act on his conclusions. Justine mocked Wesley's effort, certain he would never be welcomed back by his old friends, expecting she would be killed when he finally pulled Angel out of the sea. Instead, he let her go to live her life or remain a slave to vengeance, whichever she chose.

Justine Cooper is played by Laurel Holloman. She appears in episodes # 10, 12, 15, 16, 17, 21, and 22 of Season Three and episode # 1 of Season Four.

JASMINE (THE DEVOURER, UNSPOKEN NAME)

Unnamed at first, Jasmine emerged from the body of Cordelia Chase in a dazzling light to look upon the stunned faces of the vampire and his son who had made her birth possible. A creature of immense hypnotic power, she held them and everyone who saw her enthralled. They believed she had come to bring them peace, and she had—for a price.

"For so long, you have all been drowning in the fighting and the pain.
I'd like to help . . . if you'll have me."

An ancient being with godlike power, the humans called her Jasmine for the fragrance that pleased her. Their world was not the first she had conquered, but its technology would make it far easier than dominating a dimension of primitive insects. All she wanted in return for global tranquility was a temple and to feast on her willing supplicants.

Jasmine counted on Connor, her father, to protect her from harm. He knew her true face and didn't care. Fred and Angel, tainted by her blood, turned against her when they saw her.

"Now, if you'll please wait with the others in the banquet room, I'll be with you shortly."

For all her power, Jasmine couldn't neutralize Angel and Fred's most potent weapons, free will and determination. As she was about to broadcast her mesmerizing image throughout the world, Angel exited a portal with the one thing in the universe that could strip most of her powers: her name spoken with the dying breath of the Keeper. The vampire with a soul ruined everything—because he could. Denied the destiny she had plotted for so long to attain, she attacked the vampire. Only her own father had the power to kill her, and Connor did, with a fist through her rotting face.

"No, Angel. There are no absolutes. No right and wrong. Haven't you learned anything working for the Powers? There are only choices. I offered Paradise."

Jasmine is played by Gina Torres. She appears in episodes # 17, 18, 19, 20, and 21 in Season Four.

SAHJHAN

An interdimensional demon with knowledge of the future, Sahjhan enlisted the services of the eighteenth-century vampire hunter Captain Daniel Holtz in a twenty-first-century plot to kill Angelus. Made incorporeal, a harmless state inflicted by the being in the White Room to prevent Granok demons from creating total chaos, Sahjhan couldn't kill the vampire himself. Holtz had promised to show Angel no mercy, a vow he seemed to break when he let Angel walk away with his newborn child. Disgusted with Holtz, Sahjhan approached Lilah at Wolfram & Hart with a plan to bring Angel down.

> "'The one sired by the vampire with a soul shall grow to manhood and kill Sahjhan.' Me!"

Sahjhan hoped the taste of Connor's blood would compel Angel to kill the boy. When that plan backfired, he had to make Holtz or Lilah finish off the baby as they had both agreed. When they later refused, he ripped open reality between the human world and the darkest of dark worlds, Quor-toth. Holtz, rather than killing the child who threatened the demon's existence, jumped through. Sahjhan closed the tear, confident that Quor-toth was forever sealed and that he could safely disappear in time.

The nature of evil is to underestimate the dedicated determination of good. Sahjhan assumed Angel was responsible for the ritual that yanked him back into the human world and made him muscle, bone, and blood again. Reverting to his innate savagery, he fought Angel in his lair and overpowered the vam-

pire. He was so intent on the kill, he was caught off guard when Holtz's woman, Justine, uncapped a Resikhian urn. Dissolving into a loose line stream of pure essence, he was sucked into and trapped in the jar—where he would remain.

Sahjhan is played by Jack Conley. He appears in episodes # 7, 8, 9, 10, 15, and 16 in Season Three.

GAVIN PARK

Transferred to Special Projects from the real estate division at Wolfram & Hart, Gavin Park immediately launched a bureaucratic assault on Angel, beginning with fifty-seven code violations he reported to the city. Confident and arrogant, he did not try to hide his desire to succeed at Lilah's expense. However, he did not understand the scope of her ambitions and resourcefulness. Undeterred when she undermined his original plan with documents for the Hyperion, Gavin set up an electronic surveillance of the hotel. His superior, Linwood Murrow, was impressed, until the system failed during an infiltration to kidnap and dissect Darla and her unborn child.

Like Lilah, Gavin scrambled to protect himself when the Darla kidnapping operation ended badly. Although Linwood was willing to use his surveillance system to acquire Darla's surviving child, Gavin was held responsible for the glitches that thwarted success.

"I'm a realist."

Determined to redeem himself with Linwood, Gavin stepped up his efforts to engineer Lilah's downfall at the firm. He tricked her into mounting an expensive rescue mission when interdimensional vermin threatened Angel's hotel. Trying to save the vampire was a bad move since Linwood wanted Angel dead. With Lilah lying low, Gavin was able to launch a special ops capture mission for the vampire's newly returned teenage son. Again Linwood was impressed—until the exercise backfired. Gavin had expected Angel to protect the boy. He had not expected the boy to protect the vampire.

An eyewitness to Lilah's cold-blooded decapitation of Linwood Murrow, Gavin adopted a new MO: He kept a low profile and followed orders. He was assigned to deciphering the information pulled out of the Host's head, an effort that had zero results. When he was tied up and pressured to talk, he did not hide that fact from Angel. When the Apocalyptic Beast went on a Wolfram & Hart killing spree, Gavin decided it was time to bail. The demon caught him looking for the emergency exit in the third-floor supply room and broke his neck. He died, but experienced a brief reanimation as a zombie, a pitiful state Gunn ended by chopping off his head.

Gavin Park is played by Daniel Dae Kim and appears in episodes # 3, 4, 6, 8, 9, 10, and 22 in Season Three and episodes # 1, 7, and 8 in Season Four.

LINWOOD MURROW

"A man works hard, builds a thing, waters it, grows rich and powerful,
leaves his wife for a younger beauty. These are why we take certain blood oaths."

Linwood Murrow installed Lindsey McDonald and Lilah as competitors to run Special Projects after Holland Manners died. Having sworn a blood oath to Wolfram & Hart, he became wealthy and powerful and in a position to toy with his executives. In return for the extravagant perks, the Senior Partners would tolerate no failure. Consequently, Linwood would sacrifice anyone and anything to save himself, a downside of Gavin and Lilah's terms of employment.

The relative security Linwood enjoyed at Wolfram & Hart was shattered when Angel attacked him during a conference. Convinced the vampire's child would someday destroy them all, he had tried to have the boy killed. Angel promised to hold him responsible for any harm that might come to his son, a promise Angel didn't forget after Holtz kidnapped and fled with the boy. Helpless and humiliated, Linwood gave the vampire access to the firm's resources to save his own life, but he vowed that the vampire would pay.

"We're in a war you can never win, Lilah, full of sticky moral quandaries.
The side you choose should always be mine."

Gavin's transparent attempts to earn his approval annoyed Linwood only slightly less than Lilah's gross incompetence. She had lost the vampire's child only to have it return, practically grown, with an admirable vendetta against Angel. Despite their mutual hatred of the vampire, the boy was more valuable to him on a dissecting table than stalking the streets of L.A. Gavin's plan to capture Connor had

seemed workable, since it utilized the special ops division. No one expected the boy to side with the vampire. Oddly, Connor's presence was all that kept Angel from killing Gavin.

LINWOOD: "You spoke to a Senior Partner?"
LILAH: "He was really very helpful. Had some great tips on office furniture."

Annoyed because Lilah has been sleeping with the enemy—Wesley—and not reporting to him, Linwood called a meeting to gloat over her termination. He was stunned to learn she consulted with a Senior Partner regarding his fear of confronting Angel and his attempts to kill him. Mr. Suvarta approved the swift, neat severing of Linwood's head, abruptly ending his life and career.

Linwood Murrow is played by John Rubinstein. He appears in episodes # 8, 9, 10, 17, and 22 of Season Three and episode # 1 of Season Four.

THE GROOSALUGG (Groo)

The undefeated Champion of Pylea with a half-cow lineage, the Groosalugg left the Scum Pits of Ur to be with Cordelia, the Cursed One destined to be his mate. Cordy was attracted to the handsome, gallant, and incredibly innocent warrior, especially when he defied the priests to rescue the Host's headless body. Even so, she decided not to participate in the "Com-Shuk" mating ritual because Groo, as Cordy called him, would acquire her visions in the process. Incited by the priests to defend Cordy's honor, the Groosalugg almost killed Angel. Cordelia intervened, declaring her love for the Groosalugg and stopping the fight. Before Cordelia entered the portal to return to L.A., she gave Groo a passionate kiss and Pylea to rule.

"The tedium of government was unbearable after a life on the battlefield."

Deposed when the free people of Pylea created a republic, Groo left the demon dimension to find his princess at the Hyperion Hotel. He accepted Cordy's initial reluctance to "Com-Shuk like bunnies," deferred to Angel as the true Champion, and admitted he must learn to curb his reckless enthusiasm. Anxious to win Cordy's love, Groo had his long hair cut and borrowed Angel's wardrobe. The romantic barriers were breached with a potion to preserve Cordy's visions, a bankroll from Angel, and an extended vacation far from L.A.

Unconditionally devoted to Cordelia, Groo did not begrudge the time she spent with Angel in the shivroth, or vigil of the bereaved, for the loss of Connor. Although out of his element in modern L.A., his skills and casual input were often decisive. Still, it soon became painfully clear that he did not have Cordelia's heart. As a practical matter, and being a warrior of impeccable honor, the Groosalugg had no choice but to leave her with all his best wishes for her happiness.

"Princess, in my heart I have known the truth for some time. I have just been struggling for the courage to do what's right."

The Groosalugg is played by Mark Lutz. He appears in episodes # 13, 14, 18, 19, 20, 21, and 22 of Season Three.

He Jasmine Gavin Linwood The Groosalugg Skip The Beast Faith Gwen W
Angel Cordelia Wesley Gunn Fred The Host Connor Lilah Darla Captain Da
Just
Kn
ain Da
Faith
Darla
The
Conn
salug
The K
od T
ey G
ne G
l Cord
ne Jas

SKIP (Powerful Demon)

A powerful, armored demon with a winning personality, Skip was charged with guarding the monstrous human, Billy Blim, in a hell dimension. Although sympathetic to Angel's mission to save Cordelia, Skip fought to keep the murderous Billy contained, and lost.

"How come it smells like you work for The Powers That Be?"

When a vision put Cordelia into a deadly coma on her birthday, Skip was the emissary of the Higher Powers and made Cordy an offer he thought she wouldn't refuse: She could have her true life as a beloved Hollywood star in exchange for the demonic power that was killing her. He seemed surprised and appalled by her decision to become part demon to keep the visions. Then, just as Cordelia was about to tell Angel she loved him, Skip intervened. He told Cordy that the Higher Powers knew she had used her enormous new powers for good and could not be corrupted by them, that she *was* a higher being with no choice but to ascend to a higher plane.

"You're a great warrior, Cordelia. The battle we're all a part of is fought on many different planes and dimensions. You've outgrown this one."

When Angel figured out that Skip was a player in the plot to use Cordelia for a demon birth, Skip attacked the vampire without holding back. He was stunned to find himself captured and at the mercy of a puny woman called Fred, who could whip up a Sphere of Infinite Agonies in twenty minutes. He told Angel what he wanted to know, that Cordelia and everyone around her had been manipulated to achieve the unnamed evil's imminent arrival.

"Oh, it's [Cordelia]. She just ain't drivin'."

When the elements caused an earthquake to herald the birth, Skip fought free of his bindings. He died when Wesley shot him through an open wound Angel had put in his head.

Skip is played by David Denman. He appears in episodes # 3, 11, and 22 of Season Three and episode # 17 of Season Four.

THE BEAST

"Fire, death, and darkness have I bestowed in your name."

Rising from the exact spot where Connor was born, the Beast carried out the orders of the powerful entity that had taken over Cordelia. Following precise rituals, it brought a rain of fire, killed the Ra-Tet, darkened the sun, and killed the descendants of the Svea Priestesses. With almost all references to its existence cleansed from texts and Angel's memory, only Angelus knew how to destroy it.

Angelus had rejected the Beast's offer to join forces once before, in 1789 Prussia, when the stone creature needed him to kill the Svea Priestesses who had the power to banish it. Recognizing the Beast as a mere flunky to some greater force, Angelus let it batter Faith, then killed it with a stone knife made from a piece of the Beast itself. As the Beast died and crumbled to dust, it released the energies that restored the sun.

The Beast is played by Vladimir Kulich. He appears in episodes # 7, 8, 9, 10, 11, 12, and 13 of Season Four.

FAITH

In every generation, there is one girl called to become the Slayer. It is she, and she alone, who will fight the demons, the vampires, and the forces of darkness. . . .

Although there has always been one Slayer called in every generation, Buffy's temporary death in 1997 created a glitch in the system. Kendra was called before Buffy was revived, and Faith was called when Drusilla killed Kendra.

Upon her Watcher's death, Faith came to Sunnydale where her life began a downhill slide. A wild, spur-of-the-moment kind of girl, she resisted the authority of Giles and Wesley Wyndam-Pryce and resented Buffy's life and friends. A fugitive after she accidentally killed a human, she joined forces with the demon—wanna-be Mayor and poisoned Angel. To save him with the blood of a Slayer, Buffy fought Faith and put her into a coma that lasted eight months.

When Faith awakened, she tried to take Buffy's life by trading bodies. Defeated by Buffy again, she fled to Los Angeles where Lilah, representing Wolfram & Hart, hired her to assassinate Angel. Faith was actually trying to commit suicide by vampire, but Angel wouldn't play along. He convinced her to save her-

self, and she surrendered to the police for killing Deputy Mayor Finch. Jailed for the crime and encouraged by Angel's visits, Faith learned to control her Slayer impulses.

Sentenced to twenty-five years to life for murder two, Faith had no trouble convincing the other inmates to steer clear, and she settled in for the long haul. Then, posing as her lawyer, Wesley came to see her. He needed her to capture Angelus and save Angel.

"Angel's the only one in my life who never gave up on me. No way I'm giving up on [him]."

Without hesitation, Faith broke out of prison. Wesley brought her up to speed on the way back to L.A., where she immediately took charge. The entity within Cordelia was less than thrilled to see her, and Connor resisted taking orders until Faith proved she was stronger and had no compunction about pounding anyone who crossed her. However, her Slayer powers could not bring down the Beast. The stone creature was outwitted and destroyed by Angelus. Quick-thinking and the sun saved her from Angel's soulless self—until the next time.

"I can't risk killing Angel."

Knowing from that first encounter that she couldn't beat Angelus in a fair fight, she drugged herself with a vampire narcotic. When Angelus bit into her, he was sedated with the drug and captured, but her role in bringing Angel back did not stop there. Connected by the drug, she became part of Angelus's sub-conscious reality. She watched as he relived Angel's good deeds then fought being absorbed when Angel's soul was returned. Angel was Angel again, but her task still wasn't done. She awakened in a panic and ran to save the still-unconscious vampire from his son, Connor. With that disaster averted, she went back to Sunnydale with Willow to help fight the Hellmouth version of the Apocalypse.

Faith would always remember and cherish the look of pride in Wesley's eyes. This time, she hadn't let him or Angel down.

Faith is played by Eliza Dushku. She appears in episodes # 13, 14, and 15 of Season Four.

GWEN RAIDEN

Born with an electrically charged body, Gwen was sent to Thorpe Academy in Wisconsin in 1985, where she accidentally electrocuted a classmate. She grew up calling herself a freak, but taking exception to anyone else using the derogatory term. Making the best of her unique ability, she became an accomplished thief with a reputation for success. She met Angel across a vault when both of them were trying to steal the Axis of Pythia. Gwen wanted the multimillion-dollar mystic artifact for the commission. Angel wanted it to find Cordelia, the woman he loved. When Angel saved her from a trap set by her client, she let him have the piece. He saved her from murdering the client, an act she would no doubt have lived to regret.

Gwen looked up Angel after a huge demon killed another of her powerful clients. She joined forces with the vampire and his associates to stop the Beast from blotting out the sun, a valiant effort that failed. She left town until the danger passed, then came back to Angel's hotel when she needed help with a job.

Since a heartbeat was essential to getting past a security system, Gwen chose Gunn. He thought they were rescuing a kidnapped child. However, rather than go ballistic when he realized she had set him up as a distraction, he helped her steal LISA, a technological device that regulated bodily functions and neutralized her supercharge. She couldn't resist the feel of human contact and shared the intimate moment with Gunn.

Gwen Raiden is played by Alexa Davalos. She appears in episodes # 2, 9, and 16 of Season Four.

WILLOW ROSENBERG

The last time Willow came to L.A., she told Angel that Buffy was dead. She made a second trip to give him his soul back.

Years before, Willow had successfully recast the Gypsy curse that gave Angel back his soul a moment before Buffy sent him to Hell. She hoped to do it again, but faced a different obstacle this time: Angel's soul was trapped in a missing jar. Using her formidable brain power instead of magic, she decided the problem was easily solved by breaking the jar, or Muo-ping.

"Lotta jars out there, can't shatter them all. I mean, y'could. But good things come in jars. Peanut butter, jelly, those two-headed fetal pigs at the Natural History Museum."

As Willow began the spell to break the glass, her mind was invaded by the Beast Master's voice. Drawing on her immense inner strength and magical power, she fought the powerful evil and its effects and freed Angel's soul. With Fred's help, she channeled the soul through the Orb of Thessulah and back into Angel where it belonged. She took Faith back to Sunnydale where another Apocalypse was waiting to happen. Saving the world was so much more satisfying than trying to destroy it.

"Next time you guys resurrect Angelus, call me first, okay?"

Willow is played by Alyson Hannigan. She appears in episode # 15 of Season Four.

KNOX

A graduate of Yale with a PhD, Knox gave Fred the grand tour of Wolfram & Hart's science department, which he was assigned to run pending Fred's decision to join the firm with Angel or not. Brilliant and inventive, he seemed much too charming to be evil. . . .

Knox is played by Jonathan M. Woodward. He appears in episode #22 of Season Four.

EPISODE GUIDE

THE KEY

Crafted in the image of its predecessor, *Angel: The Casefiles,* this second volume of the episode guide is lovingly created with a slightly new formula.

FROM THE FILES OF ANGEL INVESTIGATIONS

Always start with the basics: Title of episode, writer, director, and cast.

CASE Nº: episode number

ACTION TAKEN: To remind you what you probably already knew. And if you didn't already know it, then we'll spoil the ending for you with the Resolution to every case.

DOSSIERS: A description of the Client, Civilian Support, and Suspects for each case—on those rare occasions the Angel Investigations team actually took on a client, that is.

CONTINUITY: Tracking the rich history of the show and its characters.

QUOTE OF THE WEEK: Just one of the many fun and/or meaningful pieces of dialogue from the given episode.

THE DEVIL IS IN THE DETAILS

EXPENSES: Proving that one has to spend money to not really make that much money.

WEAPONRY: A guided tour of the weapons case, highlighting the team's ability to make *anything* into a defensive device.

THE PLAN: Such as it is.

DEMONS, ETC. . . . : A guide to all that goes bump in the night, including all you need to know about the Vampire Rules.

AS SCENE IN L.A.: The City of Angel.

THE PEN IS MIGHTIER

FINAL CUT: That which did not make it to the screen.

POP CULTURE: A Who's Who and What's What of name dropping.

THE NAME GAME: The episode's title, explained.

SIX DEGREES OF . . . : Answering the question, "Why does that demon look familiar?"

TRACKS: Songs for more than just the Love-Lorne.

OUR HEROES: A word from our sponsors.

EPISODE GUIDE

SEASON 3

EPISODE NUMBER	EPISODE NAME	ORIGINAL U.S. AIR DATE
3ADH01	"Heartthrob"	September 24, 2001
3ADH02	"That Old Gang of Mine"	October 8, 2001
3ADH03	"That Vision-Thing"	October 1, 2001
3ADH04	"Carpe Noctem"	October 15, 2001
3ADH05	"Fredless"	October 22, 2001
3ADH06	"Billy"	October 29, 2001
3ADH07	"Offspring"	November 5, 2001
3ADH08	"Quickening"	November 12, 2001
3ADH09	"Lullaby"	November 19, 2001
3ADH10	"Dad"	December 10, 2001
3ADH11	"Birthday"	January 14, 2002
3ADH12	"Provider"	January 21, 2002
3ADH13	"Waiting in the Wings"	February 4, 2002
3ADH14	"Couplet"	February 18, 2002
3ADH15	"Loyalty"	February 25, 2002
3ADH16	"Sleep Tight"	March 4, 2002
3ADH17	"Forgiving"	April 15, 2002
3ADH18	"Double or Nothing"	April 22, 2002
3ADH19	"The Price"	April 29, 2002
3ADH20	"A New World"	May 6, 2002
3ADH21	"Benediction"	May 13, 2002
3ADH22	"Tomorrow"	May 20, 2002

STARRING

David Boreanaz . . . . Angel

Charisma Carpenter . . . . Cordelia Chase

Alexis Denisof . . . . Wesley Wyndam-Pryce

J. August Richards . . . . Charles Gunn

Amy Acker . . . . Winifred "Fred" Burkle

"HEARTTHROB"

CASE N⁰ 3ADH01

ACTION TAKEN

Cordelia, Wesley, and Gunn have spent the past three months keeping down the demons in L.A. while Angel was off mourning the loss of Buffy Summers, his one true love. He returns to the

city with gifts for his friends and tries to coax a reluctant Fred out of her cavelike room, where she has scribbled notes on all the walls trying to make sense out of her life.

WRITTEN & DIRECTED BY
David Greenwalt
SPECIAL GUEST STAR:
Julie Benz (Darla)
GUEST STARS: Andy Hallett (Lorne), Ron Melendez (James), Kate Norby (Elisabeth), and Keith Szarabajka (Holtz)
COSTARS: Matthew James (Merl), Koji Kataoka (Pilgrim), Sam Littlefield (Young Man Hostage), Christian Hastings (Vamp One), Dalila Brown-Geiger (Sandy), Bob Morrisey (Dr. Gregson), Bob Fimiani (Codger Demon), Robert Madrid (Rough Man)

It's not long before Angel is back on the case as Cordelia has a painful vision that sends the men of Angel Investigations to a college party while Cordy goes home to try to soothe her increasingly pained mind. The guys arrive too late to save most of the guests, but Angel gets the scent of the vampire gang and their two hostages. They catch up with the vamps and a fight ensues. Angel tears a locket from the neck of a blonde vamp as he stakes her without first seeing her face. As she turns to dust, a look of recognition crosses her eyes, and she says, "Angelus."

Angel shares a tale from the year 1767 in which he and Darla toured Marseilles with the blonde, Elisabeth, and her true love, James. Angel stops the tale just when it gets interesting with the introduction of a vampire hunter named Holtz, since the man doesn't really have much to do with the current case. Cordy notes that since Elisabeth still wears the necklace that James stole for her over two hundred years earlier, he may still be in the picture and seek revenge. But it's the parallels between Elisabeth and Buffy that prove too glaring for Cordelia to ignore.

"She was the love of your life and she died. And you weren't there when it happened, you couldn't help her fight . . . you couldn't save her . . . you couldn't die with her." —*Cordelia*

Angel refuses to discuss the matter, but he does continue the tale of his escape from the vampire hunter, Holtz. He reveals that the hunter had particular reason to go after him and Darla after horrors they performed on Holtz's family.

Meanwhile Elisabeth's love, James, goes to see a Snod demon doctor looking for "the cure." Then he goes on the attack. As Angel and Cordelia fight off the vamp at the hotel—and Fred makes a poorly timed (and brief) sojourn from her room—they are stunned to find that a

stake to the heart and direct sunlight have no effect on James. They flee to the sewers and get a garbled phone call from Wesley. Everyone's favorite demon snitch, Merl, has revealed that James had his heart removed, which makes him invincible. Wesley continues to report, saying that the good news is that it only lasts for six . . . but the cell phone cuts out before Cordelia can hear if it's six minutes, hours, weeks, or even years.

James finds the duo in the sewers and chases them into L.A.'s new subway system. Angel and Cordelia escape into a subway car, but James manages to literally catch the train and comes smashing in through the window. During the fight Angel admits that he knows what it's like to lose a love, but James asserts that if Angel really knew, then he wouldn't want to go on living—which is the point that the six whatevers (presumably hours) are up and James ceases to be.

RESOLUTION

Angel takes James's words to heart and worries why—in light of Buffy's death—he doesn't wish he were dead as well. Cordelia quickly takes him to task.

"If you were a loser, if you were a sick obsessed vampire, then you'd go to a Snod demon or whatever and get your heart cut out. But you're not. You're a living, breathing—well living, anyway—good guy who's still fighting and trying to help people. And that's not betraying her, that's honoring her."

—*Cordelia*

And with that, Angel and team go off to help the helpless. Case closed. . . .

Well, not really: At the same time, in a small Mexican town, Angel's old pal Darla sees a man about a shaman. He gives her some information and she is about to let him go, but she drains him of his life when he refuses to go. She repeats what she had told James and Elisabeth over two hundred years ago when explaining how she had once left Angel to Holtz.

"Life's full of surprises."

—*Darla*

Then comes the biggest surprise of all when Darla steps away from the bar and reveals her rather large and obviously pregnant belly.

DOSSIERS

CLIENT Cordelia's vision sends the guys to help **students at a dorm party** at Wilson College, Bonner Hall Room 918.

CIVILIAN SUPPORT Merl, the demon snitch, and **Lorne**—a.k.a. the Host—provide information on the demon doctor who helped James.

SUSPECTS Elisabeth leads the **gang of vampires** that attacks the dorm. **James** promises to avenge her death. They were both vampires who toured with Angel and Darla in the mid–seventeen hundreds.

CONTINUITY

Three months have passed since the gang returned from Pylea and learned of Buffy's death. Cordelia's visions are getting more and more painful, but only Phantom Dennis knows the truth. Cordelia suspects that James may have gotten his hands on a Ring of Amarra or something else from the "Amarra People" that makes vampires invincible. Angel reminds her that there was only one such ring, which he smashed in "In the Dark." Angel and Darla did the *really* nasty in "Reprise." Holtz, the vampire hunter seen in Angel's flashbacks, was first mentioned in "The Trial."

OFFICE ROMANCE

Angel spent three months in a monastery in Sri Lanka dealing with the loss of Buffy (and then dealing with some demon monks). Gunn suggested that he should have gone to Las Vegas.

QUOTE OF THE WEEK

CORDELIA: "I'm sticking with you."
ANGEL: "I appreciate your courage, but I don't want to see you get hurt."

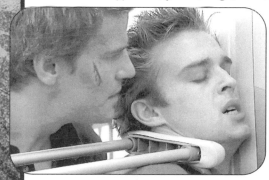

CORDELIA: "I don't either! I go home, he'll come after me because I'm home alone. That's what they do. They come after you when you're alone. Oh sure, 'Cordy go home, be a hostage!' With the torture and the fear and the torture . . ."

THE DEVIL IS IN THE DETAILS

EXPENSES

Payment for Merl the snitch.

The cost of repairs to the hotel includes a new garden railing after James is sent crashing through the old one.

Angel's shirt gets a stake hole and Cordelia's jacket tears and is left behind in the sewers.

WEAPONRY

Angel brings back a dagger from the sixteenth-century Murshan dynasty as a gift for Wesley. Cordelia has reorganized the weapons cabinet and moved some things down to the cellar because they were dust collectors. Weapons actually used for fighting in this episode include a stake, a fire extinguisher, and a pair of crutches.

DEMONS, ETC. . . .

The **Mur-ite** demon is a subspecies of the **Lur-ite** demon. The males of the Mur-ites sport a small telltale fin just behind the third shoulder blade. Both species are among the many demons worshipped by humans.

Shur-hod demons are known to be life-suckers and are prone to imitate monks.

Snod demons slough off their skin once a month and are known to be collectors. Dr. Gregson, specifically, collects rare organs, such as a vampire's heart.

Nester demons like to live in the walls of people's homes. Their offspring hatch several times a year. To rid the home of demon infestation one must kill the queen or else the Nesters will infest the place again, worse than before.

THE VAMPIRE RULES

Even though Angel owns the hotel, Fred has made her room her own personal space, so she needs to invite the vampire into it before he can enter. Also, a flyer announcing a college party in which "everyone is welcome" is considered an invitation and will allow for a group of vampires to enter the dorm room where the party is being held.

Sometimes even Cordelia needs to go over the basics when facing an invincible vamp.

> CORDELIA: "Okay, I've been doing this a while, don't stakes through the heart and sunshine usually kill you guys?"

This is the first episode of Angel to be shown in the series's new widescreen format.

THE PEN IS MIGHTIER

FINAL CUT

Cordelia continues to ramble on after making her comment on the significance of Elisabeth's still wearing James's necklace after two hundred years in lines of dialogue cut due to length.

> CORDELIA: "You see me wearing Curt Eisenthorpe's football ring or Xander's meet medallion?"
> *All three men look at her. Gunn turns to the guys.*
> GUNN: "I'd like to take this one." (To Cor) "So . . . what kind of meat did he have that earned him a medallion?"
> CORDELIA: "Not that kind of meat—swim meet, he was on the swim team. Get your mind out of the gutter. All of you!"

SIX DEGREES OF . . .

Julie Benz and Keith Szarabajka both worked on the side of the law on the television series *Roswell*. At different points in the series they played an FBI agent and a New Mexico state police trooper, respectively, investigating the "alien" occurrences in the town.

Bob Morrisey was also seen in *Buffy the Vampire Slayer* as a homeless man in "Real Me" and one of the "crazies" affected by the demon goddess Glory in "The Weight of the World" and "Spiral" (and he appeared in an episode of *Roswell*).

OUR HEROES

STUART BLATT (SET DECORATOR): "The Buddhist monastery was, by far, a phenomenal undertaking for a swing set. It being the first show of the season, we had a fairly good amount of time to build it because we knew about it coming into the season. We built it on stage five and the giant doors that open to the outside were open while my guys were building. It was such a big set that people were coming from all over the lot to peer in to see it, wondering what we were building that was so big. It was great to see faces peering around all the time and people asking, 'What are you guys doing in there? What's going on?' It was really fun and gratifying for my crew. I get a lot of the praise and attention being the production designer and I pass along all the time that I'm only as good as my crew, but they don't always get to see it and hear it. So to have people from all over the lot come and look at it, that was great."

ANDY HALLETT: "Sometimes I wander. I will never forget when Amy Acker first started here. We were on stage five and I had been here a little while so I was feeling a little more comfortable around here than she was. We were in between scenes and had a two- or three-page scene before we had to come back. We were bored and not doing anything, but we had to stick around. It was nine or ten on a Friday night and I heard some music. It turns out that in the front of the studio they were holding a party and had a band. We snuck over there . . . well, I did first and saw that there was a party and then I went back and got Amy. I said, 'Amy, honey, there is a party, let's go.' She said, 'No, we have to stay here.' I was like, 'No, this is a three-page scene, my dear. We won't be up for hours.'

"Now, I was in makeup at the time and a colorful suit with sequins under it. So the two of us strolled over into the middle of this party and of course, I'm getting a few looks. The next thing I know the cocktail waitress is going by and offers me a drink. Well, I'm not going to turn down wine. So Amy and I are sipping our wine and having a ball and then the TV cameras and lights are all on us, because the news was covering it. So I'm doing this interview with the wine and I look past the reporter and it's the guys from base camp searching for us. Evidently they had just scoured the lot for us because they were ready for the shot. I was trying to wrap the interview up, but I also didn't want the interviewer to know that I wasn't supposed to be there. So I was like, 'Listen, you know I love to speak to you, but I always want to leave 'em wanting more,' and took off. So, I'm walking toward the base camp and I'm like, 'Amy, give me the wine,' and I threw it in the bushes. I swear there was a full search party looking for us."

"THAT OLD GANG OF MINE"

CASE № 3ADH02

ACTION TAKEN

Angel makes a vamp-hearted attempt at apologizing to Merl the demon snitch for past dealings. But, even with Cordy's notes backing Angel up, Merl just isn't buying it. After securing a ride from Gunn, Merl storms home where he is met by a violent surprise.

The following morning Gunn's pager wakes him from a nightmare of his past when he killed his vamp-turned sister. He is called to Merl's place where he finds Angel and Wesley, standing among little bits of the demon, in full-on investigative mode. Gunn doesn't understand why they should concern themselves with the death of a random demon, especially since the Powers did not

put them on the case. Since he cannot get behind the action, Gunn goes off to visit his old friend Rondell and meets the gang's newest member, a particularly angry demon-hater from Miami named Gio.

The investigation continues and more random demons are found butchered. While it's true that some of the demons are evil, the majority of them are fairly well integrated and productive members of society. At the next crime scene, Gunn recognizes an arrowhead from his old ring and suspects that Gio has gone rogue. Gunn goes off to warn Rondell and learns that the entire gang is in on the killing spree.

Gunn is torn between his old gang and his new team, but eventually goes to talk to Wesley about the situation at the same time Wes and Cordelia have coaxed Fred out of the hotel for a night on the town at Caritas. When Gunn goes to the club, he is interrupted before he can talk to Wes. His old gang busts in, armed with machine guns, and kills half the demons in the place.

Rondell tries to lead the gang out of the club, but Gio reveals that Gunn—the "demon-lover"— is there, hiding behind the counter. Gio had been casing the joint for a month and knew that Gunn would probably be there during the attack. A hostage situation arises and Wes learns that Gunn knew the truth behind the killings and did not tell his boss.

WRITTEN BY Tim Minear
DIRECTED BY Fred Keller
GUEST STARS: Andy Hallett (Lorne), Jarrod Crawford (Rondell), Khalil Kain (Gio)
COSTARS: Matthew James (Merl), Giancarlo Carmona (Gang Kid), Steve Niel (Huge & Horrible), Josh Kayne (Cowering Demon), Sam Ayers (Tough Guy Demon), Heidi Marnhout (Furie #1), An Le (Furie #2), Madison Gray (Furie #3)

Cordelia is freed to get Angel while Gunn tries to defend himself to Wesley and convince Rondell that he has lost the mission—fighting demons should be done in defense, not as sport. The conflicting emotions get to Gunn and—during a heated exchange—he kills a not-entirely-harmless demon out of anger.

Angel goes off to the club, after telling Cordelia to find a trio of Furies to remove the sanctuary spell protecting Caritas from demon violence. When Angel arrives, Rondell tells Gunn that the only way out is for him to kill his vampire friend, but he refuses.

"You think I won't kill him because he's my friend . . . that ain't why. Truth is . . . he could never be my friend. That's on account of who he is. Not his fault really. Just the way things work out." —*Gunn*

The reason Gunn won't kill Angel is because the vampire understands their "mission" of helping the helpless. Fred, however, takes the offer to kill Angel, but turns Gio's weapon on him, until a distraction turns the tables on her. Fortunately Cordelia uses Angel's name—and reputation—to convince the Furies to undo the spell, and Caritas is no longer a zone free of demon violence.

RESOLUTION

A fight ensues, but ends quickly enough when a formerly sniveling demon morphs into a beast and bites off Gio's head. Caritas is left in ruins and the Angel Investigations team is nearly the same. Wesley warns Gunn that if he ever withholds information again he will be fired. Although Gunn tries to take back what he said about Angel in the club, the vampire says he knows that it was the truth. Gunn admits that someday his feelings could change, but that since he didn't kill Angel when he had the chance, it proves the vampire can trust him. Angel, however, sees things differently.

"You'll prove I can trust you when the day comes that you have to kill me—and you do."   —*Angel*

DOSSIERS

CLIENT Merl becomes a client posthumously, as do several other dead, unknown demons.

CIVILIAN SUPPORT Lorne once again gets entangled with the team.

SUSPECTS Rondell, Gio, and **Gunn's former gang** are behind the rash of indiscriminant demon slayings.

CONTINUITY

Originally, this episode aired a week after "That Vision-Thing." Angel tries to make up for his past dealings with Merl, in which he typically intimidated the snitch and didn't always pay for the information. The reputation of Charles Gunn apparently precedes him, especially considering it's been six months since he's been gone from his gang. Past events brought up during the case include the death of Gunn's sister, Alonna, in "War Zone"; and the death of Gunn's friend George, and Wesley being shot while helping Rondell in "The Thin Dead Line." Now that she's out of her room, Fred still has yet to go out in the world until her trip to Caritas.

OFFICE ROMANCE

It is implied that Angel has some kind of romantic history with the three Furies, especially since they note that he is the only one "equipped" to make good on the debt for removal of the sanctuary spell.

QUOTE OF THE WEEK

ANGEL: "Why am I at the top of this list?"
CORDELIA: "Um . . . 'A.'"
ANGEL: "Merl and I were not enemies."
CORDELIA: "Oh. Okay. My mistake."
ANGEL: "I'm the one that found the body, remember?"
CORDELIA: "Oh, and that's not suspicious. The one time you pay Merl a social visit and he ends up dead?"

THE DEVIL IS IN THE DETAILS

EXPENSES

Angel brings a box of donuts when making a second attempt at reconciling with Merl

THE PLAN

Cordelia points out the inherent flaw in Angel's plan to do what Rondell and Gio want him to do.
"We have to think of a better plan, and I'll tell you why—it's their plan! They want you to go in there where you can't fight so they can kill you."

DEMONS, ETC. . . .

A **Yarbnie** is a balancing entity. They tend to nest in urban areas under roadways and are totally nonviolent.

The **Transuding Furies** are three sisters who Lorne hires monthly to cast the sanctuary spell on Caritas to keep it safe from demon violence.

THE VAMPIRE RULES

Gio notes that vampires have a tendency to live a life counterproductive to their weaknesses.
"Why is it that places like L.A. and Miami bring out the teeth, you suppose? You'd think vamps would wanna hang out in less sunny climes. . . ."
Vampires can enter the residence of a demon without an invitation (or when the demon—or human—owner is dead).

THE PEN IS MIGHTIER

FINAL CUT

Cordelia had an even more difficult time easing into a conversation with Fred in the following exchange.

CORDELIA: "You're exactly the sort of girl who would have hated me in high school."

FRED: "Oh, I'm sure that's not true."

CORDELIA: "No, no it is. I pretty much saw to it. I was a cheerleader, had power, popularity. You didn't know me then."

FRED: "No I didn't. I knew you when you were a princess."

CORDELIA: "Uh, right. Anyway . . ."

TRACKS

Fred chooses Patsy Cline's aptly titled "Crazy" to sing at Caritas. Later Gio warbles his way through the song Bette Midler made famous, "Wind Beneath My Wings."

OUR HEROES

J. AUGUST RICHARDS: "In the episode my character is obviously having to deal with the fact that his old crew hasn't learned the lessons that he's learned while working with Angel Investigations, and that there are shades of gray in this world that we inhabit. It was a big episode for Gunn. I love the last moment where Angel says, 'I know I can trust you when you have to kill me and you do.' I thought that was pretty cool."

"THAT VISION-THING"

CASE № 3ADH03

ACTION TAKEN

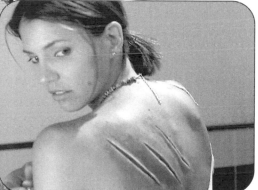

Wesley and Gunn try—and fail miserably—to act as if nothing is wrong around Cordelia when her visions hit a serious dry spell. On the one hand, she's getting a break from the painful images, while on the other it's difficult to help the helpless with no one telling them whom to assist. A visit from Gavin Park, one of Wolfram & Hart's fine upstanding young lawyers, brings a brief break to the vision discussion and a warning of city code violations for the hotel.

After Gavin is stared out of the building, Cordy has a painful vision of a coin in an herbalist's shop in Chinatown. Retreating to the bathroom to be alone, she confirms that the demons she saw hiding the coin have five claws, as evidenced by the fact that she has five bleeding gashes on her body.

The guys go to Chinatown to retrieve the coin from a nice little old couple of demons with razor-sharp claws. In the meantime Fred takes Cordy home to rest, when another vision hits hard. This time Cordy sees a key protected by a boil-covered demon, and she winds up with boils of her own.

Cordelia is in bad shape. No longer able to hide the physical manifestations from her friends, the team springs into action as Cordy wonders why The Powers That Be would do this to her. Angel reluctantly goes to retrieve the key from Cordy's vision while Wesley enlists Lorne's help to try to communicate with the Powers through their conduit, Cordelia.

Back at Wolfram & Hart, Gavin is keeping busy in light of his recent promotion out of the real estate division. He intends to bury Angel in red tape. But Lilah has a very different plan for Angel involving a Fez-wearing man and the huge brain he keeps underneath his hat.

Cordelia's next vision, of fire, scorches her skin as she flings Lorne across the room. But there is some good news. Lorne was able to read that the vision came from an earthbound source, not The

WRITTEN BY Jeffrey Bell
DIRECTED BY Bill Norton
GUEST STARS: Andy Hallett (Lorne), Stephanie Romanov (Lilah), Frank "Sotonoma" Salsedo (Shaman), Daniel Dae Kim (Gavin), David Denman (Skip)
SPECIAL GUEST STAR: Julie Benz (Darla)
COSTARS: Alice Lo (Old Chinese Woman), Ken Takemoto (Old Chinese Man), Mitchell Gibney (Innocuous Guy), Bob Sattler (Masked Guy), Kal Penn (Fez-Head), Justin Shilton (Young Man)

Powers. Angel immediately goes to Lilah, and she doesn't debate the issue. Instead she admits the truth and, using Cordelia's life as her bargaining chip, blackmails Angel into agreeing to free a young male client who has been "unfairly imprisoned."

> "This is exactly why I chose you for the mission, Angel. I needed a man of character . . . a Champion of good, a warrior . . . And I needed someone who can travel in and out of a fortressed demon dimension."
>
> —*Lilah*

Angel has no choice but to use the coin and the key to unlock a portal to the demon dimension. There he finds that the charge he has been sent to rescue has his own little private cage of flames in the hell dimension. Angel also finds a rather amiable demon named Skip who also works for the Powers. The two Champions are forced to fight, and Angel frees the man.

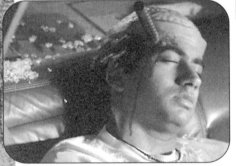

RESOLUTION

Angel returns home and meets Lilah for an exchange: her former prisoner for Cordelia's cure. Once the exchange is made, Angel sees to it that the giant-brained Fez wearer can no longer harm Cordy (with the help of a piece of rebar lying nearby).

Meanwhile the still extremely pregnant Darla meets with a shaman looking for answers to her condition. When he provides nothing helpful, she makes a decision on her own, as she rubs her tummy and tells her baby-to-be . . .

> "Time to go visit Daddy."
>
> —*Darla*

DOSSIERS

CLIENT Technically, the client for this case is **Wolfram & Hart** and the unnamed young man who will later become known as **Billy.** But it could also be argued that **Cordelia** is the client, as Angel's acting on her behalf.

CIVILIAN SUPPORT Once again **Lorne** is brought into the fold, one step closer to being part of the team. **Gavin** plays both sides of the fight for Angel (as most Wolfram & Hart employees are prone to do) and helps the vampire get into Lilah's office undetected.

SUSPECTS Of course, **Wolfram & Hart** can be considered suspects as well as clients. **Lilah** enacts her evil plan with the help of her **Fez-wearing psychic friend.** Meanwhile **Gavin** relies on a plan that's more straightforward, and we'll later learn that his exterminators weren't so much de-bugging the place as bugging it.

Other suspects who turn out to be on the side of The Powers include the aged and claw-bearing **proprietors of the Van Hoa Dong herbalist shop,** the **employee at the key shop** and the **boil-covered demon,** and **Skip.**

CONTINUITY

Fred is more comfortable coming down to the lobby, but she has yet to master some of the other rituals of civilization, like using a fork when dining. The Angel Investigation team first met Gavin Park in "Over the Rainbow," although Cordy missed out on the lack-of-pleasantries as she was already in Pylea. Gavin has recently been moved into Special Projects from real estate. Lilah is quick to point out to Gavin that she earned the right to be given Lindsey McDonald's office following his departure from Wolfram & Hart in "Dead End." Skip will play a very important role in future cases.

OFFICE ROMANCE

Both Wesley and Gunn seem to be smitten with Fred. This will develop into a love triangle as the season progresses.

QUOTE OF THE WEEK

CORDELIA: "I'm right as rain."

FRED: "I never understood that saying—right as rain. How is rain right? Or wrong for that matter? Okay, I suppose if there's a flood it's wrong, and speaking of floods, or just being overwhelmed, what's it like to have a vision?"

CORDELIA: "Wow. Y'know, next to you, I am downright linear."

THE DEVIL IS IN THE DETAILS

EXPENSES

New shirts for Gunn and Angel following their run-in with the clawed herbalists. They are also forced to provide clothes for the former prisoner and rope for tying his hands.

WEAPONRY

Gunn has a bat that's been carved into a stake, while both Wesley and Angel rely on metal pieces of rebar during the case. Angel sports a shiny sword. He later arms himself with several weapons, but they are not permitted in the prison dimension.

THE PLAN

Lilah explains why she sent Angel after the coin and the key.

LILAH: "There's a young man who's been unfairly imprisoned. And you're going to save him. Isn't that what you do? Save people? You'll need those items to succeed."

ANGEL: "I see. I do this for you and you stop sending Cordy the killer visions."

LILAH: "No, you'll do this because I tell you to."

Needless to say, Angel rewrites the end of the plan.

The demon Skip takes his name from series producer Skip Schoolnik.

DEMONS, ETC. . . .

The **Wan-shang Dhole** and **Cantonese Fook-beast** both match Cordelia's description of a five-clawed demon.

Skip keeps the man imprisoned in the fire by the sheer force of his will. His will is also powerful enough to silence the man's screams.

THE VAMPIRE RULES

As happens often in the series, vampires come across as second-class citizens when the proprietors of the herbalist shop tell Angel he is not welcome in their store. Wesley quickly comes to the rescue, explaining:

"This is a public facility and any being may enter."

THE PEN IS MIGHTIER

FINAL CUT

The stage directions make it clear that Angel's transport into the other dimension should not look derivative:

Angel, armed for bear, steps into the shimmering portal. There's a flashing column of blue light (in a totally un-Star Trek-like way) and Angel's gone.

POP CULTURE

✳ **"You're like Angel's Lassie. Sure, he does most of the saving. But it's *your* visions that tell him that Timmy's trapped in a well or the robbers are hiding in the barn."**

Fred compares Cordelia to the famed collie of film and television.

✳ **"Way outside my area of expertise, but hey . . . who knew William Shatner could sing. . . . Okay, bad example."**

The multitalented Lorne compares his abilities with that of the actor with the ever-expanding repertoire.

✳ **"'Cause I'm going to be really ticked off if I'm all Phantom of the Opera and there wasn't a key."**

Cordelia compares herself to the scarred titular character from the novel by Gaston Leroux.

✳ **"with The Powers That Be doing this whole Book of Job thing . . ."**

Cordelia refers to the book of the Bible most associated with plague and pestilence.

✳ **"You're Julie Andrews in *The Sound of Music*."**

Lorne gets a little carried away trying to get Cordy to relax.

✳ **"Now let's go looking for the Powers That Be. See if we can reach out and touch someone."**

Lorne invokes the old slogan for the Bell telephone company.

OUR HEROES

AMY ACKER: "The long rambling speeches are actually the most fun things to do. It's so much easier if I have a whole page of just babbling about something than if you're in a five-page scene where you have one line somewhere in the middle of it. For some reason if I'm just babbling and

talking about stuff, I get so excited about the challenge of learning it that it's like all I want to work on in the episode. It's always fun when you go in there and do it right the first time and everyone's like, 'Oh my God, how did you do that?' The challenge of it makes you want to be able to do it really well. I've always liked having them. At first it seemed like I had that in every episode. I would have at least one time where I would go off on some tangent that had nothing to do with anything, except in my own mind.

ROBERT HALL (SPECIAL EFFECTS MAKEUP ARTIST): "Skip was one of those times where we had something like two or three days to make the suit. He wasn't described in the script that much. Jeff wrote something like, 'He's the same color of the walls. Kind of drab.' We basically came up with Skip because we wanted to do something very different from the other demons that had existed on the show before. We didn't want to just do a guy with two big horns. We really wanted to do something out there and they liked the design a lot.

"I remember staying up till like three o'clock in the morning painting the suit. I didn't even know what color it was going to look like or how it was going to be painted until literally a few hours before it went to set. It was one of those things where we brought it, we put it on David Denman, we filmed the episode, and I thought, 'Yeah, it looks kind of neat.' But I still didn't think much of it. And it became this huge hit. I would love to take the credit for it, but I think that it was a wonderful blend of Jeff's writing, David Denman's deadpan performance, and our design. I think it was the three. It was really harmonious and probably a really wonderful happy accident that Skip was as successful as he was. It was because of Skip that I got offered *Buffy*, so it was definitely a turning point for us."

"CARPE NOCTEM"

CASE Nº 3ADH04

ACTION TAKEN

It's a quiet night at Angel Investigations, so quiet that Angel suggests going out for a Charlton Heston double feature, but only Fred—quite eagerly—takes him up on the offer. Meanwhile it's a not-so-quiet night for a young guy and two girls having some naughty fun in a hotel room—that is, until the man rather calmly disintegrates from the inside.

The next morning Cordelia tries to get Angel to realize that Fred thought their night at the movies was a date. Cordy insists that he talk to the girl, but he avoids the subject by focusing on a newspaper article about the strange case of a man whose insides seem to have "collapsed." Wesley recalls that something similar had happened the week before and agrees that it sounds odd enough to warrant an investigation, giving Angel a reason to avoid his talk with Fred.

WRITTEN BY Scott Murphy
DIRECTED BY James A. Contner
GUEST STARS: Stephanie Romanov (Lilah), Daniel Dae Kim (Gavin), Rance Howard (Marcus Roscoe), Paul Benjamin (Jackson)
COSTARS: Misty Louwagie (Christina), Marc Brett (Health Club Phil), Paul Logan (Woody), Lauren Reina (Escort #1), Magdalena Zielinska (Escort #2), Steven W. Bailey (Ryan)

"Cordelia, open up a casefile! We have to get on this right away!"   —*Angel*

While the team springs into action, Gavin Park continues his bureaucratic assault on Angel. Since the vampire with a soul has no social security number, taxpayer ID number, or even last name, the lawyer is going after the records, much to Lilah's chagrin.

After finding another story about a man molting from the inside, Angel and Cordelia go to check out the gym where all the victims were members. While investigating, Angel sees a glint of light from a window in the retirement home across the street. He leaves Cordy behind to investigate and finds an elderly man named Marcus acting rather suspiciously. Before Angel can fully question the guy, Marcus chants an ancient phrase and switches his body with Angel's.

Marcus, unaware that he's just inherited the body of a vampire, leaves Angel behind in his elderly shell. Cordy takes Angel/Marcus back to the hotel where he tries to figure out how Angel fits into this life. Meanwhile, Angel—in the body of Marcus—wakes and tries to break out of the home, only to be returned to his room by an orderly warning that the old man could have yet another heart attack.

The next morning Marcus wakes up in the body of Angel and confuses Wesley for Fred after Cordelia tells him that he needs to set Fred straight about their relationship. Marcus corrects the situation, but instead of turning the real Fred down, he suggests another outing. As Fred prepares for their "second date," Lilah slithers in with forged files that fill in Angel's missing information. Marcus decides to thank Lilah with some desktop action (on Wesley's desk no less), but things get out of hand, first when Fred sees the coupling, then when Angel's primal impulses force Marcus to vamp out.

After Lilah departs, Marcus realizes he's a vampire and goes out on the town for some real fun. When Cordelia finds Fred huddled in the elevator and hears what the girl saw, the team realizes that Angel is not himself and that the change could have happened when he and Cordy separated at the gym.

At the same time, Angel, in Marcus's body, is recovering from a heart attack, but he doesn't let that stop him from another escape attempt. What does stop him is when his "son"—namely Marcus in Angel's body—arrives to kill him.

RESOLUTION

Marcus traps Angel in the rec room, where they have their final confrontation. Even though Marcus seems to have the upper hand in Angel's body, Angel points out that it might not be enough.

"You may have the attitude, and you may have the power, but there's one thing that you don't have and never will—friends. Four of them. Standing behind you with big heavy things."　　　*—Angel*

The team captures Marcus and reverses the body switch by destroying the orb Marcus used as a conduit for the exchange. As they leave, Marcus, back in his old body, suffers one—possibly last—heart attack.

Back at the hotel Angel has his long-neglected talk with Fred, which is much easier since Cordy already prepped her for it. The talk ends abruptly when Cordelia breaks in announcing that Angel's former love, Buffy, is alive.

DOSSIERS

CLIENT As Cordelia succinctly puts it: **"Um, may I point out that no one is actually hiring us to look into this?"**

But then again, Gunn said the same thing about their investigation of Merl's death in the previous casefile.

CIVILIAN SUPPORT Gunn interviews **hotel employees** where the three victims died. Wesley uses a **contact at the coroner's office** to see one of the bodies. Angel speaks with a **health club employee,** and Cordelia speaks with **gym club members** and then **escorts** who were with the men when they died.

In unrelated events **Lilah** comes to Angel's aid by using the graphic artist/forger **Carter Williams** to create ID for the vampire.

SUSPECTS Marcus Roscoe, the seventy-six-year-old retirement home resident, was a salesman who worked alone for fifty years. His travels took him all over, and he collected many artifacts including a Nothian Herb Jar.

CONTINUITY

Cordelia reminds us that sex is a "big no-no" for Angel because if he ever experiences a moment of total bliss he will once again lose his soul. Angel has been mourning the death of Buffy since Willow came to L.A. to tell him about it in "There's No Place Like Plrtz Glrb."

Cordelia also references Buffy—and Darla—when she tries to comfort Fred by mentioning that it's weird that Angel would be with someone who wasn't blonde.

OFFICE ROMANCE

Fred has had a little crush on Angel, which makes sense considering that he was the one who rescued her from Pylea. Her interest will move on to other members of the team from this point on.

QUOTE OF THE WEEK

"She's got the big puppy love! I mean, who wouldn't? You're handsome. And brave and heroic . . . emotionally stunted, erratic, prone to turning evil, and let's face it, a eunuch . . ."

Cordelia's praise for Angel takes a sudden turn.

THE DEVIL IS IN THE DETAILS

EXPENSES

Gunn picks up breakfast burritos, which Marcus pays for using Angel's money.

WEAPONRY

When forced to fight against Marcus in Angel's body, the team comes armed with clubs and a crossbow, but it's Cordelia's stun gun that does the trick and safely takes him down without damaging the body.

THE VAMPIRE RULES

When Marcus (as Angel) chows down on a burrito, Cordelia asks him why he's eating, since vampires do not need to ingest food.

Once Marcus figures out the rules, he's quick to point out Angel's flaws.

"From what I can tell, you were the world's worst vampire. Vampires don't help people, you moron, they kill them."

THE PEN IS MIGHTIER

FINAL CUT

In a subplot that was cut due to time constraints, Angel has an awkward reunion with Marcus's estranged daughter, Madeline. After a couple of attempts to reconnect with the woman, Angel realizes that she's better off without her father and tells her as much.

> ANGEL (AS MARCUS): "I'm not your father—not in any real sense—and you have every right to cut me out of your life. You need to. But I know from experience nobody's ever gonna believe that. They'll tell you no matter what, I'm your father and that we have a bond. And on some level, you'll believe them."
>
> MADELINE: "The thought of you trying to psychoanalyze—"
>
> ANGEL (AS MARCUS): "On some level, you'll think there's something wrong. With you. Something wrong in you that I didn't love you more, treat you better. Something wrong that you're able to cut me out of your life. That ain't the case. You said I don't have a heart, but I know you do. I know how much you feel, how much you love. You need a family and you'll make one, I know. I'm not a part of that. I don't wanna be."
>
> *(She starts to tear up. And laugh a little at the same time.)*
>
> ANGEL (AS MARCUS): "What?"
>
> MADELINE: "It's just, I've been trying so hard all these years to forget you and now you're saying . . ."
>
> ANGEL (AS MARCUS): "You should."

POP CULTURE

❋ "He's probably reading too. He's so deep, you know, thoughtful. I'm guessing *The Brothers Karamazov*, Joyce, a little Goethe to round things out."
Fred suggests that Angel is into the classics.

❋ "Charlton Heston double feature at the Nu Art. *Soylent Green* and *The Omega Man*."
Angel is excited to see the films of the man who once played Moses.

❋ "Don't go all Night Stalker on me."
Lilah compares Angel to the seventies movie and TV series about modern-day vampires.

❋ "If Julia Roberts ever makes a realistic movie about being an escort, I think it should be called *Pretty Skanky Woman*."
Cordelia imagines a more true-to-life version of the film that launched a career.

❋ "It's like something out of Fitzgerald—the man who can have everything but love."
Fred compares Angel to one of the protagonists of novelist F. Scott Fitzgerald, author of *The Great Gatsby*.

THE NAME GAME

Carpe noctem is Latin for "seize the night" and is a riff on the more common phrase "carpe diem," meaning "seize the day." The original phrase refers to the philosophy of enjoying life and making the most of one's opportunities and was introduced by the Roman poet Horace, who was born in 65 B.C.

SIX DEGREES OF . . .

Rance Howard has been working in television and film for nearly fifty years, guest starring in numerous television series, including *The Andy Griffith Show*, which Joss Whedon's grandfather John

Whedon also wrote for (and Rance's son Ron Howard starred in). Rance also appeared in the film *Children of the Corn III* as did Nicholas Brendon (Xander) from *Buffy*. He was married to the late Jean Speegle Howard, who played the "Real Miss French" in the *Buffy* episode "Teacher's Pet."

Steven W. Bailey, who plays Ryan, also appeared as the cave demon in the *Buffy* Season Six episodes "Grave," "Two to Go," and "Villains."

OUR HEROES

DAVID BOREANAZ: "If I have an opportunity—like with the body switch—to really get a chance to stretch as an actor, I have fun with it. For me it was a lot of physical attributes that I wanted to put toward that character as well as inner attributes. You're playing an old man and you're trying to facilitate all those attributes and make them come alive. When the opportunity presents itself like that for me, it's great. I enjoy it."

"FREDLESS"

CASE № 3ADH05

ACTION TAKEN

While Wesley, Cordelia, and Gunn re-reorganize the weapons cabinet, Fred frets over Angel's delayed return from reuniting with his ex-girlfriend with the goofy name. She also worries that the reunion might be more permanent, but Cordelia and Wesley quickly set her straight.

WRITTEN BY Mere Smith
DIRECTED BY Marita Grabiak
GUEST STARS: Andy Hallett (Lorne), Gary Grubbs (Roger), Jennifer Griffin (Trish)

> CORDELIA: "Let me break this down for you, Fred. (Imitating Buffy) Oh, Angel. I know that I am a Slayer and you are a vampire, and it would be wrong for us to be together but—"
>
> WESLEY: (chiming in) "—but my Gypsy curse sometimes prevents me seeing the truth. Oh Buffy—"
>
> CORDELIA: "Yes, Angel?"
>
> WESLEY: "I love you so much I almost forgot to brood."
>
> CORDELIA: "And just because I sent you to Hell that one time doesn't mean we can't just be friends."
>
> WESLEY: "Or possibly more."
>
> CORDELIA: "Gasp! No! We mustn't!"
>
> WESLEY: "Kiss me!"
>
> CORDELIA: "Bite me!"
>
> ANGEL: "How 'bout you both bite me?"

Angel returns, but refuses to share with his friends the details on the real reunion and takes Fred out for ice cream. A Durslar beast interrupts their outing and they wind up tracking it through the sewers. Concerned for Fred's safety, Angel sends her back to the hotel, unaware that a more ominous threat awaits her there.

While they were out, a seemingly nice couple came looking for Fred claiming to be her parents, Roger and Trish. Cordelia, Wesley, and Gunn are suspicious from the start, especially since Fred has never mentioned her family. They also doubt the story that Fred sent the couple a letter with no return address and yet they managed to hire a detective who could track it back to the hotel. They would be even more suspicious if they knew that Fred came in while they were talking and quickly fled the hotel upon seeing the couple.

Angel returns with the Durslar beast's head and pretends that it's a movie prop so he doesn't frighten Roger and Trish. The team takes the couple up to Fred's room where everyone acts suspicious. Angel and company figures that Fred saw the couple and fled, but they don't know where she would have gone, or what to do with Roger and Trish in the meantime. Angel decides to go back to the sewers to look for her while the others hit the library where Fred used to work and take her "parents" along.

Fred goes to Caritas looking for a reading from Lorne, who basically confirms that her fears might be worth listening to. It doesn't take long for the gang to realize where Fred has gone, and eventually they get Lorne to admit she's moved on to the bus station. They arrive before Fred's bus, but she has a breakdown when she sees her parents—for they are her real parents.

The fears Fred has been experiencing have more to do with her mental state than anything her parents had done. She was afraid to see them because if she did it would make her life real again and she would have to accept that the five years she spent in Pylea did actually happen. As her parents finally get her to calm down, a giant bug demon attacks.

The group makes it outside the building where they find makeshift weapons to attack the demon. Fred takes up a golf club and attacks, but her father and Angel are forced to continue the battle for her. But it's her mom, Trish, who saves the day by running the demon over with a bus, splattering its blood and guts everywhere—including on Fred's shirt.

The whole truth eventually comes out and Fred's parents are surprisingly comfortable with it. In fact, they do everything a good parent would do to be there for their daughter. They are also thrilled when Fred decides that it's time she return to Texas where she belongs, although Angel and the team are sorry to see her (and her parents) go.

RESOLUTION

As Fred takes a cab back to her old life, she notices something odd about the demon blood on the shirt she kept as a souvenir and demands that the driver turn around. It's a good thing too, because the team is under attack by a swarm of bug demons. Fred comes in and uses a weapon of her own design to split the demon head that Angel had brought back, and little bug demon babies come spewing out. The babies are reunited with their hive, and Fred is reunited with Angel Investigations and realizes that this is where she's meant to be.

DOSSIERS

CLIENT Fred functions as the team's client in this one, as they do everything in their power to keep her safe from the imagined threat.

CIVILIAN SUPPORT Once again **Lorne** comes to the team's aid in the investigation.

SUSPECTS Roger and **Trish** act suspicious throughout the case, but it turns out that they're just suspicious of Fred's friends.

CONTINUITY

This is the first time Fred has left the hotel on her own, although it is possible she may have left to mail the letter to her parents earlier (unless, of course, she just gave it to the mailman). Caritas is still demolished from the gang attack in "That Old Gang of Mine," and Lorne holds Gunn partially responsible. While at the bus terminal Fred considers going to Las Vegas, presumably since that's where Gunn had suggested Angel go when he was mourning the loss of Buffy. The gang (and Fred's parents) paint over all the crazy writing on the wall in Fred's room.

OFFICE ROMANCE

Fred still has a little crush on Angel and reminds us that Buffy is alive. As seen in the **Action Taken,** Cordelia and Wesley explain why that romance will probably not rekindle.

QUOTE OF THE WEEK

"Sure there's the occasional demon who tries to kill us with pillows, but sadly those cases are few and far between." Cordelia tries to play things down for Fred's parents.

THE DEVIL IS IN THE DETAILS

EXPENSES

Fred will eventually need to replace the shirt that was sprayed with bug guts, and both she and Angel need some minor bandaging.

They also needed to buy paint to cover up Fred's scribbling on the walls.

Angel and Fred indulge in some ice cream.

WEAPONRY

The weapons cabinet inventory includes a Prothgarian broadsword and a third-century ceremonial Sancteus dagger. The three-pronged Scythian death spear is listed as a category six weapon, and it is on the third shelf of the newly reorganized weapons cabinet. With those weapons and more at their disposal, the team is found unarmed at the bus station and has to make do with what is around them, including a bow and arrow, golf clubs, a trash can, and a bus.

Fred's spring-loaded battle-ax contraption was developed for situations in which the combatant may have lost both her arms. The foot release pedal works to fling the battle-ax across the room. Contrary to early speculation, the contraption does not make toast.

DEMONS, ETC. . . .

A **Durslar beast** doesn't usually come above ground (unless, of course, something has laid eggs in its head), preferring to stick to sewers. Although they tend to raise a ruckus, the Durslar is typically comparatively docile.

As Wesley learned on a previous occasion, a small **Rodentius demon** can easily be mistaken for a poodle, especially by rogue demon hunters.

Lorne's heart is located in his left butt cheek.

The **bug demons** are known to lay their eggs in the heads of Durslar beasts. Their blood congeals into crystal form. They may be gender neutral and function with a hive mentality.

Both Angel and Roger have their suspicions that Spiro Agnew, the thirty-ninth vice president of the United States, was a **Grathnar demon.**

THE VAMPIRE RULES

Once again Angel gets with the basics when he explains to Fred that she only needs to invite him into her place once to allow him to enter any time he chooses.

THE PEN IS MIGHTIER

FINAL CUT

Fred's family was a bit bigger in an early version of the script.

TRISH: "I take it Fred's never mentioned us?"

CORDELIA: "Oh, sure she does, all the time. Let's see . . . there was a mother and . . . a father and . . . possibly a sibling?"

TRISH: "Two brothers and a sister."

CORDELIA: "Three siblings! Yes! A trio of siblings that Fred has mentioned to us."

POP CULTURE

✳ "**Durslar beasts are pretty Faulknerian. Lotta sound, no fury.**"
Angel compares the demon to the book *The Sound and the Fury* by William Faulkner.

✳ "**Right when Judge Judy's about to lay the smack down.**"
Lorne is watching everyone's favorite TV judge.

✳ "**It turns out massacres are a lot like sitting through *Godfather III*: once is enough.**"
Lorne refers to arguably the least popular film in the *Godfather* trilogy.

✳ "**I was kind of goin' for a Dresden-after-the-bombing sorta feel.**"
Lorne compares the demolished Caritas to that of the terror bombing of the cultural center in Dresden, Germany, in 1945.

✳ **ROGER: "I hadn't seen a stroke like that since Nicklaus took on Gary Player in the '63 . . ."**
ROGER & ANGEL: "Bob Hope Desert Classic."
The guys think wistfully back to the 1963 golf tournament held in Palm Springs, California.

✳ "**. . . Rog's always had a thing for those *Alien* movies—all that slime and teeth. He can't get enough of 'em. Except for that last one they made—he kind of dozed off.**"
Trish refers to the popular sci-fi *Alien* films, the last of which, *Alien: Resurrection,* apparently failed to satisfy her husband. It just so happens, that film was written by Joss Whedon.

SIX DEGREES OF . . .

Gary Grubbs and Jennifer Griffin both appeared in the miniseries *Heaven & Hell: North & South Book 3.*

OUR HEROES

ROBERT HALL (SPECIAL EFFECTS MAKEUP ARTIST): "It's so hard when you're doing this stuff to come up with something that A) doesn't look like a guy in a suit; and B) doesn't look like you made it in a week, which is the reality. The bug creature, in particular, was an awesome chance for us to get to do something that we've always wanted to do, 'us' being effects guys who grew up wanting to make big monster suits. That was the first big, elaborate monster suit we got to do for

either *Angel* or *Buffy.* I had just started doing the show in season three and we were only a few episodes in. I was getting all excited about it and I had my designers working on bug designs, and then I hear from either David Greenwalt or Tim Minear, someone said, well, 'Joss is thinking now it might not be a bug creature. He might want to do a slug monster, because bug creatures never really work that well, so we're scared to do it.'

"I don't know if it was brazen or crazy, but I said, 'Look, we got a couple weeks. Let us do it. It'll be bitchin'.' To their credit they really let me run with it and show them what we could do as a shop, and they were really happy with it, which made us happy. Working with Loni [Peristrere, visual effects supervisor] at Zoic really helped. Loni's awesome. We work together all the time. I was like, 'We want to do this design, but we've got to remove this guy's legs to make this thing work. Can we do it?' He said, 'Absolutely.' That helps us and frees us up, and it also gives the writers and the producers on the lot more liberties because they don't have the physical limitations."

"BILLY"

CASE Nº 3ADH06

ACTION TAKEN

Angel trains Cordelia in the art of self-defense at the same time the young man Angel helped escape from a fire cell in Hell goes missing. The lawyers at Wolfram & Hart return the man, Billy, to his uncle, a congressman, and everyone is glad that the reunion happened seemingly before he could do something to put himself back in the cell. After the congressman and his nephew leave, the typical verbal sparring between Lilah and Gavin turns physical when Gavin violently attacks her for no apparent reason.

What Wesley originally had hoped to be a romantic date between himself and Fred turns into a group outing at his place. Cordelia sees through the ruse and prompts Wesley to make his move, but he's concerned about the implications of an office romance. The conversation is thrust aside when Cordy has a vision of the brutal beating a man is giving his wife at a convenience store on the Westside. But before the team can spring into action, Cordelia puts things on hold by reporting that the incident happened a week ago.

WRITTEN BY Tim Minear & Jeffrey Bell
DIRECTED BY David Grossman
GUEST STARS: Stephanie Romanov (Lilah), Daniel Dae Kim (Gavin), Justin Shilton (Billy)
COSTARS: Richard Livingston (Congressman), Jeniffer Brooke (Clerk), Cheri Rae Russell (Female Officer), Gwen McGee (Detective), Kristoffer Polaha (Dylan), Rey Gallegos (Sanchez), Charlie Parker (Guy), Joy Lang (Amber), Timothy McNeil (Cab Driver)

The team investigates why the Powers sent a vision after the fact, and they come across a photo from the surveillance camera that shows the young man Angel released from prison in the store only moments before the attack. Cordelia blames herself for the attack since Angel had rescued Billy to save her. In turn, Angel blames himself for making the decision but says that he would do it again.

Angel goes to Lilah's home to confront her about Billy and is surprised to find her badly beaten and still willing to protect her client . . . though she does reveal a few interesting points.

"Billy never touched me and you can't touch him. Billy, as in Blim . . . as in Congressman Blim's nephew. That family's the closest thing this country has to royalty. They'd own half the eastern seaboard even if they weren't clients of ours. The law won't go near him." —*Lilah*

Angel heads out to confront Billy, but before the showdown occurs, cops show up at the door. Billy called them about another bit of his handiwork and the cops take him away.

It is clear that Billy doesn't do the attacking so much as he influences men to do it for him. As the team plans their next move Fred hears over the police scanner that Billy's escaped. Angel and Wesley find that while they were transporting Billy to jail, the male police officer attacked his female partner.

ANGEL

CORDELIA

WESLEY

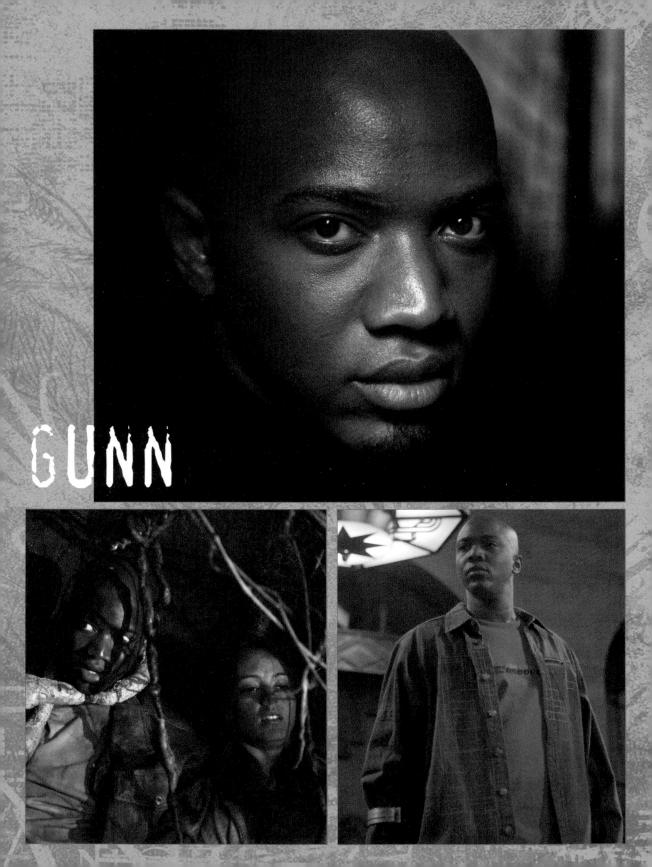

GUNN

FRED

LORNE

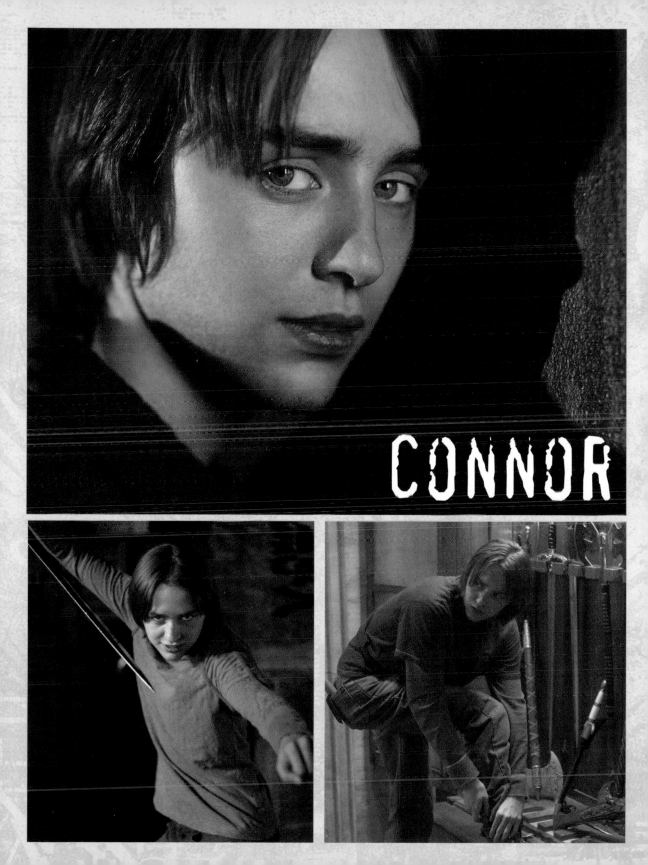

CONNOR

LILAH

DARLA

FAITH

In the resulting car crash Billy fled, leaving a bloody handprint on his escape route. Wesley tests the print to see that it's fresh and takes a sample back to the hotel to examine while Angel follows Billy's trail, unaware that Cordy is back at the hotel arming herself to do the same thing.

Following a brief yet intense discussion with Lilah, Cordelia continues her search for Billy. The trail eventually leads her—and later, Angel—to Billy as he is about to board the family jet. She threatens to kill Billy to stop him, but Angel arrives to stop her and do it himself.

Wesley and Fred's examination of Billy's blood reveals that he is part demon and that there's something in the blood that affects men and makes them act out violently against women. Wesley, having touched the blood, is also affected and chases Fred through the hotel with an ax. Luckily Gunn comes to the rescue until he realizes he has also touched the blood and will be affected. After they barricade themselves in a room, Gunn forces Fred to knock him unconscious so he won't hurt her. But that still leaves Wesley about to burst through the door.

Billy tries to use his powers on Angel, but to no avail. The surprising young man has another power that gives him the strength to match Angel blow for blow. Cordelia tries to get a clear shot with her crossbow, and just as she is about to pull the trigger, two shots echo across the tarmac as Lilah kills her client.

Back at the hotel, Fred uses her interest in building things to her advantage as she sets a trap that subdues Wesley.

RESOLUTION

Cordelia and Angel have another training session, in which he explains why Billy's touch had no effect on him.

> ANGEL: "That thing that Billy brought out in the others . . . that hatred and anger. That's something I lost long ago."
>
> CORDELIA: "Even when you were evil?"
>
> ANGEL: "I never hated my victims . . . never killed out of anger. It was always about the pain . . . and the pleasure."

But Wesley is still trying to cope with his actions. Fred manages to convince him that he was not at fault, but the events prevent them from dealing with whatever romantic feelings may have existed.

DOSSIERS

CLIENT Again, there is technically no client other than the dead ones.

CIVILIAN SUPPORT Wesley has a **source** with access to police files who usually sells the information to the tabloids if the victims are more high profile. He also relies on his **contact at the city morgue**—it is unclear whether this is the same person.

Billy's cousin, **Dylan,** also gives Cordy and Angel a lead on exactly where to find Billy. And, like Lindsey McDonald before her, **Lilah** "switches sides" in the end and takes out her own client.

SUSPECTS Billy, nephew to Congressman Blim.

CONTINUITY

The episode details the repercussions of Angel's actions in "That Vision-Thing."

OFFICE ROMANCE

Cordelia gets Wesley to admit that he has feelings for Fred, but the events of this episode interfere with his plan to tell her. He and Cordy discuss the subject:

> WESLEY: "The last thing any of us should be doing is coupling. With each other, I mean. Office romances, even under the most normal circumstances—"
>
> CORDELIA: "We don't live in 'normal circumstances.' I mean . . . what are the odds of any of us actually finding someone out there who can deal with the stuff that we deal with? I dunno. Maybe we *are* meant . . ."
>
> WESLEY: ". . . for each other?"
>
> CORDELIA: "Actually, I was going to say 'to be alone.' But what the heck. Wesley, if you like her, tell her."

QUOTE OF THE WEEK

> CORDELIA: "Angel feels responsible for this guy 'cause he brought him back from Hell. I feel responsible because he did it to save me. You, who are actually responsible for the entire thing, feel nothing at all because you are a vicious bitch."
>
> LILAH: "So you know me."
>
> CORDELIA: "Please, I *was* you. In better shoes."

THE DEVIL IS IN THE DETAILS

EXPENSES

Wesley purchased police files and photos from the liquor store crime scene.

There is a considerable amount of damage to some of the hotel's closed-off rooms. It is unclear if this will ever be addressed financially, though it is doubtful.

WEAPONRY

Wesley goes after Fred with an ax while she defends herself with nails and a rigged fire extinguisher. Gunn takes apart a chair so Fred can use one of the legs to defend herself against him.

Cordelia arms herself with a mini-crossbow and her handy dandy stun gun, while Lilah relies on an actual gun.

DEMONS, ETC....

Billy's demon origin is unknown, but he considers himself to be more human than Angel. His red blood cells are somehow "supercharged" so that his touch brings out the misogyny in men and turns them into killers. The touch works differently on different men; some lose their minds in an instant, while for others it can take hours.

The **Gurnabeast** has three horns.

THE VAMPIRE RULES

Angel can smell the blood in the police car from across the street, and he can determine that some of it isn't human.

THE PEN IS MIGHTIER

FINAL CUT

Angel's penchant for quick exits is exemplified in this piece of stage direction from the shooting script:

WHOOSH—Angel's off into the night.
WESLEY'S POV
The dark figure of Angel just disappearing over a roof (or around a corner. Point is, he ain't Superman, but we get that the cat can cook when he wants to).

POP CULTURE

* **"They already ran the THX version in my head."**
Cordy compares her very visual and aural vision to that of films screened in THX-approved theaters, which ensure that the audience has a full-on audiovisual experience.
* **"You can't just barge into a police precinct and go all Terminator."**
Cordelia warns Angel not to behave like the character portrayed by Arnold Schwarzenegger in the trilogy of films of the same name.

SIX DEGREES OF...

Justin Shilton also appeared on *Buffy the Vampire Slayer* in "Empty Places" as Officer Munroe, a cop with Hellmouth-affected anger issues that led to violence against innocents.

TRACKS

The rap song playing at Dylan's party is called "Clint Eastwood," by Gorillaz.

OUR HEROES

AMY ACKER: "I hadn't watched the show as much as I probably should have when I auditioned. I knew there was fighting and stuff, but from my sides and my audition scene it didn't seem like I would be a big fighter. Now I'm always the one who's like, 'Why can't I do any of that cool stuff?' And they'll say, 'Fred doesn't know how to do that.' I just want to kick someone. I've gotten in a few good ones. At the beginning, the physical stuff was like in 'Billy' when Wesley was chasing me around the hotel and I was crawling on the ground and falling downstairs and stuff. And now it's gotten to be more of an aggressive thing."

"OFFSPRING"

CASE Nº 3ADH07

ACTION TAKEN

The scene opens with a familiar image of Angel running through the sewers, but these are not the underground passages of Los Angeles; he is in Rome, in the year 1771. Angel is captured and tortured by his old nemesis, Holtz, until he is rescued by his former love, Darla. Flash to the future and Darla back in L.A.

Angel and Cordelia are having another training session, but the vampire seems distracted. Cordy suspects that it's because Wesley and Gunn are currently breaking into a mansion to steal the missing pieces of the Nyazian Scroll in an attempt to figure out yet another dire prediction. Angel contends that his mind is not preoccupied as they end the session. However, Fred comes in and occupies it with thoughts of Cordelia and possible Kyrumption, suggesting that the two heroes are in love.

Wesley and Fred work to decipher the prophecy, but the language and mathematics involved are very confusing. It speaks of the Tro-Clon who could be destined to bring about the end of the world very soon . . . or the previous March. But all the death prophesizing takes a back seat when the even-more-pregnant-than-she-was-before Darla shows up at their door. And not only is she pregnant, but also she is getting increasingly agitated about the unnatural occurrence.

WRITTEN BY David Greenwalt
DIRECTED BY Turi Meyer
SPECIAL GUEST STAR: Julie Benz (Darla)
GUEST STARS: Andy Hallettt (Lorne), Jack Conley (Sahjhan), Steve Tom (Mills), and Keith Szarabajka (Holtz)
COSTARS: Heidi Marnhout (Furie #1), An Le (Furie #2), Madison Gray (Furie #3), Robert Peters (Arney), Sergio Premoli (Monsignor), Van Epperson (Bus Driver), Peyton Miller (Johnny), Christian Miller (Johnny), Kathleen McMartin (Mom), Theresa Arrison (Johnny's Mom)

Cordelia instantly takes the role of protector of the pregnant Darla, angry that Angel never admitted the truth about sleeping with the vampire. Darla informs them that she has seen seers and shamans across the Western Hemisphere and now has come to them to find out what is inside her. Could it be the coming evil they had so recently read about? The gang is stumped for where to begin so they decide to start with a reading from Lorne.

The Host proves to be little help, once again focusing on the confusing destiny before them, which sends Fred off on a rant.

> "Can I say something about destiny? Screw destiny! If this evil thing comes we'll fight it. And we'll keep fighting it until we whup it. Because destiny is just another word for inevitable—and nothing's inevitable as long as you stand up, look it in the eye, and say . . . 'you're evitable!'" —*Fred*

Darla's hunger increases and she attacks Cordy, putting a bite on her and supplying her with a vision at the same time. Cordelia manages to hold the vamp back, with an assist from Angel, but Darla fights her way past the rest of the team and flees the club. As the group reassembles Cordelia reveals that her vision had to do with innocence and that Darla was unable to stop herself. She is also able to reveal Darla's present location.

RESOLUTION

Angel finds Darla about to feed on a small boy at an arcade. He rescues the boy and the two vampires do battle. Just as Angel is about to stake her, he hears something that stops him mid-thrust.

ANGEL: "The child, it has a heartbeat. It has a soul."

DARLA: "Not my child—"

ANGEL: (calming her) "Okay . . . Our . . . our child. That's why you've been craving purer and purer blood. That's why it's been driving you out of your mind: It has a soul."

Angel returns Darla to the hotel to rest under Gunn's tight security. At the same time, Fred recalculates the prophesy and comes to realize that it looks as if the coming evil is about to arrive.

Meanwhile the demon Sahjhan brings something back from the dead—Angel and Darla's former foe Holtz.

DOSSIERS

CLIENT After a truly odd set of circumstances, **Darla** becomes another one of Angel Investigations's nonpaying clients.

CIVILIAN SUPPORT A **snitch** told Gunn about the missing pieces of the Nyazian Scroll in a local mansion (although he failed to mention that they're in a safe). **Lorne** once again provides some reading support, although even he is stumped by the pregnancy.

SUSPECTS The **Tro-Clon** is definitely a suspect, though no one can be sure what it is. It seems that the unnamed demon (who will later be introduced as **Sahjhan**) has something to do with the coming evil, as the first thing he is seen doing is bringing **Holtz** back from the dead (or, more accurately, bringing him out of the past).

CONTINUITY

Holtz was first mentioned in "The Trial" and first seen in "Heartthrob," although at the time it seemed unlikely that he was going to be seen in the twenty-first century. The prophecy they are researching may be linked to what Angel learned in "To Shanshu in L.A.," when another prediction indicated that the vampire with a soul would one day live again. The vagueness of the prophecy from the Nyazian Scroll will continue to present problems for the team (and Wolfram & Hart) in the coming episodes. Angel's "friends" the three Furies are seen in Caritas reworking the sanctuary spell as Lorne rebuilds from the damage done in "That Old Gang of Mine." Cordelia refers to her mystical pregnancy from "Expecting" (which won't be her last mystical pregnancy, by the way).

OFFICE ROMANCE

Fred gets Angel thinking that he and Cordelia might have chemistry, but he's uncomfortable with the idea (and Cordy seems totally unaware). Even Fred, with her advanced degrees, has trouble tracking the love lives of her coworkers.

FRED: "Who's Darla?"
GUNN: "Angel's old flame, from way back."
FRED: "Not the one who died."
GUNN: "Yes—no, not that one—the other one who died and came back to life. She's a vampire."
FRED: "Do y'all have a chart or something?"
GUNN: "In the files. I'll get it for you later."

QUOTE OF THE WEEK

"We tried to stop her by hitting her fists and feet with our faces, but . . ."

Gunn explains how Darla got away.

THE DEVIL IS IN THE DETAILS

EXPENSES

Cordelia buys some fake flowers to brighten up the training room.

Wesley purchases steaks to distract the Dobermans guarding the mansion. He also sports a glass cutter and has a minicam in his bag of tricks.

WEAPONRY

Angel holds a stake on Darla, but doesn't use it even though she wants him to.

THE PLAN

Darla keeps it simple.

"You can get your little gang of supernatural detectives to find out what the hell is happening to me now and how to stop it."

DEMONS, ETC. . . .

It is unclear whether the **Tro-Clon** is evil (or even if it is a being as opposed to an event). The Nyazian Scroll predicts the "arriving" or "arising" of the person or being that brings about the ruination of mankind. However, that too is open to interpretation, as "ruination" could also mean "purification," which could be either a good or a bad thing. Needless to say, the prophecy is vague at best. As they continue to translate, things gets even murkier when the scroll says that the Tro-Clon will either "appear," "spring up," or "be born."

THE VAMPIRE RULES

Typically vampires are unable to conceive children. They also do not breathe.

AS SCENE IN L.A.

Darla gets off her bus in L.A. on Paramount Pictures's New York Street backlot. Later Sahjhan is seen reviving Holtz under an area of Los Angeles that also happens to be on the Paramount Pictures studio lot (where the show films).

THE PEN IS MIGHTIER

FINAL CUT

The gang realizes early on something that will come to present a problem before—and long after—Angel's child is born.

> WESLEY: "*His* child. Even if it's the Tro-Clon come to destroy us . . ."
> FRED: "It's *his* child."

POP CULTURE

* "All we can do is live each moment to the fullest and be grateful that we didn't throw too much money at the NASDAQ."
  Cordy, no stranger to financial difficulties, is glad they didn't invest in the stock market.
* "This is way beyond my ken—and my Barbie, and all my action figures."
  Lorne makes a little play on words with Mattel's most popular doll line, Barbie, and her boyfriend, Ken.

SIX DEGREES OF . . .

Jack Conley, who plays Sahjhan, also appeared in the *Buffy* episode "Phases" as the werewolf hunter, Cain.

TRACKS

Darla sings a few notes of "Oh Danny Boy," a familiar song written in the early twentieth century to the tune of an Irish folk song.

OUR HEROES

ROBERT HALL (SPECIAL EFFECTS MAKEUP ARTIST): "Sahjhan came at the point in the season for us that we were really strapped for time and ideas, frankly. We just wanted to go really old school with him; old world. We didn't try to reinvent the wheel with Sahjhan. They wanted to keep him with a very old world feeling so I came up with the twine wrapped around his neck and up into his face. They wanted him to be really expressive, so we just kept really thin appliances on the face. He's got runes dug into the skin. I don't know how much of the detail you ever really see, but he's got the runes and a twine theme. His whole hands are wrapped in twine. We just tried to do something kind of rustic and cool with him."

"QUICKENING"

CASE Nº 3ADH08

ACTION TAKEN

It is 1764 and Captain Holtz thinks he finally has Angel and Darla surrounded. When he bursts into the small house he finds it empty, except for the note that tells him where they really are. At the same time, Angel and Darla are in Holtz's home, having their way with his family. Jump to the present and Holtz is watching historical video to bring him up to date on current events, anxious to take his revenge.

Wesley's continued work translating the Nyazian Scroll reveals that the Tro-Clon is not a being but a series of events,

WRITTEN BY: Jeffrey Bell
DIRECTED BY: Skip Schoolnik
SPECIAL GUEST STAR:
  Julie Benz (Darla)
GUEST STARS: John Rubinstein
  (Linwood), Stephanie Romanov
  (Lilah), Daniel Dae Kim (Gavin),
  Jack Conley (Sahjhan), José
  Yenque (Vamp Cult Guy), and
  Keith Szarabajka (Holtz)
COSTARS: Kasha Kropinski
  (Sarah), Bronwen Bonner-Davies
  (Caroline), Matt Casper (Cyril),
  Angelo Surmelis (Tech Guy),
  Michael Robert Brandon
  (Psychic), William Ostrander
  (Commander), John Durbin
  (Dr. Fetvanovich)

of which Angel's child is only one part. But there are more immediate concerns with the baby when Darla goes into labor. The team realizes it's time to go to the hospital, so long as they stay away from the doctors.

Lilah is going over some surveillance video of the hotel that Gavin recorded when she makes the discovery that an "unidentified pregnant woman" is Darla. She immediately alerts Linwood, while a mail boy with shifting loyalties spreads the word beyond the firm. As Wolfram & Hart springs into action trying to find out how their stable of psychics missed out on predicting the coming vampire birth, a flash to the past reveals the first meeting of Sahjhan and a mourning Holtz. At that time, the demon made an offer to help him get revenge, which now plays out as Sahjhan takes Holtz to his demon team of minions, much to the human's chagrin.

Meanwhile Angel's team finds an abandoned operating theater at a teaching hospital and brings in ultrasound equiptment to find out what is inside Darla, who, it turns out, is experiencing false labor. The sonogram reveals that she is carrying a human . . . a boy.

ANGEL: "I'm going to have a son? I'm going to have a son."

FRED: "Uh, guys . . . as fascinating as the ultrasound image of an unborn child may appear to you—"

ANGEL: "Me. A father. To a son. Do you know what it means?"

FRED: "We're surrounded by vampires."

ANGEL: "No, it's a *human* boy . . . Oh. We're surrounded by vampires."

Vampire cult members, to be exact. They claim that they have come to protect the child, and prove their intentions by easily killing an assassin, who was sent by Lilah. The cultists then reveal that they not only intend to protect the child, but they also will kill all the humans . . . and Darla, too. Angel, the humans, and Darla manage to fight off the vampire cult and start to flee the city until Wesley realizes that other beings seem to have more information on the child than they do. As such, they can't just leave behind the Nyazian Scroll.

Angel parks the car several blocks from the hotel and leaves the team to protect Darla while he retrieves the scroll. As Angel leaves Darla is on the verge of telling him to be careful, but she stops herself. The child inside her is starting to affect her emotionally, but she won't admit it.

Angel heads for the hotel unaware that Wolfram & Hart has a commando team and a demon doctor at the hotel ready to take Darla and the child. But what that team doesn't know is that Holtz is on his way to the hotel too. When the time traveler arrives, he calmly tries to reason with the commandos. That quickly devolves into a massacre that leaves all of Wolfram & Hart's team dead.

RESOLUTION

Angel walks into the hotel, which he is naturally surprised to find littered with bodies. Before he can investigate or retrieve the scroll, a long-forgotten voice stops him.

"Angelus . . . I've been looking for you."   *—Holtz*

When Angel does not return in the time he allotted, Cordelia starts up the car to head somewhere safe, but Darla's scream stops her. This time the labor pains are real. Darla's water breaks, signifying that the baby is ready to be born.

DOSSIERS

CLIENT The team continues to look after **Darla** with a growing list of suspects.

CIVILIAN SUPPORT **Holtz** provides some unexpected support by taking out the commando team from Wolfram & Hart.

SUSPECTS Where to start?

The **Wolfram & Hart** team of **Lilah, Gavin,** and **Linwood** springs into action once they learn of the pending birth. Gavin enlists **Cyril** the mail boy to help bring Lilah in the loop, unaware that Cyril also brings in some other players. A Wolfram & Hart **tech guy** is in charge of the rather shoddy surveillance equipment. Linwood has all the **psychics** brought in to figure out how they could be surprised by the pending birth and kills at least one of them when he proves useless. Lilah calls in an **assassin** who doesn't last long. In the end they rely on a **special ops team** led by **Commander Burke,** along with **Dr. Fetvanovich,** the foremost specialist in paranormal obstetrics.

Sahjhan and **Holtz** enlist demons known as **Grapplers** as their minions.

CONTINUITY

This episode explains why Holtz had been chasing Angelus and Darla, as first mentioned in "Heartthrob." Angel and Darla recall the last time she was in his room—when they conceived the child, in "Reprise." The exterminators Gavin sent to the hotel in "That Vision-Thing" planted surveillance equipment that caught Lilah in a compromising position with a possessed Angel in "Carpe Noctem." Once again the concept of fleeing to Las Vegas is discussed, though quickly discarded.

QUOTE OF THE WEEK

WESLEY: "I haven't studied one of these for quite a while."
ANGEL: "Is that the head?"
WESLEY: "I think it is . . . Or is that the head?"
FRED: "Maybe you're both right . . . It's not like I'm suggesting it's an *evil* two-headed thing."

> Wesley's initial difficulty reading the sonogram leads Fred
> to a likely hypothesis.

THE DEVIL IS IN THE DETAILS

EXPENSES

Money will need to be spent on a thorough cleaning of the back seat of Angel's car after Darla's water breaks in it.

Considerable damage is done to the hotel lobby during the battle between the special ops team and Holtz's minions.

WEAPONRY

The gang uses good old reliable stakes and a broom handle against the vampire cult. Fred uses Gunn's "extra dagger" in a failed attempt to look like she's holding Darla hostage.

THE PLAN

When the team discovers they can't harm the baby while it's still in the womb, several options are considered for dealing with it postnatally.

WESLEY: "We'll wait for it to be born and we'll chop its head off."
CORDELIA: "We're gonna need a really big mallet."
GUNN: "If it skitters we should have a net or something. Maybe a flamethrower."

ANGEL: "Flamethrower?! There will be no throwing of flames. Nobody's doing anything until we know exactly what's going on."

DEMONS, ETC....

Sahjhan is able to navigate other dimensions where time behaves differently, which explains how he could be so long-lived and still look so young (although he does admit to having a little work done, especially around the eyes).

Wolfram & Hart has offices in Berlin, Singapore, and Muncie, Indiana.

Grappler demons are known to be merciless in battle, though they are not "the sharpest pencils in the box."

The **vampire cult** was sent to protect the "Special Child" that was prophesized by their Great Potentate, **Ul-thar.**

THE VAMPIRE RULES

Vampires are known to have great hearing—although that's not known by Fred.

A vampire birth is unprecedented.

THE PEN IS MIGHTIER

FINAL CUT

A place Travis Bickle might spend some time alone.

The stage directions for the episode describe the assassin's room as a place where the character played by Robert DeNiro in *Taxi Driver* may have lived.

POP CULTURE

✳ **"Did you follow this part of the history?—American Revolution, Manifest Destiny, westward expansion, the Beach Boys."**
Sahjhan lists some of the more important events in the past couple of centuries, including the pop music group with a surfer motif.

✳ **"Nothing a couple of Band-Aids and a pint of Heath Bar Crunch can't fix."**
Cordelia refers to the most popular brand of bandages and one of the many Ben & Jerry's ice cream flavors to help them deal with their wounds. (These could potentially be added to the list of expenses.)

✳ **"I agree, we need to get out of Dodge."**
Angel brings up the famous Western town of Dodge City, Kansas.

THE NAME GAME

The term **"quickening"** refers to reaching the stage of pregnancy when the fetus can be felt to move. The title parallels the way the unborn child moves Darla to feel emotions.

OUR HEROES

DAVID BOREANAZ: "With Julie Benz there was a big connection with the actress herself. I love working with Julie. I think she's fantastic. As far as the character is concerned I think that we found a really good connection between Darla and Angel. There was that angst and then conflict. There was a lot going on between those two characters. There was a lot of stuff under the radar. It was a very up and down relationship with the two of them."

"LULLABY"

CASE № 3ADH09

ACTION TAKEN

Angel's opportunity to catch up with Holtz is interrupted when Lilah enters the scene and drops the news that Angel has a soul. She also provides enough distraction for Angel to find a hand grenade at his feet and use it—and the ensuing explosion—

WRITTEN & DIRECTED BY
Tim Minear
SPECIAL GUEST STAR:
Julie Benz (Darla)
GUEST STARS: John Rubinstein (Linwood), Andy Hallett (Lorne), Stephanie Romanov (Lilah), Daniel Dae Kim (Gavin), Jack Conley (Sahjhan), Jim Ortlieb (Translator), and Keith Szarabajka (Holtz)
COSTARS: Robert Peters (Arney), Bronwen Bonner-Davies (Caroline), Kasha Kropinski (Sarah)

to help him escape. Unfortunately he cannot take the Nyazian Scroll with him, leaving Lilah to find it and take it for herself.

At the same time, Darla is experiencing intense labor pains. The team tries to take her to a more enclosed place, but find that they are surrounded by Grappler demons. As they try to fight their way out Darla tires of waiting and mows down the demons with Angel's car, then flees on her own.

In the past, the rest of Holtz's sad tale unfolds. On the night Angel and Darla attacked his home, they left a message behind—his daughter Sarah was allowed to live. But as Holtz sings a lullaby to calm the child he finds a pair of bite marks on her neck and suspects that she had been turned. He spends one last night with the child before forcing her into the morning sun, which immediately sets the little vampire ablaze.

Angel fills the team in on Holtz's arrival and goes to find Darla while the others look for a safe place for her to give birth. Angel tracks the mother of the soon-to-be child to a rooftop where she reveals her unnatural love for the child.

> **DARLA:** "I haven't been nourishing it! I haven't given this baby a thing! I'm dead! It's been nourishing me! These feelings that I'm having are not mine—they're coming from *it*."
>
> **ANGEL:** "You don't know that."

95

DARLA: "Of course I do. Angel . . . Angel . . . I don't have a soul. It does. And right now that soul is inside of me. But soon . . . it won't be and then . . ."

ANGEL: "Darla . . ."

DARLA: "I won't be able to love it. I won't even be able to remember that I loved it . . . And I want to remember."

Their conversation is interrupted by a call from Wes. He has found a safe haven in Caritas, where Lorne has nearly gotten the place rejiggered to prevent demon *and* human violence. It would seem to be the perfect place for Darla to give birth. However, the translator Lilah has working on the scroll has come to a final realization about the prophecy and reveals that "there will be no birth . . . only death."

The prophecy is already proving true when Darla's contractions stop and the labor pains are replaced by pain from a different cause. Since Darla's body is not a life-giving vessel, it is not equipped to give birth. While Angel tries to calm an emotional Darla in Lorne's bedroom, the rest of the gang tries to figure out what they can do to help.

Holtz enters and interrupts the team's discussion, but since none of them have met him before, they are unaware of the pending danger. That is, until Holtz softly sings the lullaby he sang to his

daughter as he leaves the club. Lorne reads the vampire hunter, realizes what he's up to, and tells everyone to run. Seconds later an oil drum bounces down the staircase and a bomb rolls up next to it and explodes.

RESOLUTION

The team manages to bust through the wall behind Lorne's bed and goes out into the rainy night. Darla is too weak to run and collapses in the alleyway as Holtz enters the burning club. Angel and Fred stay behind to look after Darla while the others get the car, but Darla knows that it's too late. The baby is dying.

"This child . . . Angel, it's the one good thing we ever did together. The only good thing. You make sure to tell him that for me."

—*Darla*

Darla then takes a piece of wooden debris and stakes herself, turning to dust so that the child inside her can live.

Holtz comes out of the club as Angel lifts the child off the ground. The vampire hunter sees father with child and lets them go as Sahjhan calls after him to finish the job. Although Holtz has no intention of killing Angel tonight, he does intend to keep his promise to show Angel no mercy.

DOSSIERS

CLIENT Darla continues to function as the client for Angel Investigations.

CIVILIAN SUPPORT Once again **Lorne** provides sanctuary at Caritas, and once again he lives to regret it.

SUSPECTS Wolfram & Hart is still working to take Angel's child. **Lilah** enlists the help of one of the firm's **translators** to examine the Nyazian Scroll.

Holtz and **Sahjhan** continue their plot against Angel.

CONTINUITY

This episode picks up mere moments after "Quickening" left off. Lorne is still working on getting the demon and human anti-violence spell up and running. When concerned that her baby will die in the alley, Darla recalls that Angel died in an alley, as seen in the *Buffy* episode "Becoming, Part 1."

OFFICE ROMANCE

Darla tries to apologize for turning Angel into a vampire in the past and stealing his life from him. The two share a moment of reconciliation before she kills herself to save her child.

QUOTE OF THE WEEK

"Yeah, I know. Vampire, cursed by Gypsies who restored his soul, destined to atone for centuries of evil . . . wacky sidekicks . . . yadda, yadda."

Lilah concisely sums up Angel's history and unintentionally brings Holtz up to speed on things.

THE DEVIL IS IN THE DETAILS

EXPENSES

Replacement elevator doors are added to the list of repairs necessary in the hotel lobby. Caritas was destroyed, necessitating major repairs.

WEAPONRY

Angel uses one of the commandos' grenades to blow himself out of the lobby.

The rest of the gang relies on a tire iron, baseball bats, and clubs to fight off the Grappler demons. Darla uses Angel's car to get rid of the threat.

DEMONS, ETC. . . .

The Senior Partners at **Wolfram & Hart** do not crucify their wayward employees, as that is "too Christian" a response.

THE PEN IS MIGHTIER

FINAL CUT

Gunn and Angel have a brief exchange regarding tracking Darla.

ANGEL: "She went this way."

GUNN: "You can smell her?"

ANGEL: "Tire tracks."

GUNN: "Right. I saw those."

POP CULTURE

✳ "She's free-range evil."

Lilah compares Darla to the kinds of animals left to graze instead of being pumped with chemicals before being made into meals.

✳ "So Angel has a soul. Big whoop. So did Attila the Hun."

Sahjhan refers to the evil leader of the Huns circa A.D. 450.

✳ "I can't have a baby here. I just had the booths Simonized!"

Lorne refers to a brand of protectorate that may not be tough enough to protect against birthing.

SIX DEGREES OF . . .

The translator, Jim Ortlieb, is another one of the many *Angel* guest stars who also had a role on *Roswell*. In fact, his character, Nasedo, was involved in the death of Julie Benz's character, Agent Topolski, and he is indirectly involved with predicting Darla's death here.

OUR HEROES

MICHAEL GASPAR (SPECIAL EFFECTS COORDINATOR): "Blasting Angel through the elevator doors was a little tricky to do because we had to simulate the explosion. We had a mortar sitting between the stunt double's feet that had a pyrotechnic charge in there that shot out. That one we did multiple tests [with] before shooting it. These mortars are steel tubes that are capped off on one end. You can put your charge in there and screw it to the floor, and we had it at just the angle so it blew up in front of him so you couldn't really tell it wasn't David. David started the move, but they overlapped it with the double. He stands there and we blow this thing between his legs and then toss a bunch of stuff up.

At that same time, he's being yanked by a wire so it all just fit together quickly. The good thing about TV is the cuts are quick, which helps out a lot. You can get away with a lot that way."

ANDY HALLETT: "I was really sad to see Caritas go. At that point I wasn't a regular, so I didn't know what that meant for the stability of my character. So looking at it from a total narcissistic perspective . . . I don't know . . . I just always had fun in there. Even though it had the demon and vampire crowd and it was a relatively dark crowd, it was still a lighter note on the show. My character's always been seen in that light. So I was sad to see it go. I begged for another bar . . . begged."

"DAD"

CASE № 3ADH10

ACTION TAKEN

The team returns to the hotel to find the lobby demolished, but at least Wolfram & Hart had been kind enough to remove the bodies for them. Moments later Lorne enters announcing that he's moving in, considering it's only fair since they're responsible for his place being destroyed . . . again. Lorne, like the others, tries to hold the new bundle of joy, but Angel won't allow it. The vampire father's overprotective concerns prove to be on the mark because a demon almost immediately attacks. Once the demon is killed, the team realizes that even though the baby has been born, he is still in danger.

WRITTEN BY David H. Goodman
DIRECTED BY Fred Keller
GUEST STARS: John Rubinstein (Linwood), Andy Hallett (Lorne), Stephanie Romanov (Lilah), Daniel Dae Kim (Gavin), Jack Conley (Sahjhan), Laurel Holloman (Justine), and Keith Szarabajka (Holtz)
COSTARS: Kira Tirimacco (Doctor), Stephanie Courtney (Gwen)

Angel continues to coddle his child while the rest of the team puts together an enemies list. At the same time, a pair of their enemies—Holtz and Sahjhan—argue over the seeming lack-of-plan to take out Angel. That discussion comes to an abrupt end when all of the pricey demons Sahjhan hired as minions suddenly drop dead. Holtz poisoned them because he doesn't want to work with mercenaries; he wants warriors willing to die for his cause.

The Furies put a mystical force field around the hotel to keep the baby safe, while Gunn is charged with getting more firepower for protection. Angel is getting more and more stressed over his son's safety and Lorne is hearing a strange hum throughout the place. All these events are being watched by Wolfram & Hart via the surveillance equipment previously planted in the hotel.

While Lilah tries to research information on the mysterious new player she met at the hotel, both Lorne and Cordelia try to convince Angel to share some of the responsibilities of watching the child. Cordy goes so far as to point out that he couldn't do everything on his own even if he wasn't a vampire, but that fact makes it even more difficult. Angel corrects her by holding his hand out into the sun until it starts to smoke.

"If he has to get to the hospital at noon on the sunniest day of the year, he'll get there. Even if I don't."

—Angel

Angel comes back into the hotel to be greeted warmly by Lorne just before Gunn returns with the aforementioned firepower in time to find their enemies gathering outside the magical barrier. Unbeknownst to them, the enemies list continues to grow as Holtz tries to enlist his first warrior, a woman named Justine, whose sister was killed by vampires.

Day turns to night and the enemies continue to multiply. It won't be long before a collection of demons breaks through the barrier, so Angel decides to change the plan and take his child away, leaving the others to defend the hotel. As he sneaks off, the lawyers watching at Wolfram & Hart alert their commandos. Demons attack the lobby and are held off for a moment before the bad guys realize Angel is on the move . . . and the chase is on.

Angel flees to an abandoned mine in the desert and the caravan of enemies follows. He ditches his car and takes his bundle down into the mine where he is trapped by a number of humans and non-humans. Just as it looks like there is no escape, he throws the baby to the wolves and rides a pulley out of the mine. As he drives off the vamp who caught the bundle opens it to find a teddy bear strapped with C4. The bomb explodes while Cordelia holds the real baby at the hospital back in L.A.

RESOLUTION

Linwood, Lilah, and Gavin review the surveillance tapes and realize Lorne was able to find the equipment based on the hum he had heard and pass along a message to Angel to foil the plan. As they discuss the situation, pleased that they no longer have so much competition for taking the child, Angel breaks into the law firm with a knife and a threat to Linwood.

"My son has a tiny scratch on his cheek and now by extraordinary coincidence, so do you. I'm holding you personally responsible for anything that happens to him whether it's your fault or not. A cold, sunburn, a skinned knee—whatever happens to him is going to happen to you and then some. So not only are you not coming after him, you're going to make sure he lives a long, healthy life. You just became his godfather."

—*Angel*

Angel then goes to meet up with the team at the hospital, learns that his son is perfectly fine, and, seeing that, gives him the perfectly fine name of Connor.

DOSSIERS

CLIENT Angel's son is effectively their client of primary concern.

CIVILIAN SUPPORT Lorne comes to the rescue again. He formally moves into the hotel in this episode and will be considered part of the Angel Investigations team from this point forward.

SUSPECTS The team makes a list of suspects divided into two categories. Category one is groups or individuals they know pose a threat to the baby, including **Holtz, Wolfram & Hart,** and the **vampire cult** that attacked them in the hospital. Category two is those who could pose a threat, including the **Order of Phillius, Beltar the Cremator, a Piper beast,** and **Frank,** a local mobster who specializes in kidnappings. Also on the list are **the Scourge,** an army of purebred demons dedicated to wiping out all half-demons (Angel Investigations came across the group in "Hero.") Later, they add **"more ninja guys,"** worried that the assassin who attacked them at the hospital may have friends. They are unaware of the fact that Lilah hired the assassin. Later they add a **biker gang** known to be into extortion and kidnapping and a group of **Lilliad demons.**

CONTINUITY

Once again the action picks up shortly after when the previous episode left off. As Lorne reminds the team, not only did they destroy his club in "Lullaby," but also they wrecked it in "That Old Gang of Mine." Wesley reminds Angel of the time the vampire nearly had sex on Wes's desk when he was possessed in "Carpe Noctem." During Angel's staged abandonment of the team, Gunn suggests that Angel fire them first since that's what he's good at, referencing his actions in "Reunion."

QUOTE OF THE WEEK

WESLEY: "Not to mention some bastard's blown a gaping hole in the lift."
ANGEL: "Sorry, my bastard."
WESLEY: "Oh well, it's not like we use it."

The gang takes in the damage to the lobby.

THE DEVIL IS IN THE DETAILS

EXPENSES

As the team will come to learn, babies are expensive. In this episode alone they have purchased a baby blanket, ointment, diapers, a baby book, a teddy bear (with optional C4), a stroller, and a doctor's visit.

Gunn presumably has to pony up some bucks for the additional weaponry.

WEAPONRY

The team relies on good ol' trusty crossbows and stakes as well as the tire iron from the previous episode. Gunn makes use of one of the knives left behind by the late Dr. Fetvanovich. They also get some additional firepower, including a flamethrower and a teddy that's literally armed to bear.

Angel uses a simple straight razor to give Linwood a cut on his cheek.

THE PLAN

"The plan is I go. Take the baby somewhere safe."

Ah, but that is *so* not the plan. Angel actually functions as a diversion to take out the bad guys while the others take the child for his newborn examination.

DEMONS, ETC. . . .

Lorne considers staying with a **Mulix demon,** where he has a standing offer to crash.

Wolfram & Hart's "file" on Angel fills thirty-five filing cabinets. **Gwen** in files and records also functions *as* files and records and can recall all details of the files on command. According to those records, Holtz became a vampire hunter circa 1754. He hunted Angel and Darla halfway around the world until his mysterious disappearance in 1773. After Angel and Darla killed his family in 1764 he swore to avenge their blood and pursued the vampires relentlessly for nine years, racking up a vampire body count of 378 in the meantime.

Lilliad demons make a magical broth from the bones of human children. They use strong magics and are able to break the Furies' spell. Their powers are linked directly to the lunar cycle.

THE PEN IS MIGHTIER

FINAL CUT

LILAH: "You think he has a fan club?"

GWEN: "No."

Lilah is naturally quite impressed by Holtz's accomplishments; however, Gwen—Ms. Files & Records—doesn't get the joke in these lines cut from the episode due to length.

POP CULTURE

* **"Did you know these diapers are lined with a space-age material originally developed for NASA astronauts?"**

  Wesley marvels at the technological advancements of the National Aeronautics and Space Administration.

* **"Macduff was from his mother's womb untimely ript."**

  Lilah quotes act 5, scene 8 of Shakespeare's *Macbeth,* comparing the baby's unnatural birth to that of the character Macduff, who was born delivered by cesarean section (and was therefore "not born of woman," which played into a prophecy in the play that is similar to the situation in this series).

* **"He doesn't like Smokey Robinson and the Miracles? I thought you said this kid had a soul."**

  Lorne refers to the R&B group with many hits including "Tears of a Clown."

* **"Trying to imagine myself as John Wayne in *Rio Bravo.* You?"**

  Wesley imagines himself in the 1959 western film directed by Howard Hawks.

* **"Austin Stoker. *Assault on Precinct 13.*"**

  Likewise, Gunn puts himself in the 1976 film directed by John Carpenter.

* **"What are we talking? Some kind of *Karate Kid,* Mr. Miyagi groove-thing, wax on, wax off?"**

  Justine suggests that Holtz's offer sounds a lot like the series of movies about a boy (and later a girl) and a karate mentor.

TRACKS

Angel sings "Too-Ra-Loo-Ra-Loo-Ral," the Irish lullaby written in 1913 by James Royce Shannon, while Lorne sings a lullaby of a different tune, crooning Smokey Robinson's "Ooo, Baby Baby."

OUR HEROES

MICHAEL GASPAR (SPECIAL EFFECTS COORDINATOR): "Explosions always seem to be, literally, your best bang for your buck—especially at night. They light up the sky. In season three we blew up the mineshaft. David comes running out, jumps in his car, and takes off. We were back in the desert and we set some charges on this hill to make it look like the explosion started to come from the hill and out from the mineshaft. It's nice to be able to have something that large. It was like fifty feet by a hundred feet. There was some real wood, but it was a lot of lightweight stuff . . . when it blew up it looked like it just disintegrated . . . so that while [Stunt Coordinator] Mike Massa was driving away in the car it wouldn't come down on him and hurt him. The crew gets the biggest kick out of the explosions. Everybody wants to see them at least once an episode."

"BIRTHDAY"

CASE № 3ADH11

ACTION TAKEN

It's Cordy's birthday and the team has cooked up a little surprise party to celebrate, but she comes up with a surprise of her

WRITTEN BY Mere Smith
DIRECTED BY Michael Grossman
GUEST STARS: Andy Hallett (Lorne), Patrick Breen (Nevin), Max Baker (Clerk), David Denman (Skip)
COSTARS: Heather Weeks (Tammy), Aimee Garcia (Cynthia)

own when a violently painful vision renders her unconscious. Cordelia's spirit leaves her body and tries to communicate with her friends about the girl in her vision while they worry that she is trapped in the coma-like state.

Fred and Gunn go to Cordy's place where—with Phantom Dennis's help—they find a year's worth of prescription painkillers and learn that Cordy has been keeping secret just how painful the visions have been. Cordy tries to possess Angel's body to write a note on the wall about her vision, but can't get the whole thing out when a whispering shadow crosses her path. As Angel wonders what he's doing on the floor, Wesley comes in to report that Cordelia is dying.

Cordelia's concern for herself increases exponentially when the shadow returns, crawling menacingly up the wall. A moment later a demon appears, but it turns out to be Skip, the rather laid-back guide sent by The Powers That Be (and freelance guard whom Angel had fought in order to free Billy from his little prison in Hell). Skip warns her that she will be dead soon if she does not follow him, so she does. He takes her to a "construct" of a mall where he explains that Doyle was never meant to give her the visions.

> **SKIP:** "Y'see, Cordelia, the visions are an ancient, powerful force. Demons are the only ones who can withstand them."
> **CORDELIA:** "I've had them for more than two years. Doesn't that mean I'm strong?"
> **SKIP:** "Strong, yes. Demon, no."

A journey of a different kind takes place after Angel forces Lorne to find a way for him to communicate

105

with The Powers That Be. Angel goes to a Conduit to The Powers to argue on Cordy's behalf. Unbeknownst to the vampire, Cordelia and Skip witness the part of his conversation in which he tries to convince the Conduit that Cordy is too weak to deal with the visions. Cordy and Skip leave before she can hear how deeply Angel cares for her. Cordelia accepts Skip's offer to rewrite her life, making her a famous TV star who had never met up with Angel in L.A.

As the star of the sitcom *Cordy!,* Cordelia has the life she always dreamed of, but something is nagging at her from her forgotten life. She makes an impromptu visit to the newly reopened Hyperion Hotel, where she tears back the wallpaper in what was formerly Angel's room and finds an address in Reseda. Unsure of where the numbers will lead, Cordelia goes to the city and meets a young fan who has just accidentally called up a demon.

Cordelia tries to help the girl escape when the front door bursts open, revealing Gunn and Wesley—minus one arm. They manage to defeat the demon, and Cordelia has a reunion with a very different Wesley from the one she had left in Sunnydale over two years earlier. She also learns that Angel is in L.A. but that he is also a changed man.

In this rewritten history, it was Angel who got the visions from Doyle. The visions, however, coupled with his retreat from humanity after his one human connection died, quickly drove him insane. He is a shell of his former self, babbling in a dark room. Cordelia tries to calm Angel and gives him a kiss that transfers the power of the visions back to her.

RESOLUTION

Skip pops up as soon as Cordelia remembers all that she had forgotten, and he reminds her of the deal they made. Cordelia insists that she was meant to have the visions because she was still led back to Angel. Skip insists that she's just not strong enough to harbor the power.

"Then find a loophole, Skip. I know my purpose in this world and it includes the visions. And if The Powers That Be aren't complete dumbasses, they know it too."   —*Cordelia*

It turns out there is a loophole, and Skip makes an offer to turn Cordelia part-demon. She quickly accepts the deal, even though there is no telling how her demon parts will reveal themselves.

Cordelia awakens to find her friends around her. They try to find out what happened, but Cordelia has already moved on to a new vision about a man in a park about to be attacked by a five-horned demon. The vision is not painful at all, but her friends are shocked to watch Cordelia float several feet off the ground.

DOSSIERS

CLIENT Cynthia York, who lives on 171 Oak Street in Reseda, calls forth a demon accidentally when she tries to bring her dad back home but spills some Diet Coke on the book she was using to cast the spell.

SUSPECTS The **no-eyed, three-mouthed monster** doesn't get a name or much screen time, but his arrival is much anticipated throughout the episode.

CONTINUITY

The team is in the process of cleaning up the lobby and what was left behind from the fight between Wolfram & Hart's commandos and Holtz's former demon minions in "Quickening." Angel recalls another time Cordy had problems with the visions; she was strapped to a hospital bed and Angel was told there was no hope in "To Shanshu in L.A." Lorne recalls the last time he tried to read Cordy, when she was having *other* vision problems in "Billy." Skip shows Cordy a little video clip from "Hero," when Doyle gave her the visions in a kiss before he died. He also reviews a clip from the premiere episode, "City Of," to show Cordelia what could have been. In the revised history, the last time Cordelia would have seen Wesley or Angel was in the *Buffy* "Graduation" episodes. Wesley says that it was a Kungai demon who took his arm a couple of years ago. This is likely a reference to the demon he interacted with in the original reality in his first mission with Angel and Cordelia in "Parting Gifts."

The *Cordy!* theme song is sung by *Buffy* Co-Executive Producer Marti Noxon.

OFFICE ROMANCE

Gunn has a nearly giddy reaction to Fred introducing herself to Phantom Dennis and a little sparkage seems to be flying. It is strongly implied that Doyle gave Cordelia the visions because he loved her, which is why The Powers were caught off guard, because they have no control over the free will associated with that emotion. Angel admits to the Conduit that he is more afraid of Cordelia dying than she is, implying that it is because he is in love with her.

QUOTE OF THE WEEK

"Most people who go astral, their spiritual shapes tend to be idealized versions of themselves. You know . . . straighten the nose, lose the gray, kind of a self-esteem thing. You're pretty confident, aren't you?"

Skip's reaction is understandable considering that Cordy's astral image looks exactly like her real self.

THE DEVIL IS IN THE DETAILS

EXPENSES

Cleaning supplies, presumably including the "extra-strength ick remover" Wesley used as a cover story for his shopping trip for Cordelia's party supplies and cake.

Cordelia has been paying for prescription pain medication for over a year. It's unclear whether this has been paid for through the company medical plan.

The team will have to replace the weapons cabinet.

DEMONS, ETC. . . .

Skip does not just work as a prison guard for The Powers That Be; he also serves as their guide.

Lorne's horns will regrow after being ripped off. The process takes a couple of days.

Only a Champion can speak to the **Conduit** to The Powers That Be. The Conduit refers to itself as "the gateway, the all-times, the ever." It is unseen and formless.

AS SCENE IN L.A.

All the outdoor scenes playing in the opening of *Cordy!* were filmed on the Paramount Pictures lot. Reseda is a subsection of greater Los Angeles.

THE PEN IS MIGHTIER

FINAL CUT

Cordelia deals with her fears on her own when no one can hear her.

"The last time I was this scared—I guess I was around eight or nine—and the clown just thought he was doing his job, but the way he twisted those balloon animals . . . For years I had nightmares that he'd come into my house and twist off my—"

POP CULTURE

* "Jude Law was a little busy?"

  Cordelia's birthday wish is for a visit from a certain movie star.

* "For the love of God, somebody get me a seabreeze."

  Lorne requests a cool and refreshing drink consisting of vodka, cranberry juice, and grapefruit juice.

* SKIP: "Actually, this is more of a construct of a mall. Like in *The Matrix*."

  CORDELIA: "You've seen *The Matrix*?"

  SKIP: "I love that flick. When Trinity's all 'Dodge this' and the agent just crumples to the . . . and I'm not really instilling awe anymore, am I?"

  The duo discusses the first movie in a trilogy of science fiction movies written and directed by the Wachowski brothers. And later, they have some more movie talk:

* SKIP: "It's noble, and heroic,

   and all that other Russell Crowe *Gladiator* crap."

  CORDELIA: "You've seen—?"

  SKIP: "Didn't love it . . ."

* "This process isn't easy. It'll make your vision-pain feel like a stroll through Candyland."

  Skip refers to the children's game by Milton Bradley.

OUR HEROES

SANDY STRUTH (SET DECORATOR): "The sitcom set was done on the *Dharma and Greg* set. We went in there and had it on their dark days. We took all their stuff out and dressed it all with our stuff. Then we shot it in one day and took it all away the next. They put in new walls and everything, but if you look at it again and watch *Dharma and Greg* you'll see little touches. We couldn't let anything be seen to give it away that it was *Dharma and Greg,* but we didn't switch everything out. They took out their post and all of their distinctive items. Then we brought all our stuff in, including a purple wall. We kept the windows, but we had to put in curtains. If you do just enough few things, nobody realizes. You can tell that the structure's there, but you would never know it in a million years.

"There's a lot more color in dressing a comedy and things that have a lot more fun to them. I feel you don't need to have as many reasons for things; you just put them there. In a lot of my sets, I have to know why it's there, at least in the back of my head. Because it was *Cordy!* I got to bring in modern, fun pieces. This was fun because it was colorful. There was never another set that [allowed me to] bring in as much color."

In the shooting script, an extensive scene from Cordy! was written in that had to be cut due to time constraints. Here is that sitcom scene. . . .

INT "CORDY" TV SET—NIGHT
The set's completely dark. We HEAR:

CORDY (O.S.)
O.K., turn on the lights.
The lights come on, showing us CORDELIA herself, in a hot and stylin' dress.
The studio audience bursts into applause. (Cordy's T.V. set is a loft/apt./workspace, mannequins draped with stylish clothes in various states of design.)

CORDY
What do you think?
Cordy's roommate and coworker LAUREN (who turned on the lights) checks out Cor and the dress.

LAUREN
(eh:)
Well, I guess it's all right if you go for that whole . . .
(wow)
IT'S GORGEOUS/FANTASTIC. OUR SHIP HAS FINALLY COME IN KIND OF THING! You in this dress, at the Buyer's Ball tonight, it's gonna put your label on the map. Your name's gonna be in lights.

CORDY
I don't want my name in lights, I want it sewn into that little tag that makes the back of your neck itch.

LAUREN
Oh it's happy dance time. We're doin' the happy dance.
Lauren does the happy dance—Cor joins in halfheartedly, and starts crying.

LAUREN (cont'd)
Yes, we're doin' the—sweetie, you can't cry during the happy dance, it's against the law.

109

CORDY
It's just . . . I miss Bobby. I wish he were taking me
to the stupid buyer's thing tonight.

LAUREN
He'll come around. It was just a
little misunderstanding.

CORDY
He found me in a hot tub—

LAUREN
You tripped. It could happen to anyone—

CORDY
With six male models—

LAUREN
It could almost happen to anyone—

CORDY
Everyone was naked.

LAUREN
Well that could only happen to you.
LAUGHTER from the studio audience.
The doorbell RINGS.

CORDY
Oh God, he's here.

LAUREN
It'll be fine. At least you won't have to
make conversation.

CORDY
Hey, Jack Richmond may not be a genius,
but he can make conversation.
(beat)
If you give him a topic.
(beat)
And an opinion.
(beat)
And you stick your hand up his butt and
work him like a puppet.

LAUREN
You're not going with Jack, you're going with
Helmut, the German designer.

CORDY
What? You said he said "nein."

LAUREN
He did.

CORDY
Well, that's German for no.

LAUREN
Also American for nine o'clock
More RINGING doorbell.

CORDY
But I told *Jack* nine.

LAUREN
Maybe you'll get lucky and
he'll think *you're* German.
Lauren moves to door, looks through peephole,
looks back at Cor, aghast.

CORDY
Tell me there aren't two men out there.

LAUREN
No

CORDY
Okay, that buys us a little time. Whichever
one showed, tell him I've come down with
something . . . deadly yet exotic . . . *consumption.*
I'll cough delicately in the background.
Cor heads fast for the o.s. bedroom.

LAUREN
Cordy, there's not two. There's three!
Bobby just showed up, with roses!

CORDY
Oh God, what am I gonna do? *(then, pleased)*
Bobby brought roses?

LAUREN
We're only seven floors up, you could jump.

CORDY
No. I've got to do the right thing. I'll just face them
all and . . . . do the right thing.

LAUREN
I don't like this "right thing" plan.

CORDY
Open the door.

Lauren slowly opens the door revealing:
three men. HELMUT and JACK (both in tuxes),
handsome and older than BOBBY, who's more Cor's
age, in casual clothes, a bunch of roses in hand.
Long beat as everyone looks at everyone else.
Then Cordy takes a deep breath . . . opens her mouth
to speak . . . and starts coughing pathetically.

STUDIO AUDIENCE APPLAUDS.

"PROVIDER"

CASE Nº 3ADH12

ACTION TAKEN

Now that things have settled down, Angel finally has a chance to worry about just how expensive it's going to be to raise a son. This sends him into overdrive trying to find new business. As Angel's money concerns grow into an obsession, Cordelia tries to keep him focused on their mission to help the helpless.

WRITTEN BY Scott Murphy
DIRECTED BY Bill Norton
GUEST STARS: Andy Hallett (Lorne), Laurel Holloman (Justine), Jeffrey Dean Morgan (Sam Ryan), Eric Bruskotter (Brian), Sunny Mabrey (Allison), Tony Pasqualini (Harlan Elster), and Keith Szarabajka (Holtz)
COSTARS: David Ramirez (Pizza Chef), Alan Henry Brown (Lead Nahdrah), Benjamin Benitez (Tat Vamp), Brett Wagner (Nahdrah Prince)

As the team starts fielding phone calls Holtz is busy training his first soldier, Justine, with a lesson in what happens when she doesn't listen to his instructions. Once the painful lesson is over, Justine agrees to stay, but only after belting Holtz as payback. Together, they start to build their army.

The hotel lobby is hopping and the staff of Angel Investigations is stretched to the limits just trying to speak with everyone who walks through the door. Cordelia continues to be the voice of reason, but Angel sees nothing but dollar signs as the team divvies up the caseload: Angel takes a call from a business owner that sends him running, Gunn meets with a young woman being stalked by her dead ex-boyfriend, and a group of Nahdrah come with an offer for Wesley. Lorne tries to translate the original request, though his skills are somewhat lacking.

"Can we get down to business? They want to buy your head—little rusty on the lingo, I should probably clarify that . . . They want your *mind.* They're celebrating the Prince's, uh, it's like a birthday only they're not so much born as disgorged, they need you to solve one of their traditional puzzles so they can give it to him. It's quite an honor."
—*Lorne*

But when Fred interrupts in her oh-so-cute and intellectual way, she both impresses the Nahdrah and sends them fleeing the hotel. When they return later it is to request her help instead of Wesley's, and they sweeten the deal with an offer of fifty thousand dollars.

Angel meets with an executive who complains of vampire extortion and offers Angel ten thousand dollars to get rid of the vamp gang. Angel takes out the three vamps only to find out later that the executive was a fraud and the check he wrote was worthless. Angel tracks the fake executive back to the nest and learns that the man only wanted to avenge his friend's death and has no money to offer. Angel also learns that he didn't kill the entire gang. After failed negotiations to get at least some money from the man, Angel winds up taking out the rest of the vamps, because he is a Champion, after all.

Gunn and Wesley escort their client, Allison, back to her place to protect her from her zombie ex-boyfriend. While on the case, each man realizes that the other has feelings for Fred, and the duo starts an aggressive game of one-upmanship that nearly distracts them from their mission when the ex-boyfriend, Brian, attacks. Gunn and Wesley manage to hold off Brian, which sends the zombie to sulk. Allison goes to talk to him and reveals that she had killed him since it was the easiest way to break up. Surprisingly the two reunite, leaving Wes and Gunn to simply ask if she'll be paying by cash or charge.

Fred and Lorne accompany the Nahdrah to their floating barge where Fred is put to work solving the puzzle for their prince. Lorne stumbles across the prince and learns that his original translation had been right and the Nahdrah do want the puzzle-solver's head. As it turns out, the puzzle is a test to prove that Fred is worthy of decapitation so her head can be fit onto the body of the prince.

RESOLUTION

While everyone is off on cases, Cordelia has a vision of Fred's headless future. Since she can't reach any of the team, she takes Connor and the fifty thousand and tries to return it to the Nahdrah. Just as things look their worst, the gang comes together and takes out the Nahdrah and Angel learns a valuable lesson.

ANGEL: "Money's important, but it isn't everything. I got carried away . . . I never had a life that was so totally dependent on me before, but that's no excuse . . ."

He looks back at the money. Loses his train of thought.

ANGEL: (cont'd) "Where was I?"

CORDELIA: "Money's not the most important—"

ANGEL: "No, it's not. What's important is family . . . and the mission."

He looks to Cor. They share a beat, then:
CORDELIA: "They tried to cut Fred's head off, we earned every penny."
ANGEL: "Hold the baby."
Angel hands Connor off to Cordy and heads for the dough with the others hot on his heels.

DOSSIERS

CLIENT Client #1 is originally believed to be **Harlan Elster,** although he is really **Sam Ryan,** a former employee of the real Harlan Elster and who was fired six months earlier.

Client #2, **Allison MacLaine,** hires the investigators after the police cannot help her deal with her stalker zombie ex-boyfriend.

Client #3 is a group of **Nahdrah** who originally claim to be trying to solve a puzzle as a gift for their prince.

CIVILIAN SUPPORT Lorne has to go through no small amount of firewater to loosen the tongue of his **Gar-wawk** snitch.

SUSPECTS The suspects in the case for Client #1 are the members of a **gang of vampires** who have a nest in what used to be low-income housing at the corner of 83rd and Vermont.

Brian is the aforementioned zombie ex-boyfriend stalking Client #2.

Considering their actions in trying to cut off Fred's head, Client #3, the **Nahdrah,** can also be considered suspects.

CONTINUITY

This episode serves as a perfect example of Cordelia's growth, as she was once obsessed with charging for the team's services, but now realizes that the important thing is the mission. Lorne learns that Holtz poisoned his Grappler demon minions and is now searching for human replacements. Angel is still having trouble working his voice mail but eventually gets Cordy's message.

OFFICE ROMANCE

Gunn and Wesley each realize that the other is interested in Fred. Angel and Cordelia continue to get closer, even ending the episode in bed together in a comfortably platonic fashion with Connor between them.

QUOTE OF THE WEEK

"Oooo, aren't we just the scary serial vamps with the spooky lair and the taking of trophies from our victims. Lame." Angel is less than impressed when he finds the vampires' nest.

THE DEVIL IS IN THE DETAILS

EXPENSES

Following the credo "You have to spend money to make money," Angel Investigations pays for six thousand flyers (and then an additional six thousand with the correct phone number), people to distribute both rounds of flyers, and fees associated with running a Web site (although these are lessened by the fact that Fred is the designer).

WEAPONRY

Aside from the usual stock of weapons in the cases, the team also uses the Nahdrah's silver pipe and briefcase full of money against the demons.

DEMONS, ETC. . . .

The **Nahdrah** speak in a series of clicks that Lorne sort of understands. Fred realizes that they are "puzzle people" when she sees the design on their tunics and realizes it is a series of "geometric shapes, each a prime number if you count the edges, arranged in an ascending order of exponential accumulation."

Wesley notes that it is a myth that **zombies** are flesh-eating creatures. He corrects the misassumption by clarifying that zombies merely mangle, mutilate, and occasionally wear human flesh.

AS SCENE IN L.A.

Angel's case takes him to 83rd & Vermont, which is in the heart of Los Angeles proper.

THE PEN IS MIGHTIER

FINAL CUT

Angel's love of money is perfectly captured in the following stage directions:
Angel quickly folds the check in his hand (oh yeah, he never let go of that) and stuffs it in his pocket. Then he closes the briefcase, and holds it to his chest as one would a beloved child.

POP CULTURE

✳ **"Lorne? It's all snap, crackle, pop to me."**
Cordelia compares the Nahdrah language to the sounds made by the Kellogg's cereal Rice Krispies.

✳ **"Nice décor . . . sort of Jules Verne meets Leona Helmsley."**
Lorne describes the Nahdrah's floating home as a cross between something dreamed up by the author of *20,000 Leagues Under the Sea* and the real estate tycoon who owns several posh hotels and is nicknamed "The Queen of Mean."

OUR HEROES

ALEXIS DENISOF: "The season got off and the tension began to build quite rapidly with the love triangle that was developing with Wesley, Fred, and Gunn. We had set up a nice bond between Wesley and Gunn in the second season where they really had each other's backs. Even though they were an odd partnership their first meeting, it's exactly that which makes them such fast friends later on and the fact that they can rely on each other so much. But Fred becomes an emotional wrench in the works for the relationship between Gunn and Wesley.

"A situation like that affords a lot of awkward communication and hurt feelings and embarrassment all around. That's how those things go down. Nobody knows quite how to handle it, nor should they. It is an awkward situation. Their lives do depend on each other; for all the wise-cracking and other stuff that goes on we try to always come back to the fact that these people save each other's lives regularly and rely on each other and work as a very well oiled machine. It made the emotional problems all the more poignant."

AMY ACKER ON PHYSICS-SPEAK: "I try to figure out what they're talking about. A lot of times I'll be on the Internet looking up these words and stuff. And then I'll ask, 'What is this?' And the writers will say, 'Oh, I just made that up.' So, I'm like, 'Oh, no wonder I've spent two hours trying to figure out what it meant. It doesn't mean anything.' Now I just try to memorize it, but it's so much harder to memorize something if you have no idea what you're talking about. I usually call and say, 'Is this a real thing or did you just open a random book and write out the words?'"

"WAITING IN THE WINGS"

CASE Nº. 3ADH13

ACTION TAKEN

As Cordelia works to convince Wesley that it's time he made his feelings for Fred known, Fred returns from a very friendly breakfast with Gunn. It seems like the perfect romantic evening is in store for the entire team when Angel comes in with tickets to the Blinnikov World Ballet's performance of *Giselle*. The troupe is only in town for one night and Angel still recalls their moving rendition of the same ballet back in 1890.

While Cordelia and Fred go shopping for knockout dresses they get into a conversation about a certain coworker and feelings that may exist. Unfortunately Cordy thinks Fred is talking about Wesley when she's really talking about Gunn. At the same time, Lorne is pushing Angel to open up about his own feelings toward Cordelia.

WRITTEN & DIRECTED BY
Joss Whedon
GUEST STARS: Andy Hallett (Lorne), Mark Harelik (The Count)
COSTARS: Mark Lutz (Groosalugg), Rodney Peck (Manager), Don Tiffany (Security Guard), Summer Glau (Dancer)

"You're a man of many limitations, Angel. But you're a man. You got a heart. And Cordelia is a hell of a lady. If I thought she liked to wear green I'd be elbowing you out of the way. But she's out of my league. She's a Champion, Angel. Old school. Besides, we all know you got a thing for ex-cheerleaders."
—*Lorne*

Dressed to the nines, the five members of Angel Investigations leave for the ballet, leaving Lorne to baby-sit. The first act of the ballet is quite moving, especially to Gunn, who hadn't expected to enjoy the evening. The performance is also memorable in another way—Angel is certain that he saw the exact same ballet with the exact same performers over a century ago.

At intermission Angel and a decidedly bored Cordelia check out

backstage while the others stay to watch the rest of the show. Things take an interesting turn when Angel and Cordelia hear a mixture of laughter and tears in the mazelike backstage area that is impossibly larger than the building would allow. They also stumble across a dressing room with a hot—and rather steamy—spot of energy in which their bodies are taken over by past lovers reenacting a very private moment.

At home, Lorne sings Connor a lullaby that is interrupted by a suspicious noise. When he goes to investigate, he finds something quite shocking. Meanwhile, back at the ballet, Wesley, Fred, and Gunn are concerned that their friends have been gone so long, and they make their own trip backstage. As they search the maze a pair of men with theatrical comedy and tragedy masks attack them and injure Gunn.

Cordelia realizes that she and Angel need to go back and play out the love scene because there could be important information that could tell them how to deal with the odd situation. Angel is reluctant to experience the steamy scenario since his feelings for Cordelia could be exposed . . . along with other things. Reluctantly, they go back to the dressing room and determine that the count who owned the company had a thing for his prima ballerina in spite of her love for her costar. Before they can complete the scenario, another pair of mask-faced men attacks.

Fred tends to Gunn's wounds and her concern exhibits itself in a kiss, which Wesley witnesses. As he steps away from the duo he, too, hits a hotspot and learns that the count had pulled the ballerina out of time and out of any reality beyond his theater, swearing that she would dance for him forever. After fighting off their respective masked men, the group reconvenes and determines that Angel must find the count and destroy his power source while the others distract the count by fighting the minions under his control.

RESOLUTION

As the gang fights off a growing army of mask-faced men, Angel breaks through the barrier to the theater wings and finds the prima ballerina about to take stage. She wishes that Angel could help her but is resigned to her fate.

"There's a section in the first act, during the courtship dance, where my foot slips. My ankle is turned and I don't quite hold . . . every time. He doesn't notice. He doesn't even know ballet that well. But always, at that moment, I slip. It isn't just the same ballet. It's the same performance. I don't dance. I echo."
—*The Dancer*

Angel convinces the dancer to fight against the count's power and change her dance, to distract the count. She does as requested and Angel smashes the count's medallion, allowing the ballerina her final bow.

The gang returns home, where Wesley tends to Gunn's wounds while trying to ignore the obvious attraction between Gunn and Fred. Angel finally starts to admit his feelings for Cordelia but is interrupted when Lorne comes down with a surprise visitor. The Groosalugg from Pylea has crossed dimensions to find his lost love, Princess Cordelia.

DOSSIERS

CLIENT Angel and the gang realize they have to rescue the **prima ballerina** in order to get themselves out of the theater's maze.

CIVILIAN SUPPORT It seems as if the **security guard** is going to let Angel and Cordy backstage, but when the bribe doesn't work out, Angel is forced to rely on his "Patented Sudden Burst of Violence."

SUSPECTS Count Kurskov and his **minions** with faces of either comedy or tragedy

CONTINUITY

Cordelia playfully reminds Wesley of the time he had a crush on her during the third season of *Buffy.* Gunn and Fred return from a breakfast together; they will share more of these breakfast dates in the future. Cordelia had to leave her love, the Groosalugg, behind in Pylea in "There's No Place Like Plrtz Glrb."

Amy Acker was right at home in the ballet scenes because she used to be a ballerina. A dream sequence featuring her and Alexis Denisof had to be cut from the episode for time.

OFFICE ROMANCE

All the office romances are kicked up a notch this week when Fred and Gunn get together under Wesley's jealously watchful eyes and Angel nearly admits his feelings to Cordelia as Groo shows up on their doorstep. It's also the return of "Kyrumption"—Lorne and Angel discuss the Pylean word, previously mentioned by Fred in "Offspring." Angel refers to a previous time when he was possessed, that time by the spirits of lovers from the fifties in the *Buffy* episode "I Only Have Eyes for You."

QUOTE OF THE WEEK

"Oh yeah. I saw their production of *Giselle* in 1890. I cried like a baby. And I was evil!"

Angel remembers that performance fondly.

THE DEVIL IS IN THE DETAILS

EXPENSES

Five tickets to the Blinnikov Ballet, possible tuxedo rentals (depending on whether some of the guys have their own), and possible dress purchases (if Cordy and Fred's battle-worn garments are unreturnable).

WEAPONRY

Much of the gang makes handy use of the minions' swords. Angel also uses one of their daggers and Fred uses a conveniently placed prop.

THE PLAN

WESLEY: "This kind of temporal shift can't just exist, it has to be maintained. That requires power and concentration. If we can overload him somehow, we might be able to slip back to the real world."

GUNN: "Man with a plan."

And later . . .

WESLEY: "Find his power source and destroy it. We'll try to loosen his hold."

GUNN: "By making more monsters? Man with a frightening plan."

DEMONS, ETC. . . .

Sorialus the Ravager is a six-breasted demon who will be arriving in a month to destroy the humans who killed her mate, according to one of Cordelia's visions.

Count Kurskov is a wizard.

THE PEN IS MIGHTIER

FINAL CUT

After Fred reveals a little too much of her personal history with *The Nutcracker,* she and Cordy have the following exchange:

FRED: "I often could shut up more."

CORDELIA: "It's overrated."

FRED: "*The Nutcracker?*"

CORDELIA: "Shutting up."

POP CULTURE

✻ **"Well, get it done, Johnnie Reb."**
Cordelia invokes the nickname for Confederate soldiers during the Civil War.

✻ **"Time I saw Mahta Hari at the Troubadour."**
Gunn refers to a club in Hollywood.

✻ **"You got ballet on my Mahta Hari tickets."**
Gunn does a riff on a line from the old Reese's Peanut Butter Cups commercial: "You got chocolate in my peanut butter."

✻ **". . . my family went to *The Nutcracker* every Christmas and I had my first sexual dream about the Mouse King."**
Fred refers to the holiday ballet with music composed by Tchaikovsky.

✻ **"I'm with Snoopy."**
Cordelia talks about the famed beagle from the *Peanuts* comic strip.

✳ **"You wanna wander around backstage like Spinal Tap for the next . . . ever?"**
Cordelia brings up the mock band and their tendency to get lost looking for the stage in the film *This is Spinal Tap*.

THE NAME GAME

"Waiting in the Wings" is a term used in theater to refer to performers offstage awaiting their entrances.

SIX DEGREES OF . . .

Summer Glau, the dancer, may appear familiar to fans of Joss Whedon's work, as she also appeared as River Tam, one of the main characters on the series *Firefly*.

OUR HEROES

AMY ACKER: "I was really surprised because during the first half of the season there were lines that led me to think that I was going to be with Wesley. As an actress I felt that I was playing up the sort of thing that I had feelings for Wesley. I didn't find out that I was going to be with Gunn until like episode twelve and it happened in thirteen. So I was like, 'Oh, I should have been doing something to make it seem like I liked Gunn.' It was sort of shocking to me as an actress, but once it happened and the whole story line of us being in that magical place and us kissing, it was great. I mean, there was a part of me that missed getting to play that I liked both of them and having the sort of thing where you didn't know what was going to happen. But then having those two-person scenes with just Gunn and that relationship-building stuff really was fun to do."

SANDY STRUTH (SET DECORATOR): "I think one of the highlights for me for the whole season was the ballet episode. That was wonderful. I love that whole episode. I love the fact that we did a whole show around a ballet. Who would think that an hour drama meant for the younger audiences would risk doing it? And we went all the way with it. I loved it because so much of it took place in that dressing room. And they gave me the time and the money to really work on that. We were working on that for days and creating layer upon layer of Victorian pieces. It's been sitting for a hundred years and that's where my theater background helped me because I know those dressing rooms and I know the era. I had a lot of fun with that and Joss really used that room. We saw every inch of it. He embraced it, which I think was just really wonderful for me."

ROBERT HALL (SPECIAL EFFECTS MAKEUP ARTIST) ON THE COMEDY/TRAGEDY MASKS ON THE MINIONS:
"Joss knew exactly what he wanted. I remember doing the masks and we were sculpting them and I was thinking they were kind of a little boring, a little ho-hum. And I showed them to Joss and he looked at them in a meeting, and I think he was probably visualizing them in black and white, which a lot of producers can't do. If you show them a clay sculpture they can't get it. Joss immediately looked at it and I think he just took out all the color in his mind and pictured it in black and white and said, 'Yeah, these terrify me. Go ahead, mold them.'"

"COUPLET"

CASE Nº 3ADH14

ACTION TAKEN

Lorne helps Angel out of his tux from his recent trip to the ballet and tries to get a read on the vampire's reaction to finding Cordelia's Groosalugg at the hotel upon their return. Angel tries to convince Lorne that he's fine with the surprise, but the empath has trouble buying that. Meanwhile, at Cordy's place, the Groosalugg fills in his princess on how he was deposed from his rule of Pylea, and the pair starts to get a little more personal. But a passionate kiss is interrupted when Cordelia gets a vision of a demon.

The next morning Wesley joins Angel in silent suffering from his own lost chance at romance. Wesley, however, puts his mind to use by trying to work out the question of just how Connor has come to be. As they discuss the situation Cordelia arrives—with Groo in tow—to tell them about her vision. Wesley pages Fred and Gunn away from their breakfast and the team sets about finding the demon.

Angel reluctantly takes Groo along through the sewers, where the pair takes on the demon. When it escapes into the sunlight, Angel is forced to stay in darkness while Groo goes out and rescues a damsel in distress by slaying the demon, and receives accolades as a hero.

Back at the hotel another client has come through the door, seeking help with her philandering fiancé. Although it sounds like the fiancé simply fell into an online affair, the woman swears it must be witchcraft. Wesley sends Gunn away to investigate what is probably a wild goose chase and is disheartened when Fred goes along. In the meantime Angel and Wesley go to a shop to find a rare book containing commentary on the Nyazian texts and Angel admits to feeling more and more useless with Groo around.

WRITTEN BY Tim Minear & Jeffrey Bell
DIRECTED BY Tim Minear
GUEST STARS: Andy Hallett (Lorne), Mark Lutz (Groosalugg)
COSTARS: Fanshen Cox (Anita), Bob Rumnock (Business Man), Steven Hack (Lionel), Marisa Matarazzo (Susan), Bernard K. Addison (Root Monster)

"Angel, you're the reason we all come together. It's your mission which animates us. We each contribute, it's true, but you . . . you're unique."
                                                                                    —*Wesley*

Wesley's words don't exactly ring true when Angel returns to the hotel and finds that Cordelia has given Groo a makeover including a haircut and lending him Angel's clothes. The similarities between Angel and

Groo are becoming uncanny, leading Angel to feel even more useless. Cordelia, however, finds a use for Angel. Concerned that she could pass her visions on to Groo should they ever . . . Com-Shuk . . . Cordelia has found out about a mystical prophylactic to protect her. She asks Angel to accompany Groo to the brothel where he can purchase the potion.

In the meantime Gunn and Fred are staking out their client's fiancé while he waits for his online love at a park, but they get distracted when their lips find each other in a makeout session. Once the two pull apart, they find that the fiancé is gone. Luckily they were recording the encounter and rewind the tape to see the man sucked into the ground beside a tree about a moment before they get sucked down by the roots themselves.

Beneath the tree Fred and Gunn get entangled in the roots of a tree-like monster with a DSL connection. The demon lures people to it so it can drain the life from them. Gunn calls Angel and Groo for an assist, but when the pair arrives Groo barrels in and gets caught as well.

RESOLUTION

As the root monster drains Groo's life, Angel comes in and works out his inferiority complex aloud, convincing the root monster that he's a much more worthy victim. The ruse works and the demon lashes out at Angel, sucking the life from his heart—the problem is, Angel has no life in his heart. Angel weakens the demon enough for everyone to escape and then kills it.

Back at the hotel Wesley tells Gunn that he knows about the budding relationship with Fred and that he, Wesley, will just have to accept it. Angel has to accept things too and gives Cordelia a wad of cash and tells her to take a vacation with Groo. Angel realizes that he's not alone since he has his son, but Wesley makes a much darker realization. He finally manages to decipher one last part of the Nyazian prophecy, though he doesn't share with Angel what is written out on the page in front of him.

"The father will kill the son."

DOSSIERS

CLIENT Following their rescue of an **unnamed woman** from the demon in Cordelia's vision, the team is hired by **Susan Frakes** to look into the supposed witch who tempted her fiancé, **Jerry,** away from her.

CIVILIAN SUPPORT Unrelated to the case, Cordelia gets a prophylactic potion from a demon madam named **Anita,** and Wesley purchases a rare book from a dealer named **Lionel.**

SUSPECTS The suspect, known by its screen name, **Hotblonde37159,** turns out to be a kind of **root monster.**

CONTINUITY

The episode opens at the end of the evening that began in "Waiting in the Wings" and deals with the emotional fallout from that episode. Wesley works to translate the commentary on the Nyazian Scroll, which Lilah stole in "Lullaby." The prophecy that he ultimately translates will have far-reaching effects on the team for months to come. Cordelia is concerned that having sex with the Groosalugg will transfer her visions to him, as was detailed in "There's No Place Like Plrtz Glrb."

OFFICE ROMANCE

Gunn and Fred get accustomed to the idea of shifting their relationship to a romantic level during one of their breakfasts together. They don't think anyone knows about them, but Wesley later reveals to Gunn that he is aware of the relationship and upset that Gunn didn't tell him.

QUOTE OF THE WEEK

"Everyone makes such a big deal: 'The Groosalugg, he's a Champion, he's so rugged, so emotionally available . . . look at him in the daylight.' Well, I'm smarter and stronger and I pick out my own clothes."

Angel gets to work out his aggressions toward Groo under the guise of his plan to attack the root demon.

THE DEVIL IS IN THE DETAILS

EXPENSES

Angel loses not one, but two shirts when he and Groo are attacked by the root monster.

Cordelia nearly cleans out her bank account to pay for the potion so she and Groo can Com-Shuk. Later Angel gives her a wad of cash so she can go on vacation.

WEAPONRY

While tracking the demon from Cordy's vision, Angel is given a small ax and Cordelia gives Groo Angel's favorite broadsword.

DEMONS, ETC. . . .

The demon from Cordelia's vision is known as a **Senih'D.** It manifests in its physical form only to feed. Immediately upon rising it will search for a victim. According to Groo, it resembles the **Bleaucha,** which nests in the Scum Pits of Ur. He has slain many and admits that tracking the demon will be simple, but killing it will be more difficult.

The **root crazy, tree-like demony thing** uses its DSL connection to lure its victims to it by chatting up lonely hearts online and then literally draining the energy from those hearts. Fred doesn't believe that it has any vital organs and one could probably hack at it for hours without doing any damage. However, once it is weakened, a sword to its face is quite effective.

THE PEN IS MIGHTIER

FINAL CUT

After Wesley compares Angel's uniqueness to the rare volumes in the bookseller's shop, not only does Lionel announce that he has three copies of the book Wesley requested, but he goes even further to unintentionally cut down Angel by admitting:

"Cover's coming off this one. I'll give you twenty percent off and a free bookmark."

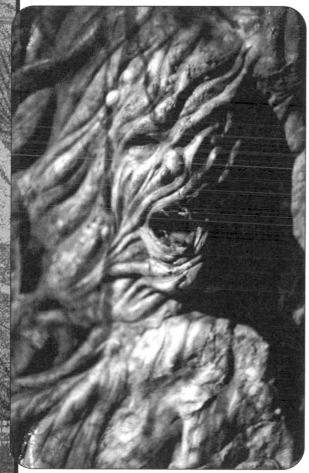

POP CULTURE

* **"Fine, Miss Garbo. Have it your way. Be alone."**
  Lorne compares Angel to the silver screen legend Greta Garbo, who chose to live her later years in seclusion.
* **"Oh wait, it's not like your strength is in your hair or anything like that, right?"**
  Cordelia is concerned that the source of Groo's powers might be like Samson's in the biblical story of Samson and Delilah.
* **"So, we lose the *Battlefield Earth* hair and get you out of those animal skins . . ."**
  Cordelia compares Groo's long locks to those of the characters in the film based on L. Ron Hubbard's book.

THE NAME GAME

A **"couplet"** is two successive lines of a poem or song that either rhyme or have the same meter.

SIX DEGREES OF . . .

Bernard K. Addison, the root monster, also played Cop #1 in the *Buffy* episode "Dead Things," which aired only two weeks before this episode.

OUR HEROES

ROBERT HALL (SPECIAL EFFECTS MAKEUP ARTIST): "The root demon was tough. That was when we were airing so many back to back and it was really just killing us time-wise. Originally we were going to do it just all animatronic, but Tim Minear was pretty specific that he wanted a guy's face in there to have him emote and say the lines. I was a little concerned about that, just because I wasn't sure it wouldn't look like Mac the Knife, with a guy's head stuck in a thing. But I think it wound up working fine for what it was. We gave him some really cool stuff with the dentures that we'd never really done before. His teeth are actually roots that are really long and twisty and they stick out of his mouth.

"With that one in particular we worked with Stuart [Blatt, production designer] a lot, telling him, 'This is our guy. This is our design. Can we make a hole here? Can we cut this stuff out? Can we give him something to stand on?' Something like that we definitely work with Stuart a lot on. He's always awesome. He's really brilliant and does great stuff."

"LOYALTY"

CASE № 3ADH15

ACTION TAKEN

Wesley wakes from a dream in which he watches Angel kill his son, and is determined not to see it become reality. He continues to work on the Nyazian prophecy and watch over Connor, even accompanying Angel on a trip to the doctor. Everything seems perfectly fine until one of the waiting mothers sneaks into the exam room after Angel leaves and takes a vial of Connor's blood.

WRITTEN BY Mere Smith
DIRECTED BY James A. Contner
GUEST STARS: Stephanie Romanov (Lilah), Laurel Holloman (Justine), Jack Conley (Sahjhan), Wendy Davis (Aubrey Jenkins), Enrique Castillo (Doctor), and Keith Szarabajka (Holtz)
COSTARS: Susan Martino (Mother #1), Annie Talbot (Mother #2), Marci Hill (Nurse), Chris Devlin (Holtzian Man), Kerrigan Mahan (Jollyburger), Thom Scott II (Holtzian Man #2)

Otherwise things have been slow since Cordelia left for vacation. When a potential client named Aubrey Jenkins walks in the door with a sad tale of her son being turned into a vampire and her having to watch as he went up in flames, the team springs into action. Gunn takes Fred along on a recon mission to the pier where the boy was known to go when he was human.

Since it's daytime Gunn decides that they can take some time to have a little fun with the carnival games. Fred, however, tries to keep him focused on their work, since she had a strange conversation with Wesley in which he made her feel guilty about dating on the job. Gunn reveals that Wes knows about their relationship and more strangeness ensues between the two of them over whether the office romance is appropriate. As day turns to night the simple recon mission turns into a trap laid by Holtz, from which Gunn escapes—just barely—thanks to an assist from Fred.

Gunn isn't the only one getting an assist when Sahjhan, tired of waiting for Holtz to finish the job, contacts Lilah at Wolfram & Hart. Although Lilah is officially forbidden to harm Angel, she unofficially offers her help by sharing some of Connor's stolen blood with the demon for his secret plan.

Wesley is also making new friends when he contacts the Loa, a powerful being that rests in the form of a Jollyburger drive-through speaker statue. Wesley tries to find a way to invalidate the prophecy that Angel will kill his son, but only learns when the event will occur.

> "The first portent will shake the earth. The second will burn the air. The last will turn the sky to blood."
> —*Jollyburger (the Loa)*

Aubrey returns to the hotel to pay for services rendered, and she uses the opportunity to ask Wesley on a date. As the pair discusses the situation, Aubrey reveals too much and Angel appears to let her know that they're on to her—she's with Holtz. With a threat to Holtz to keep away from his people, Angel lets her go, although he isn't aware that Wesley follows her to where Holtz is training his small army. Wesley tries to convince Holtz that he is going after the wrong man since Angelus is gone, but Holtz refuses to listen.

RESOLUTION

The following morning Gunn and Fred recap their conversation about workplace romance and worry that Wesley may make them choose between their love and the mission. For Gunn, it's not a difficult choice.

> "I've been fightin' vamps and demons since I was a kid. That sense of doin' good, or gettin' up in the morning and making the world safer, better . . . I've always had that . . . But I've never had a Fred before . . . If we have to . . . I choose you."
> —*Gunn*

But Gunn isn't the only one able to make choices, and Wesley finally realizes that Angel has free will and would never choose to hurt his child. Wesley even begins to laugh off the prophecy, when a huge earthquake rocks Los Angeles. As Wes and Angel navigate the debris in Angel's room, the gas stove kicks over, sending a fireball into the air. Angel manages to save Connor and Wesley, but gets a nasty cut on his forehead in the process. The blood drips off his face and colors the sky blue baby blanket red, marking the final of the three portents—earthquake, fire, and blood.

DOSSIERS

CLIENT Aubrey Jenkins comes in under the guise of being a client mourning the death of her son **Timothy.** In reality she is working with Holtz to avenge her son's death.

CIVILIAN SUPPORT Unrelated to the case, Wesley enlists the help of a **wizard,** presumably to find the location of **the Loa.**

SUSPECTS Holtz and **Justine** have a small band of soldiers all presumably looking to avenge the loss of a loved one, like Holtz, Justine, and Aubrey. **Sahjhan** and **Lilah** team up to see that the prophecy comes to fruition.

CONTINUITY

The team has not heard from Cordelia since she and Groo left for vacation. Presumably she isn't being sent visions while she's away. Angel says that he can't wait to watch Connor grow up and lose his first tooth, learn to ride a bike, and pick out his tux for his senior prom. As fate would have it, Angel will see none of those things. Lilah already knows about Sahjhan, thanks in part to the woman in files and records whom she met in "Dad."

OFFICE ROMANCE

Prior to the realization that Aubrey is working for their enemy, Fred suggests that Wesley might want to consider asking the client out. Wesley responds by pointing out that they are there to do a job, not find dates, in a not-so-subtle comment on Fred and Gunn's budding relationship.

QUOTE OF THE WEEK

"Love the whole chained-undead look you got goin' on. Really sets off your fern."

Sahjhan comments on Holtz's new digs.

THE DEVIL IS IN THE DETAILS

EXPENSES

Angel's room in the hotel is pretty much demolished by the earthquake.

WEAPONRY

Gunn and Fred rely on some broken rails at the carousel to take out the vampires.

DEMONS, ETC. . . .

Sahjhan is formally known as a "time-shifter." Although he cannot be killed in his noncorporeal form, Holtz does warn that he can trap the demon's dimensional essence in a Resikhian urn forever. Sahjhan claims to have invented daylight saving time.

The Loa is in statue form as a Jollyburger drive-through speaker from a chain of fast-food restaurants. It has the power to provide answers to Wesley's questions, but first an offering must be made. It can also shoot bolts of energy.

THE VAMPIRE RULES

"Once someone becomes a vampire, there's no turning back. No matter how much you want to believe there's some part of them you can save, all that's left is an evil thing."

Angel points out the realities of vampirism, though he stands as a testament to the fact that the rules can be broken.

AS SCENE IN L.A.

Fred and Gunn are all over the Santa Monica Pier in this episode. The carousel where Gunn and Fred battle the vampires was built in 1916, and the building housing it is a historical landmark.

THE PEN IS MIGHTIER

FINAL CUT

The following emasculating exchange was cut from Wesley's dream:

FRED: "Do we have to wake him up? He's just so cute and rumpled and puppy-like . . . Of course, I prefer big dogs."

GUNN: "You shouldn't call a guy those things. It's like neutering him."

POP CULTURE

✳ ". . . the road to Hell, right?"

Dream Angel refers to the proverb "The road to Hell is paved with good intentions."

✳ "Recruiting a bunch of paramilitary Moonie freaks to run around playing Candid Camera with Angel's buddies?"

Sahjhan refers to the nickname for the followers of cult leader Sun Myung Moon and the TV series in which unsuspected people were basically tricked on camera to make fools of themselves.

OUR HEROES

J. AUGUST RICHARDS: "What's funny is that it is an important issue in the African-American community about black men on television constantly dating white female characters. So when we were doing it, I was expecting a little bit of flack from my black female actress friends. So the first episode aired—I didn't hear a word. The second episode aired—I didn't hear a word. The third episode, I finally had to ask. I said, 'Nobody's said anything about the fact that I got this white girlfriend on the show.' And my friend was like, 'Nah. She chose you over the English guy!'"

"SLEEP TIGHT"

CASE Nº 3ADH16

ACTION TAKEN

As Angel Investigations recovers from the earthquake damage, Angel himself seems to be a little on edge. This is particularly noticeable when Kim, a human client, tells the team about the band of demons she unknowingly joined as lead singer. Angel is chomping at the bit for some action and finds it when he nearly single-handedly takes on the band and takes off one of the demon's arms.

Justine seems to be having second thoughts about Holtz's plan when she expresses concern for Angel's human coworkers. Her unease is pushed aside, however, when Wesley shows up in Holtz's training room. The conversation is tense, but Wesley does discern Holtz's true intentions toward Connor, and just how much he knows of the situation.

WRITTEN BY David Greenwalt
DIRECTED BY Terrence O'Hara
GUEST STARS: Andy Hallett (Lorne), Stephanie Romanov (Lilah), Laurel Holloman (Justine), Jack Conley (Sahjhan), Marina Benedict (Kim), and Keith Szarabajka (Holtz)
COSTARS: Jeff Denton (Lead Guitar), Jhaemi Willens (Drummer), Robert Forrest (Warrior #2), J. Scott Shonka (Commando #1)

"Your problem isn't me right now. Your problem is your friend who's going to kill his own child. You know you have to do something about it . . . Don't misunderstand me, I won't stand by while an innocent child is murdered. But I won't attack and endanger other innocent lives, unless I'm forced to."
—Holtz

The duo comes to an unspoken agreement that everyone will remain safe so long as Wesley takes Connor away from Angel, for good.

What Wesley doesn't know is that Angel's increasingly agitated behavior has a cause. After Angel freaks out one too many times, Fred examines the pig's blood he's been drinking and finds that it's been spiked with a touch of the human kind—namely, Connor's.

Angel goes for a chat with Lilah, knowing that she was behind the blood tampering. She admits to her complicity, and, in the midst of their verbal sparring, Sahjhan appears. He saw the meeting and misunderstood the situation, thinking that Lilah had betrayed him. However, he doesn't learn of his mistake until after he reveals too much to his "sworn enemy," Angel. The problem is that Angel doesn't even recognize the guy, nor does he have a clue why the demon is after him.

Wesley returns to the hotel and starts packing Connor's things when Lorne interrupts. Wes is forced into a cover story that he's taking Connor for an overnight stay, but a short serenade to the baby reveals his true plan to the empath. Wesley is forced to beat Lorne unconscious so he can escape, but not before having to get past Angel, Gunn, and Fred with more deception.

After Wesley leaves—but before the team can investigate the strange moaning coming from his office—Holtz arrives with his small army. It appears they have come to collect the baby, and attack when they find Connor is not there. The battle is brief, with Holtz ditching in the middle. As the team surveys the damage, the newly conscious Lorne reveals that Wesley has teamed with Holtz and taken Connor for good.

Wesley's plan, however, takes a dramatic turn when a limping and beaten Justine approaches him as he tries to flee his home. She plays him with the story that Holtz beat her when she asked too many questions, but it's all a ruse. She takes the child and slits Wesley's throat, leaving him to die.

RESOLUTION

Word spreads about the abduction and Lilah calls in the commandos to track Holtz, who now has the baby. Angel, in turn, follows the commandos, and everyone meets up under the Sixth Street Bridge. The commandos train their weapons on Holtz and the baby but are ordered not to fire. During the standoff Angel gets the drop on one of the commandos and takes his gun, aiming it at Lilah, realizing the only way for his child to get away safely is with Holtz. Then Sahjhan arrives to express his extreme displeasure over the fact that no one among them seems to want the child dead. Hoping to fix that, Sahjhan opens a demon dimension.

> "What you're looking into is the Quor-toth: the darkest of dark worlds. So . . . I can widen the portal and you can all be swallowed up by a world you cannot begin to imagine. Or you can keep your world and kill that child. Now."
>
> —*Sahjhan*

Lilah's sense of self-preservation immediately surfaces and she orders the commandos to fire. Holtz takes all the distractions as an opportunity and jumps into Quor-toth with Connor. Pleased by the turn of events, Sahjhan closes the portal and everyone leaves Angel to suffer . . . alone.

DOSSIERS

CLIENT Kim is a former client of Lorne's whom he set on the right life path a couple of years earlier. At the time she was in medical school, but Lorne convinced her that her voice was her calling. She hires the team to look into her band.

SUSPECTS The band of **Wraithers** she unknowingly joined. In the unrelated case, Angel has to deal with all his old enemies, including **Holtz** and **Lilah,** as well as the old enemy he never knew he had in **Sahjhan.**

CONTINUITY

Angel is still unwilling to interrupt Cordelia's vacation with the Groosalugg. Sahjhan and Lilah teamed up for the plan to spike Angel's blood in the previous episode, "Loyalty." Among Lilah's justifications for her actions includes the fact that her job allows her to take care of a mother who doesn't recognize her, as evidenced during a phone conversation in "Loyalty."

QUOTE OF THE WEEK

"Hey . . . *vampire* . . . need to drink something red. It doesn't make me a . . . blood-aholic."

Angel tries to justify his recent behavior.

THE DEVIL IS IN THE DETAILS

EXPENSES

The team is still in the midst of cleaning up the earthquake damage, for which Wesley reminds Angel that they have no insurance. Later the lobby experiences more uninsured damage during Holtz's attack, including yet another smashing of the weapons cabinet.

The cell phones used by the team are company phones, a point that Wesley reminds Gunn and Fred of when they use them for their cutesy romantic phone calls.

WEAPONRY

Aside from the usual complement of weapons against the Wraithers and Holtz's men, Lorne's high-pitched singing voice also does some damage. Wesley pulls a gun when protecting Connor from an unknown person approaching them.

DEMONS, ETC. . . . .

Kim unknowingly joins a band comprising **Wraithers,** demons who can make themselves look human for a period of about two weeks before reverting to what they really are. The only way to deal with the demons is to kill them. Kim's proximity to the demons has infected her and is turning her demon, though it isn't permanent. Fred suggests a mystical antibiotic of twenty milligrams of cylenthium powder twice a day for a month to combat the infection.

THE PEN IS MIGHTIER

FINAL CUT

The following stage directions humorously describe the battle between the team and the Wraithers:

During the fight—Gunn mostly watches Angel go insane; he should hit or kick one guy and eventually get a shot off, taking out one of the demons with an arrow through the neck (hey, you're in a hurry? Lose the shot through the neck); Fred gets the girls outside, comes back in, watching in shock as Angel tears these guys apart (quite literally, at one point, pulling one of the guy's arms off.)

The fight will include belting someone on the back with a guitar, etc. We've never seen Angel fight with this much pure animal carnage (all right, not since he was a beast at the end of last year, anyway; who am I, Shakespeare?).

POP CULTURE

* **"You look like hell—and not the fun one where they burn you with hot pokers for all eternity, but the hard-core one, with Nixon and Britney Spears."**

   Angel jokingly refers to a form of damnation worthy of the likes of former President Richard Nixon and bubblegum pop sensation Britney Spears.

* **"The Wreck of the Hesperus, I know!"**

   Angel compares the damage to his hotel to the wreck found in Henry Wadsworth Longfellow's famed poem.

* **"... the Lakers, the music ..."**

   Gunn lists the championship L.A. Lakers basketball team among the attributes of the city.

* **"I like nuns. How did the Flying Nun fly, anyway? Was it God or magic?"**

   In Angel's blood-induced ramblings, he references the character played by Sally Field in the 1960s series of the same name.

* **"Wait, are you the A & R guys?"**

   The drummer mistakes the team for artist and repertoire personnel, the record label people responsible for finding new talent.

* **"So Sammy's at the Flamingo and Frank, Dino, Peter, Joey, and Shirley are all front row center. Sammy starts singin' 'I Did It My Way.' Then he suddenly stops and says, 'I can't sing this in front of you, Frank.' And the crowd loves it, they're laughin'. So then ... then, Frank calls out, 'You're short and you're one-eyed, and I heard somewhere you're Jewish, don't be intimidated.' And the crowd goes wild."**

   Lorne regales Connor with a bedtime story about the Rat Pack.

* **"... then you went all Tyson on those demons ..."**

   Gunn compares Angel's fighting techniques to that of Mike Tyson, who has also been known to get a little wild in a fight.

Series cocreator David Greenwalt wrote the song that Kim sings while Lorne is reading her.

SIX DEGREES OF ...

Jeff Denton, who plays the demon lead guitarist, also played a vampire in the *Buffy* episode "Lessons."

OUR HEROES

ALEXIS DENISOF: "There was a lot of discussion among audience members where it was perceived that Wesley did the wrong thing. To me, I always felt—of course, I'm biased, because I'm playing the part—but I always felt it was an extraordinary sacrifice he made. He knew that he was risking everything in his life and his relationships because it was worth it to him to prevent the fulfillment of the father killing the son prophecy and saving Connor, the child who had come into the world in such an extraordinary way. That starts the journey into the dark place. Now all of the things, all of the signposts are gone that point him which way is right, which way is wrong, and all of the things that matter are gone, and gone instantly. It becomes a confusing time for him and he makes morally ambiguous decisions, and he doesn't always make the right decision at the right time, which is, to me, very important, not only for him, but for the show."

"FORGIVING"

CASE № 3ADH17

ACTION TAKEN

Fred and Gunn search Wesley's place for evidence of where he may have gone, but don't realize that Wesley's dying body is just across the street in the park. The pair returns to the hotel to learn the fate of Connor as Justine returns to Holtz's troops to tell them that their leader is gone, but their mission to kill Angelus lives on.

Angel enters the hotel in a rage against everyone, but mostly Wes. He instructs the remaining team to find out all they can about the demon world known as Quor-toth, and find a way for him to get there. Lorne eventually learns that there are no portals to Quor-toth; Sahjhan had to use extremely dark magic to rip right through the fabric of reality.

At the same time, Lilah is writing up her report on the recent events for Linwood, who is quite angry about being left out of the loop. Angel quickly remedies things for Linwood and brings him up to speed by kidnapping the lawyer and threatening him with torture.

WRITTEN BY Jeffrey Bell
DIRECTED BY Turi Meyer
GUEST STARS: John Rubinstein (Linwood), Andy Hallett (Lorne), Laurel Holloman (Justine), Stephanie Romanov (Lilah), Jack Conley (Sahjhan)
COSTARS: Tripp Pickell (Holtzian), Kenneth Dolin (Bum), Kay Panabaker (Girl), Sean Mahon (Truck Driver)

Gunn and Fred corner Justine and try to get her to admit what happened to Wesley, but Holtz's men arrive and overwhelm them. The encounter seems to be a total loss, but the conversation inspires Fred to go back to Wesley's and find his missing journals.

Linwood sends Angel to Wolfram & Hart where Lilah takes him to the mysterious White Room to meet a being of incredible power, in the form of a little girl. The girl recounts the history of Sahjhan and the decision to make him and his kind immaterial. She reveals that the demon can be trapped in a special urn, but she knows that Angel wants to kill it. Since the only way to do that is by making the demon flesh once again, the little girl instructs Angel in how to do just that.

Fred and Gunn reconstruct their friend's notes, unaware that he is still lying, near death, across the street. Once they see the prophecy that "the father will kill the son," everything falls into place for them and explains why Wesley did what he did. But Gunn suspects that no explanation will be good enough for Angel.

In spite of Lorne's warning against using dark magic, Angel conjures Sahjhan in corporeal form, but the demon does not appear in the hotel. Lilah gets out a call to confirm that something big has just turned up in town, sending Angel off to find the demon. Before Angel can leave, however, Fred and Gunn arrive and force him to listen to the truth about the prophecy. The truth doesn't stop Angel from his mission, nor does Justine and her soldiers, who lie in wait outside the hotel.

Gunn and Fred are surprised to see bodies littering the hotel exterior, but are even more shocked to see Justine driving away in Wesley's SUV. They follow her back to Sahjhan's lair where she admits that Wesley did not willingly give Connor to Holtz. Sahjhan and Angel soon join in, and even more truths come out when Sahjhan reveals that he worked his way through time to rewrite the prophecy and create the fictional one that read "the father will kill the son." In doing so, he also reveals that Angel was never really his enemy . . . it was Connor.

"The one sired by the vampire with a soul shall grow to manhood and kill Sahjhan."
—*The Original Nyazian Prophecy*

Naturally a battle ensues, and just when it seems that Sahjhan has gained the upper hand, Justine opens up Holtz's Resikhian urn, trapping the demon inside.

RESOLUTION

Justine tells the team where to find Wesley, but his body is no longer in the park. While Gunn and Fred search the hospitals, Lorne tries to get Angel to understand that Wes had no choice but to do what he did. Angel gets a call that sends him to Wesley's bedside.

"I just . . . I want you to know I understand why you did it. I know about the prophecies and I know how hard it must have been for you to do what you did. You thought I was going to turn evil and kill my son. I didn't turn into Angelus. It's important to me that you know that. This isn't Angelus talking to you, it's me, Angel. You know that, right?"

Angel then lashes out and tries to smother Wesley, screaming that he will never forgive Wes. It takes several orderlies and Gunn to finally pry the enraged vampire off Wesley.

CONTINUITY

Upon learning of Connor's fate, Fred immediately feels for the little guy, having been pulled through a dimensional portal once before herself. Gunn reminds

Angel that the last time they opened up a portal, it was Wesley who did the actual opening (in "Over the Rainbow"). In spite of recent events, Angel still insists that Cordelia's vacation should not be interrupted. As Angel promised in "Dad," he brings Connor's "godfather," Linwood, in for torture when something bad happens to the baby. This is the first visit to the Wolfram & Hart's soon-to-be-infamous White Room. Justine uses the Resikhian urn that Holtz mentioned he had in "Loyalty."

QUOTE OF THE WEEK

ANGEL: "Tell you what, take me to the Quor-toth world, help me find my son . . . we'll call it even."
SAHJHAN: "Really? You and me, buddy cop summer release? We iron out our wacky differences and bond? Don't think so."

THE DEVIL IS IN THE DETAILS

EXPENSES

Wesley's wallet is stolen by the bum who eventually saves him.

WEAPONRY

Gunn knows that Wesley has left his apartment for good when he notices a number of items are missing, including the Mossberg twelve-gauge shotgun Wesley kept in his closet.

DEMONS, ETC. . . .

According to the script, Sahjhan is a member of a race of demons called **Granoks.** As the little girl explains, they were all about torture and death in the past and caused a lot of trouble before Wolfram & Hart's Senior Partners made them immaterial.

THE PEN IS MIGHTIER

FINAL CUT

Linwood makes the following implied threat to Lilah in a line cut due to length.

"It's not like I'm going to get my feelings bruised and yank your mother out of that very expensive clinic you had her in . . . Don't worry. She's safe as a baby. Well, not the baby you lost, 'cause that one's gone to Hell forever . . . you might want to keep me updated in the future. I look forward to that report."

POP CULTURE

✳ "Whatever it was flipped a two-ton truck like a Tonka toy."
Lilah compares the vehicle Sahjhan upended to the popular brand of toy trucks and construction vehicles.

OUR HEROES

DAYNE JOHNSON (MAKEUP SUPERVISOR): "We do strategically placed bruises that kind of end up in the same general area every time we do them. As far as the adding any kind of injuries or anything to the actors, about half the time the director may point and say, 'There, put it there.'

Or we kind of watch and see where the fight was. Sometimes when we shoot the end of the show before we ever see the fight, I can go to the stunt guy and ask if the fight's been rehearsed. If it has, I'll ask, 'Where's he going to get hit?' before I put a bruise on the left side and he gets hit on the right side. So if they do that, then I'm going to say, 'Well, I put a bruise on that side so you'd better incorporate a hit. A really bad one from this side.' So we kind of play that game."

"DOUBLE OR NOTHING"

CASE N° 3ADH18

ACTION TAKEN

Cordelia returns from vacation in time to sit with a despondent Angel while he mourns the loss of his son. In the meantime Fred and Gunn are busy trying to keep the place running in light of the now-lost-to-them Wesley. Their clients, an extremely elderly demon couple that has been married for hundreds of years, has them wistfully wondering what their own future together will entail. At the very same moment, a demon from Gunn's past—a casino owner named Jenoff—is also concerned about Gunn's future, or more specifically, the future of his soul.

Jenoff sends his repo man to find Gunn. A business card leads the repo man to the hotel where the Groosalugg leads him to Gunn. After Gunn successfully closes the elderly couple's pending casefile, the repo man finds him and his errant soul.

The story shifts backs to 1995, when a young Gunn signed away his soul to Jenoff in exchange for something or someone of great importance. Flashback to today and Jenoff's man tells Gunn it's time to collect since they know he was about to invalidate the deal by giving his soul to someone else—namely Fred.

WRITTEN BY David H. Goodman
DIRECTED BY David Grossman
GUEST STARS: Andy Hallett (Lorne), Mark Lutz (Groosalugg), Jason Carter (Repo Man), Patrick St. Esprit (Jenoff), John David Conti (Syd Frzylcka), P.B. Hutton (Monica Frzylcka)
COSTAR: Nigel D. Gibbs (Doctor)

REPO MAN: "Now listen good: you got twenty-four hours to get your house in order and get your ass on down to the casino. And if you're thinkin' about runnin' or cheatin', don't. 'Cause then we take your soul and the girl's too."
GUNN: "She's got nothing to do with this."
REPO MAN: "Well you can keep it that way or you can get her killed. It's up to you now, Slick. See ya' tomorrow."

Gunn and Fred take off for a fun-filled day of adventure—and food—around Los Angeles. In fact, the day is so overly fun-filled that Fred begins to suspect that something is wrong. What she doesn't expect is Gunn telling her that she's the problem. He rails on her for reasons that seemingly defy explanation, but it's all a ruse so that she won't hurt as badly once his soul is taken away from her.

In his burned bedroom, where he'd been keeping watch over Connor's empty crib, Angel finally breaks out of his near-catatonic state. After he admits how deeply the loss pains him, Cordelia tries to comfort him the best she can even though she knows she can't even imagine how he feels. As they talk Fred interrupts, worried that something is seriously wrong with Gunn.

Angel is not about to lose another member of his family and springs into action, planning to scour the city in search of Gunn. Only after the plans are set does Groo show them the business card left by the repo man who came looking for Gunn a day earlier.

Gunn goes to Jenoff's casino to make good on his deal, but just as his soul is about to be sucked away, Angel and team burst into the club. The battle is short since the bouncers and demon casino patrons have them massively outnumbered. With their backs against a wall, Angel makes a double-or-nothing deal with Jenoff. A simple cut of the cards will determine if Jenoff will let Gunn's soul go or take Angel's as well.

RESOLUTION

Cordelia agrees that Angel's plan is the best course of action, in spite of the fact that the vampire is not too pleasant to be around when he doesn't have a soul. Knowing this, Angel gives Cordy a stake and tells her not to hesitate to use it should he lose the cut of the cards . . .

Angel loses.

Before Jenoff can collect, Cordy stakes the demon's hand to the table and Angel chops off his head. The day, it would seem, is saved, until Gunn points out that killing Jenoff isn't so easy. The demon starts to grow a new head right in front of them. Angel takes in the situation—they're still surrounded by bouncers and patrons—and he realizes the only logical course of action.

"So who else in here owes this guy?"
—*Angel*

It takes about a half second for the dozens of demons in the room to realize that Angel and his team are not their enemies—Jenoff is. As the demons attack the soul sucker, the team leaves the casino unscathed.

Gunn apologizes—repeatedly—to Fred for hurting her and admits that he sold his soul for his truck, explaining that when he was younger his truck was a necessary weapon in his battle against demons, and back then he didn't imagine himself having a future worth saving. Now he sees things differently because he loves Fred.

But the ending is not so happy as Angel returns to the hotel and realizes it's time to end his mourning, and he starts to take apart Connor's crib.

DOSSIERS

CLIENT Syd and **Monica Frzylcka** are a demon couple who have been together for over three hundred years. Later, **Gunn**'s actions result in his becoming the team's client.

SUSPECTS A **Skench demon** is squatting in the client's home. **Jenoff** and his **repo man** are ultimately taken care of when they try to collect on Gunn's debt.

CONTINUITY

Cordelia and Groo return from the vacation they left for in "Couplet." She hasn't had a real vision since before they left. Fred brings Wesley up to speed on recent events—most notably the false prophecy.

OFFICE ROMANCE

Cordelia admits to Gunn that she had originally seen Wesley and Fred as possibly getting together, but that she fully supports the coupling that occurred. Angel is the last of the group to learn that Gunn and Fred are dating, which is understandable considering he has been so preoccupied of late.

QUOTE OF THE WEEK

"If there's one thing I learned living on a hellmouth: every day is precious, you never know when it may be your last."   Cordelia imparts some wisdom to Gunn.

THE DEVIL IS IN THE DETAILS

WEAPONRY

The team uses the traditional accoutrements and Gunn uses a machete to deal with the Skench demon.

DEMONS, ETC. . . .

Skench demons take over a house and drive the people living there out with constant shrieking and projectile phlegm. The way to get rid of one is by lopping off its head.

According to Syd, **leprechauns** don't exist.

Jenoff is known formally as **The Soul Sucker.**

THE VAMPIRE RULES

Angel reveals the darker side of eternal life when reflecting on his missing son.

ANGEL: "You live as long as I do, eventually you lose everyone. I'm not saying you get used to it but you expect it, you deal. But he was just a little . . . just a little . . . You think you know something about living 'cause you have this really long life. And that's really all you have . . . I mean, in my case anyway. Then one day you wake up and you have something else . . ."

CORDELIA: "A future."

AS SCENE IN L.A.

The park where Gunn "dumps" Fred is located on the lot of Paramount Pictures.

THE PEN IS MIGHTIER

FINAL CUT

The following exchange between Lorne and Groo while going through Wesley's things was cut for time:

LORNE: "'The Propoxil Codex'? Ugh. Sounds like a cure for male pattern baldness."

GROOSALUGG: "On no, my friend—the Codex is a valuable description of the Klarpath conquest by the Great Wizard Urd."

LORNE: "I'll wait for the movie."

GROOSALUGG: "Ah, yes, movies—talking pictures with no substance."

LORNE: "Last couple decades? You're not wrong."

SIX DEGREES OF . . .

P. B. Hutton, who plays Monica Frzylcka, also portrayed Mrs. Kalish in the *Buffy* episode "What's My Line? Part 1."

TRACKS

Coolio's "Gansta's Paradise" opens up Gunn's flashback to 1995.

OUR HEROES

SANDY STRUTH (SET DECORATOR) ON MAKING ANGEL'S ROOM BABY-FRIENDLY: "We moved Angel's bed out and we made a little area where we put his desk so he could be in there working when Connor was there. That was kind of fun because you wouldn't normally do that. We went shopping like crazy for cribs, looking at pictures and pictures of cribs. Then I wanted to have the bedding be very childlike, but I also wanted to have the sense of the outdoors and this little ethereal thing of Angel's not being able to be outdoors. So I had clouds and stars and things that had enough of the grounded quality to Angel that it wasn't too cutesy, but it also . . . there's this wish, in my mind, that he always wants to get out in the sun. You yearn for him to be able to do that, to be in the sun and experience it. So whenever I can do that without disrupting the design, I like to put that in there."

"THE PRICE"

CASE № 3ADH19

ACTION TAKEN

Angel and the gang spend a Sunday afternoon putting his earthquake-ravaged room back together when a client walks in off the street and into an empty lobby. The man is about to leave when a translucent, slug-like creature appears and dives into his body. Angel comes down to find the man, who is suddenly incoherent, saying "we" have to leave.

Once the man leaves, Cordelia finds Angel by what remains of the pentagram he painted on the floor when he used

dark magic to bring Sahjhan back to his old solid self. Later she tries to scrub away the pentagram, but it won't budge. Then *she* refuses to budge when Fred asks her to speak to Angel about Wesley. She does, however, try to talk to Angel about a very recent vision of him being flung across the lobby, but Lorne interrupts with news of a big brouhaha (minus the ha-ha) at the juice bar across the street.

WRITTEN BY David Fury
DIRECTED BY Marita Grabiak
GUEST STARS: Andy Hallett (Lorne), Stephanie Romanov (Lilah), Daniel Dae Kim (Gavin), Mark Lutz (Groosalugg), John Short (Phillip Spivey)
COSTARS: Vincent Kartheiser (Teenage Boy), Waleed Moursi (Manager), Wayne Ford (Kid)

The team finds the man Angel met earlier trying to drink every liquid in the place. His skin is cracked and dry and he is threatening everyone so he can get some water. The team takes their new client back to the hotel and tries to figure out what's wrong. The client points to Angel and says that it's all his fault before falling to the floor and breaking apart into dust in the center of the pentagram. They realize it wasn't the guy talking at all when the translucent slug-like being pops out of the remains and slithers away.

The team arms themselves and locks down the hotel so the creature can't escape. Angel sends Fred to research Thaumogenesis because he suspects the creature's arrival was probably a result of his using dark magic—something Lorne had warned him against. Fred is overwhelmed by the text and once again tries to convince Gunn that they need Wesley's help.

Angel finds the creature drinking from a toilet tank, and when Lorne accidentally knocks out the light, the creature starts to glow. Angel flings a dagger through the center of the creature, but that only slows it down. In the meantime Cordelia and Groo have their own run-in with a similar creature, and the team realizes there's more than one.

In an attempt to gain the upper hand, they turn off the power in the hotel to set the creatures aglow. Fred keeps reading but is interrupted when one of the creatures attacks and gets into her body.

The events transpiring inside the locked-down hotel don't go unnoticed by Wolfram & Hart. Lilah is concerned when Gavin reminds her of how it will look if Angel died on her watch, particularly since she was involved in the dark magic that led to the current events. But when Lilah prepares a contingent to go into the hotel, Gavin returns with a message from Linwood telling her to let Angel die.

Angel, Cordy, Lorne, and Groo explore the closed-off south wing of the hotel when Gunn rushes in with an increasingly incoherent Fred. He insists that they take her to the hospital, but Angel refuses to let the creature inside her out of the hotel. It's a standoff as Gunn blames Angel for putting them in the situation in the first place by acting so recklessly with dark magic to save the son he had already lost. The argument is interrupted when they find dozens of the creatures drinking from the pool under the hotel.

The team flees to the industrial-size kitchen where Fred realizes that Gunn is missing. Angel decides it's time to go on the offensive and withholds water from Fred, hoping the being inside her will give her information. It does talk, but Angel wasn't expecting to hear what it has to say.

FRED: "Have to flee. It brings pain . . . such pain."

LORNE: "'It'? What happened to 'we'? What's with the pronoun switcheroo?"

ANGEL: "What are you fleeing from?"

FRED: "The bringer of torment . . . agony . . . death . . . The Destroyer."

CORDELIA: "Oh, that is just not the name you want to hear."

ANGEL: "Why is this 'Destroyer' after you?"

FRED: "It's not . . . It's coming after you . . . Aaaangel."

Gunn turns up at Wesley's door begging for help that Wes refuses to give—until he finds out that Fred is the one in danger. He gives Gunn a bottle of vodka and tells him to never come back.

RESOLUTION

Angel and Cordy stay behind to fight off the dozens of demons while Lorne and Groo try to take Fred to the hospital. Before they can leave the hotel, Gunn arrives and forces Fred to drink the alcohol to dry out the creature. Meanwhile Angel and Cordelia are about to be overwhelmed. When a creature latches on to Cordy her body begins to glow, sending a bright light throughout the hotel that kills all the creatures.

The gang reconvenes in the lobby, where the air over the pentagram starts to crackle and a huge monstrous demon bursts out. Moments later a young man emerges and, with a single slash, kills the monster. He then surveys the shocked people around him, locks eyes with Angel, and speaks. . . .

"Hi. Dad."

—*Connor*

DOSSIERS

CLIENT **Phillip J. Spivey** from Inglewood originally comes for help finding his lost dog, but needs more specialized attention when he is infected with the parasitic creature.

SUSPECTS The creatures that came through the portal Angel created with dark magic.

CONTINUITY

Angel has finally decided to fix the earthquake damage that all but destroyed his room in "Loyalty." When looking at the snow globe Angel bought for Connor, he mentions that it never snows in Southern California. Cordelia reminds him that it did snow once, likely referring to the snowfall in the *Buffy* episode "Amends" that The Powers That Be had sent to cloud the sky and save him from taking his life at dawn. The events of this episode are a result of the spell Angel cast in "Forgiving." The concept of Thaumogenesis was introduced on the *Buffy* episode "After Life" when the Scooby Gang was attacked by an invisible being that was a result of the dark magic Willow used to resurrect Buffy. Wesley has regained his power of speech, though his voice is soft and scratchy.

OFFICE ROMANCE

Groo overhears Cordelia telling Fred that Angel is her only priority. Cordelia tries to clear things up by explaining that Angel is her *work* priority, though she does not seem too convincing.

QUOTE OF THE WEEK

GROOSALUGG: "'Sunburst Splendor' is a hue more worthy of a Champion. Or perhaps this unique one called 'Purr-pleh.'"
ANGEL: "Purple . . . And yet you have no problem pronouncing 'Pomegranate.'"
GROOSALUGG: "It was my mother's name."

THE DEVIL IS IN THE DETAILS

EXPENSES

Angel must outlay the expense of painting and fixing his room without having to pay "real, dishonest-to-goodness, overpriced contractors" for more professional services.

WEAPONRY

The team loads up with swords, a shiny crossbow, an ax, and daggers.

THE PLAN

It's a rather simple, yet scary plan that Angel puts into action, and Cordelia reacts accordingly.
"What, they glow in the dark? How's that supposed to help us, unless we shut off all the lights in the holy crap you're not serious."

THE PEN IS MIGHTIER

FINAL CUT

Though the creatures are never named in the episode, the script does develop a shorthand way of referring to them.

A TRANSLUCENT, TENTACLED, SLUG-LIKE CREATURE (or for brevity's sake, "SLUK") slithers quickly past . . .

POP CULTURE

* "No question, we got ring around the lobby."

    Cordelia echoes the famous phrase "you've got ring around the collar" from the classic ad campaign for Wisk laundry detergent.

* "Exactly how do we know that slicing and dicing will do the trick on Mr. Sluggo?"

    Lorne makes reference to the mortal enemy of the classic Saturday Night Live character, Mr. Bill.

OUR HEROES

LONI PERISTERE (VISUAL EFFECTS SUPERVISOR): "The sluks, as described by David Fury, were like half jellyfish, half cockroach. It needed to move very, very quickly and it needed to be able to change its body shape and mass so that it could squeeze itself through the nostrils or mouth of a given character, and once inside it would dry them out to a husk and from that

husk they would shatter. That being said, we had a big red flag in the visual effects department, because we were like, 'Well, I don't think Rob Hall can make that. And if he can make that, it's going to be pulled around on a string.'

"This was going to be expensive and difficult, but the producers were interested in trying, for an episode, a very feature approach to one of their bad guys. They are really good about this. When they have an opportunity to try something that's a little beyond their reach and if they can make it happen, they'll make it happen. So we went ahead and we started designing almost six weeks in advance for this sluk creature. We started doing an illustration phase with Rob Hall. He designed the creature and what it looked like; even though he wasn't making it he was still designing it because that's what he does. So he draws those out and that gets approved, and the creature gets modeled in 3-D."

SANDY STRUTH (SET DECORATOR): "Wesley's apartment was nice. It took us some time to do because we wanted to show another side of Wesley. We wanted to show a masculine side of him and that he wasn't what you expected. So we gave him a lot of modern pieces mixed in with some historical pieces. We had a lot of brushed aluminum, refinished pieces that you get at antique stores, but we also had some classic art. Alexis was very much a part of that decision. He would tell me the kind of things that he wanted, like the painting of St. George fighting the dragon and pictures of England. He helped me out.

"I speak to all of the actors about their spaces. If I have time, I do it before and let them know I'm doing it, and ask if there's anything they want to tell me. Usually they say, 'Do what you want.' Then once I have it done I ask them because sometimes there are things that they're not happy with—not very often—but once in a while there will be something and I like them to know that we can change that. In fact, Alexis was one of those people. He didn't like curtains. He didn't feel they were right, so we took out the legs and left in the roman shades and it actually looked much better."

"A NEW WORLD"

CASE № 3ADH20

ACTION TAKEN

Angel barely has time to register that the intruder called him "Dad" before a set of stakes is flying toward him from a weapon on the boy's arm. Time seems to slow down as Angel twists his body so the stakes do not find his heart. The team joins in to fight back, but the teen puts up a fierce battle until Angel is finally able to subdue him. One look in the boy's eyes confirms that it is indeed Connor. The fighting resumes and Connor flees the hotel, hopping a bus downtown.

WRITTEN BY Jeffrey Bell
DIRECTED BY Tim Minear
GUEST STARS: Vincent Kartheiser (Connor), Andy Hallett (Lorne), Stephanie Romanov (Lilah), Mark Lutz (Groosalugg), Erika Thormahlen (Sunny), Anthony Starke (Tyke), Deborah Zoe (Mystress Myrna), Keith Szarabajka (Holtz)

Fred confirms the bus's destination online and Angel hits the sewers to find his son. While Cordelia hands out marching orders for the rest of the team to track the boy above ground, the dimensional rift starts to crackle with energy again. Cordelia tries using her new demon powers to close the rift, but when that doesn't work Fred suggests calling Wesley. That idea is quickly rejected as Lorne suggests that he may know someone who knows someone who could help. Cordy doles out new assignments for Lorne to contact his contact, Gunn and Fred to track Connor above ground, and she and Groo to guard the rift for whatever might come out.

Although Wesley's friends are respecting his wishes and leaving him alone, he does get a surprise visit from Lilah bringing a not-entirely-unexpected surprise offer of a job with Wolfram & Hart. Wesley declines, but he does accept her gift of a copy of Dante's *Inferno*.

As Connor explores the strange streets of Los Angeles he stumbles across a drug deal gone bad and comes to the aid of a damsel in distress. Connor takes on the dealer, named Tyke, and his muscle. One of the men dies in the process and as Connor is about to kill the dealer, the damsel, Sunny, tells him to stop. Connor does as he's told but cuts off the guy's ear so he won't forget what happened. Sunny takes Connor back to the hotel she's squatting in and the two bond over a pile of junk food.

Fred, Gunn, and Angel follow Connor's trail to what is now a police scene. Since nightfall is approaching Angel sends the others back to the hotel so he can track Connor on his own. When Gunn and Fred get home they find Cordelia and Groo sprawled out on the floor, having received a strong jolt from the dimensional rift. Cordy and Groo regain consciousness and they all worry that something else may have come through while they were out.

Lorne arrives with help in the form of Mistress Myrna, who specializes in dimensional magic and—as a result of her interaction with the subject matter—has an annoying habit of disappearing and shifting herself across the room. Mistress Myrna expresses her concern over the recent use of dark magic in the hotel, but manages to seal the rift. Unfortunately she is unable to tell them if anything else has come into this dimension.

Angel finds Connor in the hotel room. Connor is ready for more of a fight because Sunny died from a drug overdose, and the boy blames the dealer for her death. He is planning to track and kill the dealer, but Angel tries to stop him. However, his appeals to his son fall on deaf ears as the boy explodes when Angel calls him by his name.

"Stop calling me that! My name's Steven." *—Connor*

Angel pleads with his son to understand the situation, but the boy's mind has been poisoned by years of listening to Holtz's version of the story. Connor sees things simply: Angel is a vampire, and therefore evil and must be killed. He forces the vampire to reveal his demon face, but Angel tries to convince his son that it is only a part of him. Connor rejects the idea, and the conversation abruptly ends when the dealer, Tyke, arrives.

RESOLUTION

Angel tries to talk their way out of the situation, but the discussion devolves into violence when the cops arrive. Angel convinces his son to escape through the window as he takes a bullet for the boy. The cops burst in as Angel flees as well. As he and Connor run through the streets Angel tries to talk his son into coming back to the hotel with him, but the offer is refused. Instead the boy goes off and finds an aged Holtz waiting for him.

"Hi. Dad." *—"Steven"*

DOSSIERS

CLIENT Connor functions as a reluctant client in **Angel**'s missing person case.

CIVILIAN SUPPORT Sunny briefly supports Connor in his first day in L.A.

SUSPECTS Holtz's reappearance—though unknown to Angel and Co.—works counterproductively to Angel reclaiming his missing son, while **Tyke,** though evil, gives the boy a reason to bond with his biological father.

CONTINUITY

The final scene of the previous episode, "The Price," is replayed at the opening of this episode, and the story continues from that point. Cordelia reminds Angel of the vision she had the previous day, in which he was flung across the lobby floor. It comes true in the opening battle sequence of this episode. Due to the time difference between Earth and Quor-toth, Connor has aged sixteen years in a matter of weeks. He was taken to Quor-toth in "Sleep Tight." Fred learns that Gunn went to speak with Wesley to save her from the parasitic creature inhabiting her body in "The Price." Although Wesley does not accept the offer of a job at Wolfram & Hart in this episode, he and the rest of the team (minus Cordelia) will take over the Los Angeles office of the law firm at the end of Season Four.

OFFICE ROMANCE

Lilah and Wesley's initial contact in this episode will pave the way for a future "romance." Groo effectively admits to Cordelia that he is upset with the way she constantly brings up Angel and how the vampire is her primary concern. Cordy tries to put his mind at ease, but Groo's jealousy over the situation will continue to grow.

QUOTE OF THE WEEK

GUNN: "He was wearin' diapers coupla weeks ago, now he's a teenager?"
CORDELIA: "Tell me we don't live in a soap opera."

THE DEVIL IS IN THE DETAILS

WEAPONRY

Connor has a stake-shooter strapped to his arm that is capable of firing several stakes at one time.

DEMONS, ETC. . . .

The Pylean **Burrbeasts,** when engorged, will couple with anything that moves.

THE VAMPIRE RULES

Connor succinctly summarizes the ways to kill a vampire.
"Decapitation, stake in the heart, daylight, fire . . . I forget anything?"

THE PEN IS MIGHTIER

FINAL CUT

The team's original discussion regarding Connor's return had to be trimmed due to time constraints.
CORDELIA: "You think he's here for revenge?"
GROOSALUGG: "He did attempt to kill us all a number of times."

POP CULTURE

✳ **"Angel, if Peter Pan here doesn't stop . . ."**
Considering the way Connor is dressed, Gunn compares the boy to the titular character from the

story by J. M. Barrie made famous by numerous interpretations on stage and screen.

* **"What're you wearin' to the Oscars? My shammy suit!"**
Tyke makes a not-entirely-funny comment playing off the idea that many people are concerned with what the celebrities will be wearing to the Academy Awards.

* **"What I wouldn't do for a lasso and some Krazy Glue."**
Lorne mentions the incredibly strong adhesive that's well known for getting people to stick around.

To ensure that the viewers would be surprised by Holtz's return, Keith Szarabajka's name did not appear in the opening credits. Instead it was held until the end credits.

OUR HEROES

DAVID BOREANAZ: "I enjoyed working with Vincent. He's a talented actor. We really had a great time. We'd get into our scenes pretty heavily. The one that Tim Minear directed when Connor comes back and I'm confronting him in the apartment—there's a really sweet 360-degree steadicam move when we have this big emotional scene. It was one of my favorite scenes."

DIANA ACREY (HAIRSTYLIST): "When I'm doing fantasy characters, I get with the costumer and find out what the character's wearing so I can get a visual of what I want to do. For instance, Mistress Myrna's gown was very Gothic and it was kind of . . . well . . . Middle Ages. So I wanted to do the hair up with a lot of ropey work and buns incorporated. Then they said, 'We want blue hair.' So I said, 'Okay. Any preference of blue?' 'No. Just blue.' They didn't say what style or anything and they let me go, and it came out good. I used four cans of hairspray. It was shocking blue."

"BENEDICTION"

CASE Nº 3ADH21

ACTION TAKEN

Angel returns to the hotel without his son, but confirms that it was Connor who came through the portal—though the boy prefers to be called Steven now. The team disagrees over how to handle the situation, and Fred is upset with the idea of Connor being totally alone in the city. What none of them realizes is that he's not wandering the streets alone; he's checking into a motel with Holtz, the man he calls father.

Holtz expresses paternal pride for his son's success at freeing them from Quor-toth, but he knows that the escape was not solely because "Steven" wanted to kill Angel. Holtz knows that it's perfectly natural for the boy to want to see the man who was his biological father, and he sends "Steven" to be with that man, though with the warning to be careful.

Groo has a private chat with Lorne and confirms his worst fear: Cordelia may not feel the same way about him that he feels about her. Fred cobbles together a sort of demon detector to read the para-plasmic radioactivity unique to Quor-toth to see if anything else came through the rift, and she follows the signs to a real hot spot when Connor walks through the door.

WRITTEN & DIRECTED BY Tim Minear
GUEST STARS: Vincent Kartheiser (Connor), Laurel Holloman (Justine), Mark Lutz (Groosalugg), Andy Hallett (Lorne), Stephanie Romanov (Lilah), and Keith Szarabajka (Holtz)

Angel and Connor's reunion is short-lived when Cordelia interrupts with a vision of a woman in a nightclub about to be attacked by vampires. Angel decides to take his son on the mission, unaware that Wesley is already there. Lilah summoned Wesley to the club and set up the situation so she could watch how he would react when he learned the woman in jeopardy was Justine. Once again Wesley refuses to join Wolfram & Hart, but his momentary hesitation when faced with the choice of just leaving or warning Justine of the danger is all Lilah needed to see.

Father and son fight well together and manage to take out most of the vampires and save Justine, who recognizes the boy as Angel's son, which she realizes means Holtz may not be far. Connor follows a vamp out to the alley, but Angel is the one who winds up rescuing his son from the evil. The two then share a moment of father-son playfulness, unaware of the fact that they are under Holtz's watchful eye.

Once again Angel and Connor go their respective ways. When Connor returns to Holtz, Holtz sends the boy back to Angel again, explaining that only Angel can provide the answers Connor is looking for. As Connor reluctantly goes back to the hotel, Gunn and Fred see him with Holtz, since their little portable tracker led them there. Connor gets back to the hotel first and has a tense exchange with the "filthy demon" Lorne. Cordelia interrupts to calm Connor, but when he learns that she is also part demon, he lashes out with his blade.

Cordelia manages to hold him back as a warm white glow issues from her body and disintegrates the blade. The glow continues to grow and envelopes Connor's body, cleaning his soul of the poisons of living in Quor-toth. When Fred and Gunn return they find a calmer Connor, but an agitated Angel, who has learned that Holtz is back too. Gunn and Fred tell Angel Holtz's location, then agree to watch over Connor while the two fathers have a heart-to-heart. Cordelia begs Angel not to go without telling Connor, but he is too focused on Holtz to listen.

Justine finds Holtz, and the two reunite and hatch a plan before Angel arrives. The two fathers discuss their situation and Holtz ultimately gives over Connor to Angel, but reveals that he still got the vengeance he had longed for.

> "Every time you look upon his face, every time he calls you 'father,' you will be reminded of that which you took and can never give back. And if that is vengeance, I've found I have no taste for it."
>
> —*Holtz*

Holtz gives Angel a letter for Connor and then bids the vampire farewell.

RESOLUTION

As it turns out, Holtz does still have a taste for vengeance; when Justine returns, he has her kill him by stabbing him in the neck with an ice pick. Connor learns where Angel went and goes off to find him. As Angel reads the note Holtz left for Connor, the boy finds Justine holding the body of his father. With two puncture wounds in Holtz's neck, Connor makes the only logical conclusion as to who killed the man.

> "Angelus."   —*Connor*

DOSSIERS

CLIENTS Connor still functions as a reluctant client in **Angel**'s missing person case. **Justine** also becomes an unwilling client.

SUSPECTS Justine later joins **Holtz** following **Lilah**'s plot against her.

CONTINUITY

The action picks up shortly after the previous episode, "A New World," left off. Angel still does not know how to use his cell phone, as established earlier in the season. Holtz discovers that he and Connor have only been gone for days since their disappearance in "Sleep Tight." Though the creatures went unnamed in "The Price," Connor notes that he followed the sluks through the rift into this dimension. Lilah tries to gauge Wesley's desire for vengeance on Justine, considering the woman slit his throat in "Sleep Tight." Apparently Justine has been continuing Holtz's mission of killing vampires. Connor wonders if he is a demon because his parents are. It is a question that will haunt him throughout the fourth season. Cordelia's demon powers continue to grow. Now she can go back into her visions to watch Angel fight, and she even gives Connor a kind of "mystical colonic."

OFFICE ROMANCE

Groo's jealousy over Cordelia and Angel's relationship proves to be more and more justified as the episode wears on. When he talks over the situation with Lorne under the guise of speaking about Angel's relationship with his son, Groo tricks the green demon into putting his own feelings into words:

"Just because somebody hops a dimension or two is no guarantee things will work out."

QUOTE OF THE WEEK

"Okay, so he survived an unspeakable hell dimension—who hasn't? You just can't leave him alone on the streets of Los Angeles."

Fred tries to keep things in perspective where Connor is concerned.

THE DEVIL IS IN THE DETAILS

EXPENSES

Fred and Gunn were able to pick up a standard-issue Geiger counter at a yard sale and turn it into a demon locator using an enchanted Cedrian crystal.

WEAPONRY

Connor has a roughly made blade that came with him from Quor-toth.

DEMONS, ETC. . . .

A **Six-horned Lach-nie Hag** owed Lorne a favor and gave him—free of charge—a Cedrian crystal, which is said to contain millennia of stored mystical energy, though it needs to be enchanted before it can be used.

THE VAMPIRE RULES

Vampire bites are marked by two puncture wounds in the neck. To the uninitiated, a pair of puncture wounds from an ice pick can look similar enough. Vampires can enter motel rooms because they are public accommodations.

AS SCENE IN L.A.

Fred and Gunn take Connor to Santa Monica beach, which is right beside the pier they were set up at in "Loyalty."

THE PEN IS MIGHTIER

FINAL CUT

The following exchange was cut after Lorne suggested that maybe they should be wearing lead when using Fred's radioactivity-tracking device.

CORDELIA: "Good point. Fred, how worried should we be about contamination?"

FRED: "I wouldn't be. I mean, not now. Not after we've been sucking this stuff up all day."

GUNN: "Nice."

POP CULTURE

✳ "Who's the boy wonder?"

Lilah likens Connor to one of the most famous young sidekicks in history, Batman's sidekick, Robin.

THE NAME GAME

"**Benediction**" is a form of blessing that usually comes at the end of a church service.

OUR HEROES

ALEXIS DENISOF: "I like the new look. We took the big fight and the slitting of the throat and going to the hospital as there was an obvious couple of episodes where he wasn't wearing his glasses and he wasn't shaving, again, for obvious reasons. They just liked the look in the head office. They said, 'Well, this kind of matches where he is internally. Let's keep this for a little while and assume that you're wearing contacts or had laser surgery with all the time off while you were in the hospital.' It was kind of, 'Could you zap the retinas for me while you're stitching up my larynx?' We didn't go to great pains to explain it. The beauty of drama is you can make these little jumps and people fill in the gaps for you."

DIANA ACREY (HAIRSTYLIST): "Holtz progressed into an old man so I combed gray into his hair. He had a big prosthetic on his face so I wanted his hair to look as real as possible to make people believe his face was like that. If he had a wig with it, they probably wouldn't have bought it as much. So we just painted gray streaks through his hair."

"TOMORROW"

CASE № 3ADH22

ACTION TAKEN

Things are definitely looking up as Angel shares the news that Connor will be coming home for good. What he doesn't know is that Connor is at that same moment cradling Holtz's dead body in his arms, mistakenly under the impression that Angel is to blame.

Angel can barely contain his glee as he and Cordelia try to pick out the perfect room in the hotel for Connor. The joyousness takes a brief break when Lorne interrupts to share his plans for leaving the team, and the city. He's got an offer of a gig in Las Vegas and plans to fly out the following day.

Connor and Justine see to it that Holtz gets a proper burial. Justine looks on as Connor beheads his father in case the man was turned, although she knows that Angel had nothing to do with the death. At the same time, Lilah approaches Wesley with yet another offer to join forces. The pair has a join-

WRITTEN & DIRECTED BY David Greenwalt
GUEST STARS: John Rubinstein (Linwood), Vincent Kartheiser (Connor), Laurel Holloman (Justine), Mark Lutz (Groosalugg), Andy Hallett (Lorne), Stephanie Romanov (Lilah), Daniel Dae Kim (Gavin), David Denman (Skip), and Keith Szarabajka (Holtz)

ing of a different kind as they wind up in bed together, an event that Wesley immediately regrets.

Gunn and Fred return to the hotel to tell Angel that after Connor overheard them talking about Angel's planned visit to Holtz, the distraught boy ran away. However, Connor shows up only moments later, acting as if he is fine with the new arrangement while secretly plotting to make Angel pay for what he supposedly did.

Angel tries to bond with his son, suggesting a movie outing for the next evening. Connor agrees, but first he wants to learn how to fight from Angel; or, more specifically, he wants to learn how Angel fights. The team works together for a training session that Angel takes to be another good sign. During the session Angel asks Cordelia to join them for the movies, but she begs off because of plans with Groo.

Cordelia's evening with the Groosalugg does not go as planned when she returns home to find him looking quite sad. Groo explains that he knows she is in love with Angel, a fact that even Cordelia wasn't entirely aware was true. Meanwhile Lorne bids farewell to Angel, telling him that it's obvious Cordelia feels for the vamp. Lorne and Groo's conversations intertwine as they both convince their respective scene partners that it must be love.

Angel puts aside his feelings for Cordy and enjoys an evening at the drive-in with Connor, Fred, and Gunn. The action on screen suddenly turns all too real when a helicopter comes bursting onto the scene and commandos attack. Linwood and Gavin watch the fight on a video screen, safe in a nearby van. While they're not surprised to see Angel defend his son, they are intrigued by Connor's desire to protect his father.

The fight ends and Angel realizes that the van with the shaded windows in front of him looks rather suspicious. He rips open the doors to find his nemeses. Amid threats and accusations, Connor steps in to defend Angel. Seeing an opportunity, Linwood tries to appeal to the boy, referring to him as Steven, but is immediately shut down.

"My name is Connor." —*Connor*

Angel heads back to the hotel, thrilled over the seeming connection he has finally made with his son, when things take an even more joyous turn: Cordelia calls, asking him to meet her at the bluffs so they can discuss their feelings for each other.

RESOLUTION

As Cordelia drives to the meeting her body begins to glow and the world around her stops. Her demon guide, Skip, joins her in the middle of the freeway with a new offer. The Powers That Be are so impressed with how she handled her new abilities that they want her to take the next step in fighting the battle against evil by becoming a higher power and moving on to another plane of existence. Cordy is reluctant to accept because it would mean leaving immediately, without having the chance to tell Angel how she feels. That, it turns out, is her final test, and she ultimately chooses the mission over love.

Angel sits at the beach, unaware of what is keeping Cordelia, when Connor arrives and attacks his father. The fight is intense, and Connor gets the upper hand with the help of a Taser, rendering Angel unconscious before summoning Justine, who is on a boat offshore. Angel reawakens to find that he is on a boat and is being sealed into a metal box so he can live forever on the bottom of the ocean. Angel tries to convince Connor that he has the story wrong, but he fails to move the boy.

"Someday you'll learn the truth. And you'll hate yourself for this. Don't, it's not your fault. I don't blame you." —*Angel*

Gunn and Fred are back at the hotel, where they find that Connor is missing once again. They try calling Cordelia and Angel, but can't reach either of them. With Lorne and Groo gone as well, potentially for good, the two of them realize that they are alone. But they don't realize just how alone they truly are as Cordelia's body is lifted up into the heavens and Angel sinks into the sea.

CONTINUITY

As before, the action picks up where the preceding episode, "Benediction," left off. Holtz used to tell Connor every night about his dream to live in Utah together. That was the original plan hatched by Holtz and Justine in "Sleep Tight." Wolfram & Hart's attack on Angel is largely motivated by Linwood's need for revenge after being kidnapped and threatened with torture by Angel in "Forgiving." Skip introduced himself to Cordy as her guide in "Birthday."

OFFICE ROMANCE

The Groosalugg leaves his princess for parts unknown as Cordelia and Angel finally realize they were meant to be together—until fate gets in the way.

QUOTE OF THE WEEK

LILAH: "I'm starting to like you, Wes. But don't go making more of this than it is. I'm not one of those doe-eyed 'girls of Angel Investigations.' Don't be thinking about me when I'm gone."
WESLEY: "I wasn't thinking about you when you were here."

THE DEVIL IS IN THE DETAILS

THE VAMPIRE RULES

Connor knows that one way to ensure Holtz does not rise again if he was turned to a vampire is by cutting off the man's head.

THE PEN IS MIGHTIER

FINAL CUT

Lilah enjoys the potential for irony in her conversation with Wes.

"Cheer up. Angel finds the kid with blood on his hands, he might just prove you right about that prophecy: 'The father will kill the son.' OOO! Maybe he'll slit his throat!"

POP CULTURE

* "Yeah, if you're Tom Sawyer paintin' a fence!"
  Cordelia refers to one of the more memorable scenes from one of Mark Twain's most famous works and its titular character.
* "Leavin'. On the midnight train to Georgia."
  Lorne refers to the song made famous by Gladys Knight & The Pips.
* "You're a vampire, you're not in *Cats*."
  Angel corrects Fred's interpretation of the undead, which seemed rather similar to a character from the Andrew Lloyd Webber musical.
* "You are the prince of lies."
  Connor compares Angel to Lucifer.

OUR HEROES

MICHAEL GASPAR (SPECIAL EFFECTS COORDINATOR): "The water stuff at the end of [season] three, beginning of four was fun. At the end of three we threw Angel in a coffin. We built a metal coffin that had a dummy inside and we took belt wheel racks that sat on top of this box and fastened it to the deck of the boat and we just rolled off the box. The box was actually hooked up to a cable

that we were pulling from the other end so that the actors weren't doing any pushing; we had manpower pulling that box off. It floated for a couple seconds and then it sank into the water. We had a cable on it so that it could only go down twelve or fifteen feet. Then we had to haul it back up with a crane that was on another boat.

"They had to drop a hook down, and we had a couple divers in the water who swam the hook from the crane down to the box so we could pull the box back up, which is what we did at the start of four. We started with the box on the crane and just put it down in the water and pulled it back up. I don't know if you've ever been to the L.A. harbor, but it's not the most clean water to dive in. It's pretty nasty. There's no visibility during the day, and it was at night."

EPISODE GUIDE

SEASON 4

EPISODE NUMBER	EPISODE NAME	ORIGINAL U.S. AIR DATE
4ADH01	"Deep Down"	October 6, 2002
4ADH02	"Ground State"	October 13, 2002
4ADH03	"The House Always Wins"	October 20, 2002
4ADH04	"Slouching Toward Bethlehem"	October 27, 2002
4ADH05	"Supersymmetry"	November 3, 2002
4ADH06	"Spin the Bottle"	November 10, 2002
4ADH07	"Apocalypse, Nowish"	November 17, 2002
4ADH08	"Habeas Corpses"	January 15, 2003
4ADH09	"Long Day's Journey"	January 22, 2003
4ADH10	"Awakening"	January 29, 2003
4ADH11	"Soulless"	February 5, 2003
4ADH12	"Calvary"	February 12, 2003
4ADH13	"Salvage"	March 5, 2003
4ADH14	"Release"	March 12, 2003
4ADH15	"Orpheus"	March 19, 2003
4ADH16	"Players"	March 26, 2003
4ADH17	"Inside Out"	April 2, 2003
4ADH18	"Shiny Happy People"	April 9, 2003
4ADH19	"The Magic Bullet"	April 16, 2003
4ADH20	"Sacrifice"	April 23, 2003
4ADH21	"Peace Out"	April 30, 2003
4ADH22	"Home"	May 7, 2003

STARRING

David Boreanaz . . . . Angel

Charisma Carpenter . . . . Cordelia Chase

J. August Richards . . . . Charles Gunn

Amy Acker . . . . .Winifred "Fred" Burkle

Andy Hallett . . . . . .Lorne/The Host/Krevlornswath of the Deathwok Clan
(Starting with "Release")

Vincent Kartheiser . . . . .Connor

Alexis Denisof . . . . .Wesley Wyndam-Pryce

"DEEP DOWN"

CASE Nº 4ADH01

ACTION TAKEN

Angel hosts a lavish dinner for the entire team and his beloved Cordelia. It's a perfect night, except for the fact that it's all a hallucination and Angel rests at the bottom of the ocean.

Fred and Gunn have done everything in their limited power to locate Angel and Cordelia, but have met with nothing but dead ends. Even Lorne seems to be too busy to help from his hit engagement in Las Vegas. Finally their luck pays off when they track down a vamp who used to live by the bluffs where Angel was last seen. She did witness the events of that night, but Connor—who has been living and working with Gunn and Fred as if nothing happened—kills the vamp before she can squeal.

WRITTEN BY Steven S. DeKnight
DIRECTED BY Terrence O'Hara
SPECIAL GUEST STAR: Andy Hallett (Lorne)
GUEST STARS: John Rubinstein (Linwood), Laurel Holloman (Justine), Stephanie Romanov (Lilah), Daniel Dae Kim (Gavin)
COSTARS: Noel Guglielmi (Driver Vamp), Ingrid Sonray (Marissa), Rod Tate (Bruiser)

Wesley, however, has a far better lead, and, after Lilah departs following a not-so-romantic encounter, he opens up his closet to reveal that it has been turned into a prison for Justine. She has admitted to her complicity in both Holtz's and Connor's plans against Angel and reluctantly "agreed" to help Wes.

"Not much of a plan, though, was it really? Easy to figure out which door to kick in when Angel went missing. And not much harder to 'persuade' you to betray everything Holtz gave his life for. Not that it was worth very much. You should know. You're the one that ended it."
—*Wesley*

Following nights of searching the deep water, they locate Angel's aquatic tomb and bring him back up into the night air. Wesley is quick to feed the vampire some animal blood, but when that fails to quench the thirst, Wesley opens a vein and lets Angel take directly from him.

Lilah's relationship with Wesley is brought out in the open at Wolfram & Hart. Linwood lets her know that he is very much displeased with Lilah's performance of late—much to Gavin's glee—and he intends to discuss that topic at the evening's staff meeting. Lilah manages to turn the tables—or actually, boardroom chair—on him by contacting one of the Senior Partners about Linwood's own lack of action. After decapitating her boss with the lethal office chair, she announces to the staff that the Senior Partners have put her in charge.

RESOLUTION

Fred uses her growing bond with Connor to lull him into a sense of security before zapping him with a Taser. Wesley has called and told them of Connor's misdeeds, but Gunn and Fred are upset that their friend didn't tell them sooner. When Wes arrives he simply drops off the vampire, revealing that he donated his own blood so Angel could begin to heal.

Connor tries to escape, but Angel stares his son down and confirms that the boy had nothing to do with the missing Cordelia. Following an impassioned speech about the meaning of being a Champion, Angel tells his son to get out. His only focus now will be finding Cordelia.

Up in the heavens above, in a dimension of light and untold joy, Cordelia waits with only one thing on her blessed mind.

"God, I am so bored." —*Cordelia*

DOSSIERS

CLIENT The Angel Investigations team (now down to just **Fred** and **Gunn**) functions as its own clients trying to find the missing **Angel** and **Cordelia**.

CIVILIAN SUPPORT Wesley (who is no longer on the team) obtains the reluctant support of **Justine** to find Angel. **Lorne** (who left to pursue his dream in Vegas) provides very little support and is actually quite difficult to get on the phone. A **gang of vamps** directs Gunn and Fred to a vampire named **Marissa**, who used to live by the bluffs where Angel was last seen. She could provide help, but Connor kills her first.

SUSPECTS Although Fred and Gunn don't realize it until the end, the person who's had all the information on one of their missing persons is **Connor**.

CONTINUITY

Gunn and Fred have spent the last three months chasing leads in Angel's and Cordy's disappearances.

Wesley has been busy too, though it is unclear how long he has been keeping Justine prisoner during that time. Lorne is still in Las Vegas and tries to pass along a secret message to Fred, although it won't make any sense until "The House Always Wins."

OFFICE ROMANCE

Angel dreams of a happy life with Cordelia and—when awake—vows to do everything in his power to find her. Wesley and Lilah continue their strange affair of mutual distrust and sexual liaisons.

QUOTE OF THE WEEK

"I'll take away your bucket."

Suspecting that Justine is about to attack, Wesley threatens to take away the one "luxury" in her cell.

THE DEVIL IS IN THE DETAILS

WEAPONRY

The usual. Fred has taken possession of Angel's wrist-strapped retractable stake.

THE VAMPIRE RULES

Wesley lays out the reality of vampire nourishment:

"A vampire can exist indefinitely without feeding, but damage to higher brain function from prolonged starvation can be catastrophic."

AS SCENE IN L.A.

Angel dreams that he and Cordy are back on the bluffs of Point Dume, which is located in Malibu off the Pacific Coast Highway.

THE PEN IS MIGHTIER

FINAL CUT

The vampire Marissa makes a desperate attempt to act innocent in a line cut due to length:

"I didn't see nothing, I swear. You know how dark it is down by the bluffs? And hey, my eyes were never that good. Sure, the creature of the night thing helps, but . . ."

POP CULTURE

✳ **"Mr. Big-Hit-In-Vegas is too busy Danke Shoening the tourists to care about us."**
Fred refers to the Wayne Newton hit.

✳ **"Evil Dead was probably just messing with us."**
Gunn refers to the 1981 horror film written and directed by Sam Raimi.

✳ **"His nickname back in Quor-toth was 'The Destroyer,' and unless you put 'Conan' in front of that I'm guessing it's not a good sign."**
Gunn naturally is referring to the mythic film *Conan the Destroyer,* which starred Arnold Schwarzenegger.

* "Not a peep. But if I Miracle-Ear anything I'll send up a smoke signal."
  Lorne turns noun into verb, referring to the hearing aid advertised as being so small it's nearly invisible.
* "Been playing a little Ahab."
  Gunn compares Wesley to the captain in *Moby Dick*.

SIX DEGREES OF . . .

One of the vamps Fred and Gunn fight off, played by Noel Guglielmi, also played one of Xander's coworkers in the *Buffy* episode "Life Serial."

Rod Tate, the bruiser, will later play a security guard in "The House Always Wins."

There's a little in-joke when Linwood tells Lilah, "This is my corner of the sky." John Rubinstein starred in the original Broadway production of the musical *Pippin*, and one of the songs he sang was titled "Corner of the Sky."

OUR HEROES

ALEXIS DENISOF: "Because Wesley became ostracized from the group as a result of the kidnapping and the subsequent tension with Angel, it created space and time around the character where other people and events could take place for him. It kind of solidified the things that had started in season two with the gradual growing up and shedding of the foppish, pedantic Watcher that had arrived on *Buffy*. It was always Joss's intention, and mine . . . that the character would have to evolve. But that was really going much further than I had ever anticipated and initially I was afraid. It's good to alienate the character and at times alienate the audience, but I didn't want to be the guy everybody hates.

"It really tested the character. You send him into new situations, away from the field of play that he's used to, and it gives you a chance to test the limits and explore some other areas. He did get very dark, but rightfully so. The plot points supported it. You have to make each step, and then the next step becomes plausible. But when you're looking at a giant leap, that's impossible."

DAVID BOREANAZ: "That story line as it unfolded of Angel becoming a father and having a child and having to bring him up and then losing him and having him come back as a teenage angst-ridden son—he went through a lot of levels with that as far as the character was concerned. Did I [use] a lot of my personal experiences of having a child with that? Not really. I just kind of played the scenes and what it pertained to. For me, it's always been what we're looking at as the whole of the scene and then taking it that far."

"GROUND STATE"

CASE № 4ADH02

ACTION TAKEN

Angel goes over Cordy's apartment with Gunn and Fred, hoping that he can pick up on something they missed on their previous searches before the landlord rents the place to someone else. When the search turns up nothing, Angel contacts Wesley, hoping to mend some fences, but finds that Wes has moved on and now leads his own team of demon fighters. A much colder Wesley gives Angel all the information he had collected on Cordy's disappearance and tells the vampire to contact the demigoddess Dinza for information on what he has lost.

Dinza's words are cryptic at best, but she does reveal that Cordy is far from Angel and no longer needs him. She reluctantly reveals that he can find Cordelia using the Axis of Pythia, a statue imbued with mystical qualities including the ability to find souls or entities across dimensions. Dinza then dismisses Angel with a haunting prophecy.

WRITTEN BY Mere Smith
DIRECTED BY Michael Grossman
GUEST STARS: Stephanie Romanov (Lilah), Alexa Davalos (Gwen), Rena Owen (Dinza), and Tom Irwin (Elliot Caspar)
COSTARS: Belinda Waymouth (Ms. Thorpe), Heidi Fecht (Mrs. Raiden), Michael Medico (Mr. Raiden), Easton Gage (Boy), Megan Corletto (Young Gwen)

"I'd *love* to keep you . . . but you have so much more to lose."   —*Dinza*

Angel and team prepare to take the $33 million Axis from the high-security auction house where it is stored, but they are not the only ones interested in the piece. A buyer is scheming his way through a deal with a high-end burglar with some high-voltage powers of her own. The thief, Gwen, breaks into the building first, incapacitating some of the guards and making her way to the vault.

Angel, Fred, and Gunn also break in, unaware that they are not the only ones on the case. They split up and go to their respective spots, and find clues that someone is already ahead of them. Angel finds the biggest clue when he reaches the vault and a gate comes crashing down in front of him. Gwen pops in from an air duct and bends the laser light sensors, revealing her self-proclaimed "freakish" power.

Fearing that the thief will take his only link to Cordy, Angel tries to plead his case, but to no avail. Fred manages to release the gate, and a fight for the Axis ensues, with Gunn severely wounded in the process. After she accidentally kills Gunn, Gwen pauses in her escape to give Gunn the electrical volt his heart needs to get it beating again. Angel and Fred have to get him to the hospital right away, so they let Gwen go.

Suspecting that the buyer is one of Wolfram & Hart's clients, Angel tracks Lilah and is not surprised to find her tracking his son, Connor. After threatening to punish her if she doesn't stay away from the boy, Angel gets the information he needs.

RESOLUTION

Angel meets up with Gwen at the buyer's office and tries to convince her one more time to let him borrow the Axis. They fight, and Gwen uses her powers on him. At first it has no effect on the vampire, but when it temporarily jump-starts his heart, the two share a passionate kiss that is interrupted by Gwen's buyer.

The buyer is there for a double-cross and traps Angel and Gwen in an elevator, forcing them to work together to escape. Angel takes down the buyer before Gwen could do so with an electrical action she would eventually regret. Gwen lets Angel have the Axis as the two part company.

Angel returns from his Axis journey with news. Although he did not speak with Cordelia he could tell she was in a much happier place.

"All those months underwater . . . the whole time I'm thinking, 'I gotta get home to Cordelia.' I come back and she's gone. So, then all I can think is 'I gotta get *Cordy* home.' Finally I find her, I realize . . . she already is home . . . where she belongs."   —*Angel*

But what Angel doesn't realize is that Cordelia is watching over them right that moment . . . and she's bored out of her mind.

DOSSIERS

CLIENT Although Angel has been found, **Cordelia** is still on the missing persons list.

CIVILIAN SUPPORT **Wesley** helps out, though he's not interested in rejoining the team. The demigoddess **Dinza** provides useful information for locating Cordelia. Angel beats the auction house's building plans out of a snitch who thought Angel was dead. **Gwen Raiden** first works against the Angel Investigations team but eventually joins forces with them and hands over the Axis of Pythia. **Lilah**, though still an enemy, provides useful information to Angel for reclaiming the Axis.

SUSPECTS Gwen's buyer, **Elliot**, tries to get in the way, though he neither knows Angel nor cares why the vampire needs the Axis.

CONTINUITY

Gwen will make return appearances in "Long Day's Journey" and "Players." Gunn confirms to Angel that they tried enlisting Lorne's help, as they did in "Deep Down," to no avail. They show Angel the photos and stuff Cordelia had been going through on the night she went missing in "Tomorrow." When Angel refers to his past experiences breaking into places to steal, Gunn asks if he's including the time they stole the "crazymakin' death shroud that nearly killed [them]." Of course, he refers to "The Shroud of Rahmon."

OFFICE ROMANCE

Lilah and Wesley continue their mating game, and Angel can smell them on each other. When Gwen meets Gunn, she throws a flirtatious line his way, paving the way for their future coupling in "Players." Fred has a minor breakdown after Gunn briefly dies, worried about what she would do without him.

QUOTE OF THE WEEK

ANGEL: "Tell me you're not here for the Axis."
GWEN: "I'm not here for the Axis."
ANGEL: "You're lying."
GWEN: "I'm fibbing. It's lying, only classier."

THE DEVIL IS IN THE DETAILS

EXPENSES

Gunn and Fred paid Cordelia's rent for the first couple of months she was missing, but when money got tight, they had to let the landlord show the apartment for new tenants.

Items that may have been purchased for the attempted heist include rappelling hooks, flashlights, and aerosols.

THE PLAN

The plan involves the team scaling the auction house's wall to the roof and disabling the external security system. Once the get inside they split up so Fred can access the internal security, Gunn can take care of the guards, and Angel can find the Axis. Things go slightly amiss when they discover that someone else is in the building.

DEMONS, ETC. . . .

Dinza is considered one of the Eleusian mysteries. She is the dark demigoddess of the lost. Only the dead can enter her presence, and those who do she often traps there for eternity.

The Axis of Pythia is an ancient power that bridges all dimensions. It was forged from the tripod of the Delphic oracle into a metal arch set into a marble base. It stands approximately two feet high and weighs eighteen pounds.

Not technically a demon, **Gwen** has power over electricity, including the ability to excite subatomic particles with energy and bounce them off one another before they hit ground state. She has been struck by lightning fourteen times.

THE PEN IS MIGHTIER

FINAL CUT

Angel's unexpected reaction to Gwen's powers appears in the stage directions as follows:
ZAP! CGI SPARKS leap from her hands, and we go into a SPECIAL FX SHOT: AN INTERNAL-ORGAN VERSION OF ANGEL'S BODY, as we see his SHRIVELLED DEAD HEART CONVULSE, as though zapped with electricity, before FILLING WITH BLOOD and beginning to BEAT. We HEAR: THA-DUMP. THA-DUMP.

POP CULTURE

* "... all quiet on the psychic front."
  Fred riffs on the name of the book (turned movie) *All Quiet on the Western Front,* written by Erich Maria Remarque.
* "Really ... City of Atlantis? Holy Grail? Jimmy Hoffa?"
  Angel lists some missing things that Dinza may know the location of, including the ancient city that reportedly sunk into the sea, the cup used by Christ at the Last Supper, and the former leader of the Teamsters union.
* "Do I look like a blue light special to you?"
  Gwen is offended when Elliot tries to bargain down her rates as if she were an item on sale at Kmart.
* "But if it's at an auction house, can't we just, you know, eBay the thing?"
  Gunn refers to the popular auction Web site where one can pick up rare collectibles.
* "Looks like Connor's gonna need someone who cares—like a big sister or . . . hey, Mrs. Robinson, if that's what he's into."
  Lilah suggests that she can fill the role of the mature seductress from the film *The Graduate* in taking care of Connor now that he's on his own.
* "Damn, this is so much harder than it looks on *Batman*."
  Gunn compares the team's wall scaling to that seen on the sixties TV series.
* "... that's fun for a girl and a boy."
  Gwen sings part of the classic ad for Slinky when discussing the Axis.
* "Hey there, Denzel."
  Gwen compares Gunn to the Academy Award–winning actor.
* "Being dead. Gone. See anything interesting? White light? Shirley MacLaine?"
  Fred inquires about the actress known for her belief in paranormal experiences.
* "Then Angel woulda picked me up and Flash Gordon-ed me to the ER."
  Gunn changes noun to verb referring to the titular character from the series of science fiction comic strips.
* "What are you, Lex Luthor?"
  When Elliot traps Gwen (and Angel) in the elevator, she compares the man and his crazy elevator-gas plan to Superman's archenemy.

THE NAME GAME

"Ground state" is a physics term referring to a condition in which the least energy is produced in a physical space.

OUR HEROES

ROBERT HALL (SPECIAL EFFECTS MAKEUP ARTIST): "I remember being really excited when we got the script for 'Ground State,' which was the episode we made Dinza for. Dinza is probably one of my favorite characters that we've done, to date, and is highly underused in the episode. I thought for sure they were bringing her back. I thought, 'Oh, wow, you didn't get to see her much.' She's kind of veiled, but she was super, super elaborate. She wasn't wearing a body suit so her arms had big arm appliances. . . .

Her feet even had foam feet with long nails on it and hydraulic wings. There was a full chest and back prosthesis. It was one of the most elaborate things we'd ever done, and I really loved that character.

"She was probably the most time-intensive makeup application we'd ever done. It was over five hours. I thought Rena Owen was amazing. You didn't get to see her that much, but being on set I was like, 'This is cool. They're going to be bringing her back.' And they never brought her back. So that one I was a little bummed out about, but Dinza was one of my favorites."

"THE HOUSE ALWAYS WINS"

CASE Nº 4ADH03

ACTION TAKEN

Following another morbid evening of Angel watching over his estranged son, the vampire realizes that it's time for him, Gunn, and Fred to have a little retreat. . . . And what better place for a spiritual journey than Las Vegas?

The trio is surprised to see Lorne's demon face lighting up a billboard on the strip promoting his headlining act at the Tropicana. They are even more surprised when Lorne blows them off during his show as he goes to different audience members and gets them to sing into the mic. He even blows past his friends when they're waiting backstage for him among his many adoring fans.

Lorne retires to his plush dressing room and is soon joined by the hotel owner, Lee DeMarco. Through violence—and threat of further violence—the businessman forces Lorne to reveal the bright futures of some of the people he read during his act, including that of a student chef named Vivian who will open three five-star restaurants within a decade. Minutes later Vivian is offered a special chance to "Spin to Win."

WRITTEN BY David Fury
DIRECTED BY Marita Grabiak
SPECIAL GUEST STAR: Andy Hallett (Lorne)
GUEST STAR: Clayton Rohner (Lee DeMarco)
COSTARS: Brittany Ishibashi (Vivian), Morocco Omari (Spencer), John Colella (Croupier) Rod Tate (Bruiser), Gloria Alexander (Lornettes), Tom Schmid (Well-Dressed Man), Diana Saunders (Bejeweled Woman), Jennifer Autry (Lornette #2) Matt Bushell (Security Guard #3)

As Gunn watches Fred clean up at blackjack, Angel tries to get a message to Lorne but winds up being thrown out of the hotel for his efforts. There he finds a zoned-out Vivian, who had seemed so lucid when he saw her earlier. Angel puts two and two together and busts into the "Spin to Win" game, only to lose his own lucidity after he is tricked into playing the game.

Fred sneaks into Lorne's dressing room and—after realizing that her friend is being held against his will—helps him escape. She, Gunn, and Lorne try to get Angel to flee with them, but he's more focused on slots than fleeing. The trio—sans vampire—head out into the bright lights of Vegas where Lorne finally has a chance to recap his last three months. He was being forced to tell Lee about audience members' futures so the evil owner could use his tricked-out "Spin to Win" game to steal their destinies. The game is rigged so the players always lose, and their destinies are sold on a global black market.

FRED: "Futures trading."

LORNE: "Can't get more literal than that, crumbcake."

At first, Gunn is angry that Lorne would play along, but the demon explains that Lee killed one of his dancing Lornettes right in front of him and threatened to kill others each time the demon refused. Then they realize that Angel had that same hopeless look that most "winners" at the game had once they lost their futures, and they go back to the hotel to save him. Angel doesn't know he needs to be saved, though, and the others are captured and brought to Lee's futures exchange room where they learn they're about to die.

RESOLUTION

Luckily all this has been watched from above by the higher being Cordelia. Though she can't directly interfere, she does use some very literal powers of deus ex machina to tweak Angel's slot machine into making him a winner. Lee brings the vampire into his back room, because nobody ever wins in his casino. As Angel sees his friends about to be marched off to their deaths, he springs into action. During the fight, Lorne smashes the mystical destiny collector and everyone's futures are restored.

As they return to L.A. Lorne explains that Angel was able to break Lee's spell because he saw that his friends' destinies were in jeopardy, and no magic can take away his concern for his friends. Lorne then runs ahead leaving Angel, Gunn, and Fred to make a surprise discovery in the hotel lobby—Cordelia has returned. But what's even more surprising than her appearance is the first thing that she says.

"Who are you people?"   *—Cordelia*

DOSSIERS

CLIENT

Lorne becomes the gang's client when they seek to free him from his captor.

SUSPECTS

Lee DeMarco, the owner of the Tropicana, his right hand man, **Spencer**, and various **security guards** work to keep Lorne in his place. DeMarco used to be a second-rate lounge magician until he got his hands on the power to steal peoples' futures.

CONTINUITY

The gang finally makes that trip to Las Vegas that Gunn has been talking about since the third season. Wes and his newly formed band of demon hunters handle Angel's clients while the gang is out of town. Among the things DeMarco learns about Angel's destiny is the fact that he's to be a major player in the Apocalypse, which was established in "To Shanshu in L.A." Cordelia still watches from above and is apparently forbidden to interfere directly in her friends' lives. She finally comes home, after having ascended into a realm of higher beings in "Tomorrow."

QUOTE OF THE WEEK

FRED: "Frankly, Lorne . . . we weren't aware you needed rescuing."

LORNE: "Weren't—? I told you!"

FRED: "When?"

LORNE: "Well, every time you called me I kept asking about 'Fluffy.'"

FRED: "Oh, I just thought you were using some show business catchphrase I wasn't hip enough to get. Who's Fluffy?"

LORNE: "*Fluffy!* Fluffy the dog! The dog you don't have! The universally recognized code for 'I'm being held prisoner. Send help!'"

THE DEVIL IS IN THE DETAILS

EXPENSES

Costs for the impromptu road trip include gas for the ride to and from Vegas and tickets to Lorne's show (although they probably could have gotten those comped if they hadn't helped Lorne escape).

WEAPONRY

Once again Lorne finds a defensive use for his singing voice.

AS SCENE IN . . . LAS VEGAS

The cast and crew actually went on location to Las Vegas for this episode. Though the action was set at the Tropicana, much of the filming took place inside the Riviera Hotel.

THE PEN IS MIGHTIER

FINAL CUT

The revelation that Lorne isn't as incognito as he is normal in Vegas reads as follows in the stage directions:

Angel and Gunn follow [Fred's] eyes up to
THEIR POV—LORNE'S FACE on a BIG-ASS BILLBOARD in front of the huge, impressive TROPI-CANA HOTEL AND CASINO.
A marquee in front reads: "Exclusive engagement—17th Straight Week—The incomparable song stylings of LORNE!" and underneath that: "The Green Velvet Fog—Las Vegas Review-Journal."

POP CULTURE

✳ "Argh! Think, bobble-head . . ."

Cordy compares her floating head and torso to the fad toy figurines with bouncing heads.

TRACKS

Lorne's set includes the song "It's Not Easy Being Green" (originally performed by fellow green guy,

Kermit the Frog), and "Lady Marmalade" (the Aretha Franklin song recently updated for the soundtrack to *Moulin Rouge*). As the team escapes through the city, they do so to the sounds of the Elvis Presley hit "Viva Las Vegas."

OUR HEROES

ANDY HALLETT ON HEADLINING IN VEGAS: "That, I have to admit, that took the cake. I was in heaven. It was like a real show for me. We were at the Riviera Hotel, which was wonderful, but we were saying that we were at the Tropicana. First when we pulled in it was fun because we all flew there together, pretty much. Just being on a plane with all your work friends has a whole different dynamic. It was like we were on a field trip. From the time we took off it was great. Getting there and pulling up and seeing Lorne's name on the marquee— that was wild. We were all screaming in the van and just cracking up. But, they did screw something up, which is hilarious. It was supposed to say, 'Lorne, The Green Velvet Fog.' The people at the hotel who do the billboard, they screwed it up so it said 'The Green Velvet *Frog*.' And I could see why they would think that.

"It was really fun. I got to sing up there. I had the three gals who did the backup singing and they were jammin' to the left and to the right. And there were twelve real showgirls. Those were the real showgirls from the house show at the Riviera, which is called 'Splash.' So those girls can dance. They were so sweet to me. We just rehearsed several times to see where I would be and where they were. And it was a full audience, which to me it felt like a real audience, but then I realized, 'Wait a minute, they're getting paid to sit there.'"

DAYNE JOHNSON (MAKEUP SUPERVISOR): "It was a great episode. I think it was well received, but it was a lot of work. There was a lot of green makeup going on in that episode, especially with the Lornettes and Amy. Amy was cute as she could be as a Lornette. Everybody loved her. When I did a convention in London a fan asked me if I changed Andy's makeup during that episode because when he was singing they had a blue spotlight on him that turned him that milky gross color. I've had more than one person ask me about that. I didn't change it, but it's a perfect example of what lighting will do."

This episode highlights many of the attractions in the rich history of Las Vegas. In addition to setting the action in the famous Tropicana, the gang also makes the following Vegas references:

"And maybe afterwards we can check out that Danny Ganz guy I keep seeing billboards for."

Angel refers to the multitalented Vegas headliner.

GUNN: "Man, it has been a while. They tore the Dunes down ten years ago."

ANGEL: "Not the casino. I mean actual sand dunes. Bugsy used to call 'em 'dung piles.'"

Gunn refers to one of the more famous old Vegas hotels, while Angel brings up mobster Bugsy Siegel, the man who made Las Vegas the gambling capital city it became.

"They must think it's all makeup. Like the Blue Man Group."

Fred compares Lorne's green act to the guys in blue with a unique brand of performance art.

ANGEL: "I thought it was a little overproduced. It's like I told Sammy Davis at the Sands: 'When you, Frank, and Dean are the meal, you don't need the trimmings.'"

GUNN: "Wait a minute. Hold it. You knew the Rat Pack?"

ANGEL: "Know 'em? No. I met 'em. Once or twice. For drinks."

Gunn and Angel discuss the famed group of entertainers.

"What, you were living so large, blaring Tony Bennett so loud in that suite of yours that you couldn't hear your conscience screaming at you?"

Gunn refers to another famous singer often associated with the city.

"Now I remember that room! Elvis and Priscilla's wedding reception. 1967."

Angel contends that he was in attendance when the King found his queen.

"SLOUCHING TOWARD BETHLEHEM"

CASE Nº 4ADH04

ACTION TAKEN

Connor takes a break from patrolling the streets and sneaks into the hotel, surprised to find that Cordelia has returned. He watches from above and discovers that he is not the only one shocked by the turn of events.

Angel tries to calm a frightened Cordelia who reveals that she doesn't know her friends, or even her own name. The gang scrambles to keep Lorne out of sight and figures it's best to reintroduce Cordelia to her strange life slowly, leaving the demon dealings for later.

While Gunn and Fred tend to a client, Angel takes Cordy to visit her stuff (that was moved to the hotel) hoping it will jog her memory. Angel tries to convince her she's among friends, but Cordelia asks to be alone as she goes through photos and mementos trying to remember who she had been. After that fails to produce results, she wanders through the hotel, seeing and hearing strange things that send her fleeing out to the street, where a pair of Wolfram & Hart commandos lies in wait.

Cordelia's training kicks in and she and Angel fight off the bad guys, but she refuses to calm down around her suspicious-acting friends. Angel tries to answer her questions, but when she dumps a pile of crosses in his hand and he bursts into vamp face, he is forced to tell her the overwhelming truth.

The gang convinces Cordelia to sing a tune for Lorne so he can read her and try to figure out what's going on. Her song hits more than a few sour notes, but that's not what sends Lorne fleeing from the room. Angel follows Lorne and learns the frightening truth.

WRITTEN BY Jeffrey Bell
DIRECTED BY Skip Schoolnik
SPECIAL GUEST STAR: Andy Hallett (Lorne)
GUEST STAR: Stephanie Romanov (Lilah)
COSTARS: David Grant Wright (Dad), Steven Mayhew (Teen Boy), Carol Avery (Mom), Thomas Crawford (Humanoid-Looking Demon), Nynno Ahli (Tech Guy)

> "What I saw was . . . jumbled. Pieces, flashes . . . It was just enough to make my skin crawl away and scamper under the bed. Evil's comin'. And it's plannin' on staying, Angel." —*Lorne*

Cordelia insists on spending more alone time, and this time when she wanders through the hotel, she crosses paths with one of Lorne's clients, who has a nasty habit of eating humans. Connor rushes in with a rescue, saving Cordelia and taking her to his new home in a museum warehouse. Cordy feels safer with the boy, especially after he honestly reveals some of his past misdeeds to her.

While Angel worries that Cordelia is missing again, Wesley learns her whereabouts. He overhears Lilah on a call telling the office to put together an extraction team. Once she leaves, Wes reports the news to Angel.

RESOLUTION

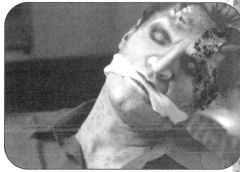

The Wolfram & Hart team attacks and is about to overwhelm Connor and Cordy when Angel, Fred, and Gunn rush in. The fight shifts in their favor, but a camera is placed in the warehouse and Lilah confirms that another mission has been accomplished. After the commandos retreat, Cordelia tells Angel that she wants to stay with Connor because the boy is the only one who has been totally honest with her.

The gang returns to the hotel to find Lorne tied up and bleeding. While they were out, another team from Wolfram & Hart came in and burrowed Cordelia's visions right out of his head.

> "What we do know is that Wolfram & Hart may now know more about Cordy's doom and gloom thing than we do . . . And that's a problem." —*Angel*

Wesley realizes that Lilah had set him up to pass along the false information and he confronts her about it, but they accept that the deception was all part of the nature of their relationship.

DOSSIERS

CLIENT In the midst of helping **Cordelia** readjust, Gunn and Fred take off to help **Murray, down at the spa,** with his demon problem.

SUSPECTS Although the demon Fred and Gunn deal with is never clearly identified, it appears that the main problem was that she gave birth to a number of skittering creatures.

Lilah and agents of **Wolfram & Hart** pop up a few times, unrelated to the case at the spa.

CONTINUITY

This episode starts up roughly where the last left off, opening with the evening from Connor's perspective. Cordelia's past is demonstrated in several ways to jog her memory. Angel holds up the shoe she wore to the ballet in "Waiting in the Wings," recalling that it was a special night. She looks through her high school yearbook from Sunnydale High. The song Cordelia sings, "The Greatest Love of All," is the same song she sang on the *Buffy* episode "The Puppet Show" so many years ago. Connor tells Cordy that she was nice to him once, referring to "Benediction," which was the same episode in which he tried to kill her.

OFFICE ROMANCE

Angel moves in for a kiss when he suspects that Cordelia is beginning to feel some semblance of her past romantic stirrings for the vamp . . . but he's wrong. Wesley loses the dollar bet he has with Lilah when he is the first to refer to their coupling as a "relationship." Although they originally joke about the subject, it seems clear that they both want it to be one. In the end they realize that their mistrustful natures are basically what are keeping them from making it a relationship.

QUOTE OF THE WEEK

Cordelia is a little thrown by the odd entries in her high school yearbook, including:

"Homeroom was fun, too bad it burned to the ground."

"Hey, how 'bout that giant snake."

"Dear Cordelia, thanks for the flaming arrows."

THE DEVIL IS IN THE DETAILS

EXPENSES

One can assume the large amount of demon goo Fred and Gunn got on their clothes will require a hefty laundry fee.

WEAPONRY

Connor has his own sword and rigs his room with a few booby traps, including a stake launcher.

THE VAMPIRE RULES

As amnesiac Cordelia is surprised to learn, a pile of crosses can burn a vampire's hands.

THE PEN IS MIGHTIER

FINAL CUT

The following exchange was cut when the gang was trying to convince Cordy to sing for Lorne so he could read her. The pop culture reference is from Elton John's tune "Your Song."

 FRED: "It's his gift."

 LORNE: "Au contraire, ma petite frite. My gift is my song . . . Sorry, I can never walk away
  from that one."

POP CULTURE

❋ **"Okay Jughead, that's enough."**
Lorne calls his client by the name of one of the characters in Archie comics after the guy sings "Sugar, Sugar," a song associated with The Archies.

❋ **GUNN: "So, I look Russian to you?"**
CORDELIA: "Black Russian."
ANGEL: "That's a drink."
CORDELIA: "Says the head spy."
They are, of course, referring to an alcoholic beverage made of vodka and Kahlua.

❋ **"Seabreeze?"**
Lorne offers a sip of his signature drink.

❋ **"You're the one who decided to take what you overheard and give it to the Good n' Plentys™."**
Lilah references the Good & Plentys candy-coated licorice bits often sold in movie theaters.

THE NAME GAME

The phrase **"Slouching Toward Bethlehem"** comes from a poem about the apocalypse by William Butler Yeats entitled "The Second Coming," the final lines of which read: "And what rough beast, its hour come round at last, / Slouches towards Bethlehem to be born?"

OUR HEROES

ALEXIS DENISOF: "The relationship with Lilah was very interesting. It was such a signpost for where the character Wesley was at that time that it became a plausible relationship, and the fact that he was willing to sleep with the enemy was just fascinating to me."

"SUPERSYMMETRY"

CASE № 4ADH05

ACTION TAKEN

Fred screams for joy over the publication of her article on the theory of "Supersymmetry and P-Dimensional Subspace," while Gunn struggles to keep up with the big words and focuses on the effect the article has on Fred. The next morning Fred shares her news with Angel and Lorne. The excitement is only temporarily put aside when she learns that Connor had made a secret visit the previous night to collect some of Cordelia's things.

Fred's article does not go unnoticed by Wesley, who goes to see Fred speak on her theories at the university. Lilah sees the article too and jealously follows her lover to the school. There Fred runs into Professor Seidel, the mentor who had put her on her life path to study physics. It's beginning to look like Fred can regain the life she had lost when she was pulled into Pylea, when another dimensional portal opens above her during her speech and a demon's tentacles grab her.

WRITTEN BY Elizabeth Craft & Sarah Fain
DIRECTED BY Bill Norton
SPECIAL GUEST STARS: Andy Hallett (Lorne), Stephanie Romanov (Lilah), Randy Oglesby (Professor Seidel)
COSTARS: Jerry Trainor (Jared), Jennifer Hipp (Laurie)

Angel and Gun fight off the tentacled demon, and the portal closes. Having noticed Lilah sneak out before the attack, Angel goes on his own attack, only to find that the evil lawyer had nothing to do with it. Meanwhile Fred goes back to the hotel and tries to get over the horror of a close call with another hell dimension.

The next day Angel tries to recreate the events of the dimensional demon attack and realizes a suspicious student was sitting behind him. He and Gunn track the kid to a comic book store and learn that Fred was not the first student to go missing in recent years. Further investigation reveals that all the missing students had one thing in common: Professor Seidel—the man Fred is visiting at that very moment.

Fred reveals to her former mentor the truth about her missing years. He seems surprised to learn that theoretical dimensions are real, but not as surprised as Fred is when she stumbles across his notes for calling up the dimensional portal from the previous day. That leads her to the more painful revelation that Professor Seidel was the one who had sent her to Pylea years earlier because the star student was threatening to overshadow her mentor. Stunned, she returns to the hotel where she meets up with Angel and Gunn and tells them that she knows about Seidel and wants him to pay for what he did.

She wants him to die.

> **FRED:** "We kill monsters every day."
>
> **GUNN:** "We help people. Fred, if you do this, the demons you'll be livin' with won't be the horned fangy kind. They'll be the kind you can't get rid of."

Fred seems to take Gunn's words to heart and says she's going to bed. Instead she goes for help from an unlikely source: Wesley.

RESOLUTION

Wesley points Fred in the right direction for taking her revenge, but he knows she must do it alone. However, Angel and Gunn figure out her plan and hurry to stop her. Using his vampire speed, Angel gets there first, but Seidel distracts the vamp with a dimensional demon attack. By the time Gunn arrives, Fred is already holding Seidel at crossbow point. She has opened another hell dimension and is forcing the professor in. Gunn tries to reason with Fred, but when that proves fruitless, Gunn snaps the professor's neck and dumps the body into the portal to save Fred from living with her own regret.

Angel finally gets the best of the demon and enters to find the fight over. When he asks about the professor, Gunn's response is simple.

"It's taken care of." *—Gunn*

They allow Angel to believe that the professor fell into his own portal and they go home to find Cordelia waiting. She finally understands why Angel had lied to protect her, but she wants to know one other truth. She wants to know if they were in love.

DOSSIERS

CLIENT Fred is the one whom all the focus is on this week.

CIVILIAN SUPPORT Comic book fan (and online Angel aficionado) **Jared** helps point the guys in the right direction.

SUSPECTS Lilah is briefly considered a suspect because of her suspicious appearance at Fred's lecture, but **Professor Seidel** turns out as the man of interest in this and several other unsolved missing persons cases.

CONTINUITY

It has been "a couple of days" since the previous episode, in which Cordelia went to stay with Connor and Lorne was brain-drained by Wolfram & Hart. Lorne tells Angel that he has no intention of reading Cordelia again for fear of Wolfram & Hart attacking him a second time. Following her nearly being sucked into another demon dimension, Fred reverts to her post-Pylea self by writing her theories out on the hotel room wall.

OFFICE ROMANCE

Connor and Cordelia continue to bond while trying to discover her memory. Connor suggests that he train her to fight, and the two take on a vamp. After the kill they find themselves in a kiss that Cordelia pulls out of. She later tells Connor that things are moving too fast—she still has to figure out who she is. However, this sets up the strange father-son triangle with Cordelia at the apex. Speaking of triangles, it is clear that Wesley still has feelings for Fred and is keeping track of her. He even tries to undermine her relationship with Gunn. However, it is Gunn's "noble" act of killing Seidel so Fred doesn't have to that proves to be the beginning of the end for the couple.

QUOTE OF THE WEEK

"You know what they say about payback? Well, I'm the bitch."   Fred makes an entrance.

THE DEVIL IS IN THE DETAILS

WEAPONRY

Angel keeps a dagger in his boot and can make handy with a microphone stand when necessary. Fred goes through the weapons cabinet for something to hurt Professor Seidel with and comes out with a halberd and a flail for a good whipping that could last hours. She ultimately settles on a crossbow supplied by Wes, as well as a chant to open another dimensional portal.

DEMONS, ETC. . . .

Voynok demons are incredibly difficult to kill and possibly have nine lives. If the demon's head is cut off it will grow a new one.

THE PEN IS MIGHTIER

FINAL CUT

The following exchange was cut from Fred and Gunn's talk over the open portal before Gunn kills the professor.

FRED: "I can't live in this world knowin' he's in it and not go crazy."

GUNN: "Baby, I know about mistakes that eat you up from inside out. Please . . ."

POP CULTURE

✳ **"Oh God, I'm between Ed Witten and Brian Green . . . Think Nomar Garciaparra and Sammy Sosa."**

Fred compares a couple of first-string physicists to all-star baseball players.

* **"If this is about the Jolly Green Demon . . ."**
  In discussing her past actions against Lorne, Lilah compares him to the mascot for Green Giant vegetables.
* **"Tragedy struck Gidget?"**
  Lilah refers to the "Girl Midget" from the surfer movies and TV series when expressing false concern for Fred.
* **"Yeah, yeah . . . Hulk smash."**
  And Lilah continues her reference-fest by mentioning the not-so-jolly-green Marvel Comics character known for his simple commentary.
* **"Think Daredevil. One-eighty-one. I'm Bullseye. You're Elektra. One wins. One dies."**
  Gunn uses terminology Jared will understand by referencing a set of Marvel Comics characters from the *Daredevil* series.
* **"But we're crushing the Dark Horses."**
  Dark Horse is another Comic Books line . . . that just so happens to publish the *Buffy* and *Angel* comic books.

THE NAME GAME

"**Supersymmetry**" is a theory of particle physics that tries to link the four fundamental forces that emerged separately during the big bang.

OUR HEROES

AMY ACKER: "When Gunn killed the professor and I'm almost mad at him for doing it, we were trying to decide if I was angry at him because I wanted to do it and he had done it or if it was the fact that now I felt guilty that he had done this. So it seemed that they sort of went more with the second option in writing, but we were kind of interested in the fact that it was like 'This isn't your place.' And it was the first time that Fred was standing alone doing something that was totally different. It was sort of the first fight scene that I had on my own where I was in some sort of physical confrontation with someone and wasn't just hiding under a table or with Angel there, that I knew that he was going to be in charge. That was interesting and we were just curious to see how that was going to break us up."

J. AUGUST RICHARDS: "It was a very difficult scene to play. I found that I got a little upset that day because I felt like there was a particular moment in that scene that was kind of breezed over that I didn't feel that anybody was giving weight to, which was the difference between me trying to convince her not to do it and then me doing it myself—that sort of unwritten moment, that unspoken moment. I was trying really hard to capture that moment, so I found myself getting really protective of the scene and of that moment. I don't think it ever really got on film, to be honest, but that scene was difficult to shoot."

LONI PERISTERE (VISUAL EFFECTS SUPERVISOR): "Those stand-alone episodes are always fun because usually they're very, very unique. It's rare that you use the same effect over and over again. I mean, there's always a vamp, there's always a dusting. But when you come up with things like the tentacles that we had to do, to have them come down, grab the people and just start flailing around, that was just so much fun. All the actors, of course, had to react to nothing in the scene, which is a little bit scary when you're trying to go ahead and take a look at their

performance and actually create an object within the scene. That for us was a lot of fun. You have to tell the actors, 'Okay, there's this huge tentacled creature hanging up there, its tentacles come down, grab you, and you're going to be lifted up there, and you have to react to all that stuff and there's nothing there.'"

"SPIN THE BOTTLE"

CASE Nº 4ADH06

ACTION TAKEN

Lorne sets the mood with a song in a club, then he tells the tale onstage of how Cordelia regains her memory. It begins with a spell from one of his clients. Although Angel is reluctant to trust magic, Cordelia's willing to do what it takes. The spell requires six people, so Lorne puts in a call to Wesley. He agrees to come, and inquires as to how Fred is doing following her run-in with her professor. No one realizes how much the encounter has come between Fred and Gunn.

Lorne sets up the spell as Wesley arrives. Gunn can't help but notice that Wesley seems a little too interested in Fred's well-being. It doesn't take much for Gunn to realize Wesley's part in Fred's attempted murder and the two men have it out.

GUNN: "Angel's the man on the card, it's his world. I'm not a leader no more. Don't got that Champion's heart like Cordy—and the brains, well that was you. So that leaves the muscle."

WRITTEN & DIRECTED BY
Joss Whedon
SPECIAL GUEST STAR: Andy Hallett (Lorne)
GUEST STAR: Vladimir Kulich (The Beast)
COSTARS: Sven Holmberg (Delivery Guy), Kam Heskin (Lola)

WESLEY: "What about Fred?"

GUNN: "Well, that's the question, isn't it. She's pretty brainy too. Maybe you two are kindred souls. Maybe that's why she went to you for help gettin' revenge on that Professor. Killin' takes brains."

WESLEY: "I did what you weren't prepared to do."

GUNN: "You have no idea what I've—what I would do for her."

The gang gathers to enact the spell and things immediately get trippy. Lorne crawls away behind the desk before collapsing, and the others walk about the lobby in a haze until Cordelia smashes the bottle at the center of the spell. As the world comes back into focus, Cordelia is no longer the only one who doesn't know what's going on.

Actually, Cordelia's memory is back, but she's stuck as a teenager, as are Gunn, Wesley, Fred, and Angel . . . or Liam. The group struggles to figure out what's going on since they don't remember anything about their adult lives—or about one another. Things get even more complicated when they find an unconscious demon—Lorne—lying on the floor.

Wesley and Gunn reveal to the others that vampires are real, although they don't really know *what* the green-skinned demon is. It's all a little too much, especially for Liam, who is over two hundred years out of his time. Wesley thinks it may be a test he has heard of and that they may be locked in with a vampire. Although their situation doesn't exactly fit the test, the group splits up to search the hotel and Liam is shocked to find that he is the vampire in question.

When their search proves nothing to anyone else, Wesley suspects that the vampire might be one of their group. Liam does his best to hide his true self from the others, but when Lorne awakens, unaware of what's going on and unaffected by the spell, he outs the vamp. Liam tries to stop Lorne with a smack that sends the demon across the room.

RESOLUTION

Liam goes from the defensive to the offensive, figuring he can use his vampire strength as a weapon, chasing Cordelia through the lower levels. Just as he is about to capture his prey, Connor comes in and knocks his father to the ground, happy to be Cordelia's savior. Connor takes on his dad and slowly realizes that Angel doesn't know what's going on. Rather than ending the fight, Connor comes on stronger.

Lorne revives once again and convinces Fred to let him go so he can reverse the spell. He does, and sends everyone back to normal. When Cordelia gets a taste of the potion to reverse her memory spell she sees everything—including a menacing demon—and runs away. Angel follows and confirms that her memory has returned, and asks her the same question she had asked him at the start of everything.

ANGEL: "Were we in love?"

CORDELIA: "We were."

DOSSIERS

CLIENT All the action this time revolves around regaining **Cordelia's** memory.

CIVILIAN SUPPORT One of Lorne's clients, a **wraith** who deals professionally in memory magic, provides the spell to regain Cordy's past.

CONTINUITY

Once again the action in Lorne's tale picks up where the previous episode, "Supersymmetry," left off. In fact, the entire story takes place in one night. Angel reverts to the life he had before being turned into a vampire, as seen in "The Prodigal." Wesley, having been trained at the Watchers Academy, knows of a ritual test—the Cruciamentum—that Slayers have been put through in which they are locked in a house with a vampire. This was seen in the *Buffy* episode "Helpless." Cordelia echoes the line "Hello, salty goodness" when she sees Angel, which is the same thing she said when she saw him for the first time in the *Buffy* episode "Never Kill a Boy on the First Date." As will be learned later in the season, when Lorne brings back Cordelia's memory he awakens the being inside her that will ultimately become known as Jasmine.

OFFICE ROMANCE

Angel is quick to point out that nothing of a romantic nature ever occurred between himself and Cordelia in the workplace prior to her time spent missing, except for when they were under a spell in "Waiting in the Wings." He and Connor get into a fight over Cordelia. The Gunn-Fred-Wesley triangle intensifies as they all adjust to the happenings in "Supersymmetry."

QUOTE OF THE WEEK

"Oh good, symbols on the floor. That always goes well."

Gunn has an understandable reaction to seeing Lorne prepare for the spell.

THE DEVIL IS IN THE DETAILS

WEAPONRY

Wesley is testing a weapon from an arms dealer named Emil. The contraption is strapped to his forearm and can eject a stake or turn into a sword with a flick of the wrist.

DEMONS, ETC. . . .

Young Wesley thinks Lorne is a demon of the Karathmamanyuhg family, which are known to be nocturnal and feed on roots, or possibly human effluvia.

AS SCENE IN L.A.

"Connor and I are not exactly staying at the Mondrian."
Cordelia refers to the trendy hotel located on Sunset Boulevard.

THE PEN IS MIGHTIER

FINAL CUT

The spell to regain Cordy's memory originally had a bit more explanation that was cut due to time constraints:

LORNE: "Now, we represent the six spheres of consciousness, the six gifts from the Lords of Shah-teyaman, the six walls of the house of truth. We're all one with Cordelia, we bring to this circle only trust and imagination. The bottle in the center of the circle contains the liquid essence that has passed through the wraith and been gathered here—"

GUNN: "We're curing Cordy with a urine sample?"

CORDELIA: "Okay, not drinking it . . ."

LORNE: "Hush, puppies. All we do is join hands and concentrate. On the bottle, on Cordy, on calling her back to the way she was."

✳ **"Okay! We've heard from Scarlett O'Please-shut-me-up."**

Taking Fred's accent into account, Cordelia brings up another Southern belle with a riff on the name Scarlett O'Hara from *Gone with the Wind*.

✳ **"Well, maybe it's *Motel Hell*."**

Fred calls up the title of the "classic" horror movie from 1980.

✳ **"Slayer? The band?"**

Fred confuses vampire slayers with the heavy metal band.

TRACKS

Fittingly, Lorne sings "Memory" from the Andrew Lloyd Webber musical *Cats*.

OUR HEROES

DAVID BOREANAZ ON REVERTING TO ANGEL'S (OR LIAM'S) YOUTH: "You get an opportunity to get in deeper with your character—with Angel—and see where he came from. You learn little idiosyncrasies that you can take from that experience to playing him presently the way he is now. There's so much about this character that I still don't know and that I probably won't fully understand, even when the show is over. For me, it's always been a learning experience to get into that and dive into that realm."

ALEXIS DENISOF: "Well, that was thrilling. Not only because Joss wrote and directed it, but because it afforded us all a chance to go back to the very roots of the character, prior to them even being in the world that was created for them. Before they all know each other. So, some very obvious hilarity ensues as a result. It isn't that you could transform . . . your bodies didn't become fifteen years younger. You tried to infuse the spirit of that time in the character's life.

"It was such fun to dust off the awkward, uptight, bombastic Wesley that eventually went to Sunnydale. That was the fun of him, in the early days of the show. *Buffy* was at a point that it needed a very light, silly character, so that it didn't suffer too much from self-consciously being dark. And then as the years have gone by, we've found other needs for Wesley to fulfill. It was such a stroke of genius for Joss to come up with a way that we all could have the fun of going back to the original characters and having them interact and having characters meet that had never met before in a sense."

"APOCALYPSE, NOWISH"

CASE Nº 4ADH07

ACTION TAKEN

Lorne tries to convince Angel to ask Cordelia about the horrific visions in her head, but the vampire is reluctant to push his friend—her memory is just newly regained. On the other hand, Cordelia *wants* to talk about what's up there plaguing her dreams but can't seem to find the words to warn anyone.

WRITTEN BY Steven S. DeKnight
DIRECTED BY Vern Gillum
SPECIAL GUEST STAR: Andy Hallett (Lorne)
GUEST STARS: Stephanie Romanov (Lilah), Daniel Dae Kim (Gavin), Vladimir Kulich (The Beast)
COSTARS: Tina Morasco (Mrs. Pritchard), Molly Weber (Waitress)

The tension rises when Gunn and Fred are called to a house with what turns out to be an extreme rat infestation. But that's nothing compared to the tension continuing to rise between Fred and Gunn in light of their actions against Professor Seidel. Fred goes off to be alone as Angel Investigations experiences other portents of biblical proportions.

While one couple drifts apart, another gets closer as Cordelia is impressed with Connor's more mature (and Angel-like) ways. Connor is worried about Cordelia and asks his dad to speak with her, but Angel does not like what he hears.

> **CORDELIA:** "What I remember when I was a higher being . . . I remember seeing you. Your past. When you were Angelus."

> **ANGEL:** "I've never tried to hide who I was. Or what I've done. You already knew."
>
> **CORDELIA:** "Knowing's different than living it. When I was up there, I could look back and see everything you did as Angelus. More than see. I felt it. Not just their fear and pain. I felt you. And how much you enjoyed making them suffer . . . I love you, Angel. But I can't be with you. It's too soon."

Before they can talk further, Cordelia is struck with a powerful vision that a Beast is about to rise to slaughter them all.

Angel pays a surprise visit to Lilah intending to have that promised talk about her theft of Lorne's memory, especially since he's already gotten Gavin to squeal. The law firm hasn't been able to decipher what was pulled from Lorne's mind because every time one of their psychics gets close, his head explodes. Knowing that Lilah's bosses wouldn't want someone muscling in on their coming Apocalypse, Angel convinces her to share what she pulled out of Lorne's brain.

Cordelia and Connor go in search of her Beastly vision and come across a huge stone demon as it bursts up from the ground in the exact same spot that Darla gave birth. Connor tries to fight against the Beast, but it is too powerful and escapes.

In the meantime Wesley goes to the hotel hoping to check on Fred and pool their resources. When Angel returns with pages of undecipherable info, he, Wes, Gunn, and Lorne get to work. Gunn finally manages to put it all together when he discovers the pages all link together like a puzzle forming one huge prophecy in the Eye of Fire. At the same time, Lorne has laid out all the strange disturbances on a map of the city and found that the symbol of the Eye and the map are a match.

RESOLUTION

The guys follow the map to the center of the Eye at a club atop a hotel. There they find the Beast standing among the slaughtered bodies of patrons that have been arranged in the symbol of the Eye. The gang attacks, but the Beast proves too much as he beats down the group and sends Angel flying off the roof. The Beast slams his fist down in the center of the symbol and a bolt of energy shoots up to the sky. Moments later the night begins to rain fire.

Knowing they have lost, Wes, Gunn, and Lorne retreat while Angel lies bloody and broken on the ground below. Fred watches the burning sky from a diner, trying to reach Gunn but getting no answer, and Cordelia tries to calm Connor.

CONNOR: "It chose the place where I was born. Is that why it's here? Because of me?"
CORDELIA: "No."
CONNOR: "I was never supposed to happen. The child of two vampires. What if—"
CORDELIA: "Connor. It's not you."

When her words do not prove enough to calm him, Cordelia gives Connor the kiss he has been wanting since she turned to him for help. Worried that this might be the beginning of the end, Cordelia then gives herself to Connor, unaware that Angel is watching from above.

DOSSIERS

CLIENT Mrs. Pritchard, a woman with a very nice home in the Hancock Park area of the city, calls with a complaint of odd noises in the pipes that turn out to be caused by a rat infestation. Other potential clients are dealing with snakes, swarms, and other weird occurrences.

CIVILIAN SUPPORT Lilah and **Gavin** are forced into providing Angel with the information Wolfram & Hart extracted from Lorne.

SUSPECTS The Beast rises to lay waste to the land.

CONTINUITY

Lorne is pushing Angel to find out what was stolen from the empath's mind in "Slouching Toward Bethlehem." The Beast that Cordelia had a flash of in the previous episode, "Spin the Bottle," appears live and in living color. Cordelia also tells Angel what she meant when she said it was all too much for her after she regained her memory—specifically seeing all that he had done as Angelus. The Beast rises in the same spot where Darla "gave birth" to Connor in "Lullaby."

OFFICE ROMANCE

Lilah dresses up—sort of—like Fred (complete with Southern accent) to seduce Wesley, knowing that the little physicist is what he really wants. As they get hot and heavy, Wesley insists that she keep on the "Fred" glasses, and a brief flash of hurt crosses Lilah's face. Fred continues to pull away from Gunn. She is both angry that he did not let her kill the professor, and upset to know that Gunn had that kind of thing in him.

QUOTE OF THE WEEK

LILAH: "Couldn't you have at least tortured him a little more?"
ANGEL: "Really wanted to. But he wouldn't stop talking long enough for me to get into it."

Lilah and Angel stand over a bound Gavin.

THE DEVIL IS IN THE DETAILS

EXPENSES

Cleaning of the hotel exterior, which is littered with dead birds after they commit mass suicide.

WEAPONRY

The crossbows, mace, and sword used on the Beast all prove ineffectual, but it is Gunn's favorite hubcap ax that fares the worst when the Beast crushes it. Bullets from Wesley's two .45 hand cannons and sawed-off assault shotgun also prove useless. The Beast uses Angel's own retractable stake against him.

DEMONS, ETC. . . .

A **Glurgg** is made up of ninety percent pus.

THE PEN IS MIGHTIER

FINAL CUT

Cordelia tries to explain the odd sensation she has following her vision of the Beast in dialogue cut due to length:

CORDELIA: "It's kind of like . . . you ever had a toothache?"

CONNOR: "No."

CORDELIA: "Super teeth. That explains the Colgate smile . . . Okay, let's see, umm . . . It's a throbbing pain, like somebody squeezing you really hard, only it's inside your tooth. Now imagine that feeling, but it's connected to something outside you. Something far away. And every time it moves . . . you squirm."

POP CULTURE

* "Chocodiles . . . and some other stuff."

    In a dream Connor brings Cordy some snacks, including the chocolatey snack made by Hostess.

* "Casper's dealing with the big boys now."

    Gunn, thinking the client's house has a ghost infestation, refers to the friendliest ghost of them all from the cartoon by Harvey Comics.

* "Or some consecrated Drano."

    Fred suggests that some holy clog-clearing products might be more useful at their client's home.

* "Whatever Lorne gleaned from Wonder Girl, it's protected."

    Lilah compares Cordelia to the junior version of DC Comics's Wonder Woman.

* "Chanel?"

    Lilah wears only the best perfume.

* "It might be a couple of days. You're the fifth on the bleeding walls list. Spritz it with a little 409."

    Lorne suggests using an all-purpose cleaner for some unnatural stains.

* "Maybe we could save the three rounds until after the Chuck Heston plague-a-thon cools off."

    Lorne refers to the actor who played Moses in the plague-infested film *The Ten Commandments*.

* "Hate to be the little demon who cried apocalypse nowish, but . . ."

    Lorne brings up the story of the little boy who cried wolf, and the episode's title, which is explained under The Name Game.

THE NAME GAME

"Apocalypse, Nowish" is a play on the 1979 Francis Ford Coppola Vietnam war film *Apocalypse Now*, which was based on the Joseph Conrad book *Heart of Darkness*.

OUR HEROES

MICHAEL GASPAR (SPECIAL EFFECTS COORDINATOR): "That was the most challenging episode we've ever had. We started by making little pieces of clay and stuck feathers in them so they looked like birds and made these special pneumatic guns that shot out these little pieces of clay against the windows. After a while there were so many feathers. We're hitting Plexiglas doors and putting blood on them so they looked like they were smashing.

"Then, the visual effects guys came to us and said, 'We need elements. We don't have any fire that looks like it would [work] in this instance. We need shots of fire coming down out of the sky. What can you do?' I said, 'How much?' 'Tons.' We took some burlap, tied them up with stovepipe wire, soaked them in lighter fluid and got a bunch of guys up above the backdrop with gloves on and just lit them up and threw them down on the ground. When we were doing it, I thought, 'God, this is going to look hokey.' But the finished product was pretty cool."

ROCCO PASSIORINO (DIGITAL EFFECTS SUPERVISOR): "The fire raining was beautifully done. A lot of that had to do with taking the existing plates that they gave us and augmenting them a little bit to show that the sky was burning and on fire. We had shot some cloud elements and some smoke elements and we'd done particles for enhancing the clouds. When it came down to actually having the rain go through, we shot practical elements, and we used a lot of those shots and then created digital versions of all the fire that was coming through. So we created digital rain just passing through all the shots."

ROBERT W. ANDERSON (PROPERTY MASTER): "We destroy a lot of stuff. Gunn used to have that big battle-ax he made ghetto style out of hubcaps and all that stuff. They wanted a shot where the Beast was crushing it and that was a tricky thing to work around. I was like, 'How are we gonna crush this?' We ended up having a few made of soft lead, which they then crushed. It worked out pretty well.

"A lot of times, we'll just cheat things. We'll have breakaway glass made to look like something and dress it up nice enough that you can't tell when it's going to break. We get a pretty good heads up on what's going to break so we know in advance what we have to manufacture. Although, there are often times when we don't get a lot of time to manufacture stuff. We need to have two days and don't always get that."

"HABEAS CORPSES"

CASE № 4ADH08

ACTION TAKEN

As Angel watches Cordelia and Connor coupling, Fred waits back at the hotel for some sign of her friends and loved ones. Gunn, Wesley, and Lorne return to the hotel, beaten

WRITTEN BY Jeffrey Bell
DIRECTED BY Skip Schoolnik
SPECIAL GUEST STAR: Andy Hallett (Lorne)
GUEST STARS: Stephanie Romanov (Lilah), Daniel Dae Kim (Gavin), Vladimir Kulich (The Beast)
COSTAR: Kay Panabaker (Girl)

but alive. After they brief her on events, Gunn is ready to go back into the field, even though Wesley insists that's not what Angel would want. The vampire agrees when he returns still wearing the shock of seeing the woman he loves with his son. Angel retires to his room, leaving the Beast for another day.

The next morning, Cordelia wakes and realizes that she made a mistake. She tells Connor that they cannot be together and he thinks it's because he's somehow linked to the demon. Even though Cordelia insists that's not true, Connor runs off looking for answers. But that's not the only relationship to come to an abrupt halt when Wesley finally tells Lilah that he can no longer be with her.

Cordelia goes to the hotel and finds a very uncivil Angel, though she doesn't know why. She tells him about the Beast rising in the same spot that Connor was born and the fact that the boy believes that they're somehow linked. At the same time, Connor is searching for answers in the most unlikely place: Wolfram & Hart.

As Connor and Lilah work out their arrangement, the building shakes and the power goes off. As the emergency lights kick in Connor realizes that the Beast has come to the law firm. Gavin is sent to check things out, but as he cowers in a supply closet, the Beast finds and kills him. The Beast then faces off with Connor and Lilah in a third-floor conference room. It wounds Lilah and is attacked by . . .

"Connor."   *—The Beast*

. . . who is surprised that the Beast knows his name. The Beast knocks Connor through a stone column, bringing the ceiling in on the boy. Lilah flees the Beast and runs into Wesley, who has come to rescue her thanks to a tip from a source in the building. Lilah takes Wes to the same supply closet where Gavin was killed. They use an escape hatch to drop out of the building into the sewers below. Wesley tells Lilah to flee the city for safety and she, in turn, warns him that Connor is trapped in the building.

Wesley immediately goes to the hotel and Angel rallies the troops. Lorne offers to stay behind and Cordelia is forced to wait with him when Angel jealously decides he doesn't want Cordy along. Angel, Wes, Gunn, and Fred get into the building the same way Wes and Lilah got out, but meet up with a welcoming committee of zombie lawyers.

RESOLUTION

The gang manages to hold off the zombies until they find Connor, but the dozens of dead lawyers are about to overwhelm them. Short on options, Angel decides to flee to the White Room. He uses his photographic memory to remember the code that brought him there on his first visit, and the team is beamed to the interdimensional space where the Beast is already waiting . . . and draining power from the powerful being Angel met once before.

As the being in the form of a little girl is drained of life, she turns to Angel with her final words.

"The answer is among you."   —*Girl*

The Beast turns toward the team. As it approaches the girl uses her remaining energy to send them safely home. The happy reunion is short-lived, however, when Angel quietly tells Cordelia to take her boyfriend, Connor, and leave.

DOSSIERS

CLIENT The gang puts together a rescue mission to get **Connor** out of Wolfram & Hart.

CIVILIAN SUPPORT Lilah provides the needed intel to let them know Connor is in the building.

SUSPECTS The Beast is the big bad threat that everyone believes Connor needed to be rescued from.

CONTINUITY

The episode opens with Angel watching over Cordelia and Connor as he was at the end of the previous episode, "Apocalypse, Nowish." The Wolfram & Hart Senior Partners try to have Lilah broker a deal with the Beast so they can share in the disaster and cut down on the expenses of their anticipated end of the world. Zombies have popped up occasionally in this dimension such as the one Gunn and Wesley fought in "Provider" and in the *Buffy* episode "Dead Man's Party." Angel first visited the White Room in "Forgiving." Though the staff and offices of the L.A. branch of Wolfram & Hart are pretty much decimated, they'll be back and better than ever by the Season Four finale, "Home."

OFFICE ROMANCE

Fred is relieved to see that Gunn is alive and seems to have moved past her desire in the previous episode to be alone. When Cordelia wakes she immediately regrets her actions with Connor and tells him that what happened was because of the odd set of circumstances and that it can't happen again. Lilah was worried about Wesley and left a bunch of messages on his machine before going over to his place to make sure he was okay. When he breaks up with her, it is clear that they were both more invested in the relationship than they had intended to be.

QUOTE OF THE WEEK

CONNOR: "What's a zombie?"
ANGEL: "An undead thing."
CONNOR: "Like you?"
ANGEL: "No. Zombies are slow-moving, dim-witted things that crave human flesh."
CONNOR: "Like you—"
ANGEL: "—No! It's different. Trust me."

DEMONS, ETC. . . .

The offices of **Wolfram & Hart** automatically shut down and seal themselves off under a full-scale attack so that nothing can get in or out of the building.

The only way to kill a **zombie** is to stop brain activity by cutting off its head or smashing its skull. They are conveniently slow and stupid. Their bites do not result in their victim being turned into a zombie.

THE PEN IS MIGHTIER

FINAL CUT

Even in the midst of an overwhelming battle, Gunn manages to lighten the mood in an exchange cut for time:

Gunn takes an awkward step toward Wes.
GUNN: "Eiyii . . ."
Wesley raises his sword. Ready to put Gunn down if necessary.
GUNN: (con't) "Iiiyyiii . . ." (then completely normal) "You're not gonna fall for that, are you?"
—Zombie fake out.

POP CULTURE

※ **"I believe he's referring to the big, bad, possibly invincible, demony thing that nearly killed us all before it ringmastered tonight's 'Cirque de Flambé.'"**
   Lorne makes a riff on the theatrical experience that is *Cirque du Soleil.*

※ **"Listen up, Daddy Dearest."**
   Cordelia compares Angel to Joan Crawford—or at least how she was portrayed in the film *Mommie Dearest.*

※ **"I don't care if you have to LoJack the damned thing."**
   Lilah suggests using the car locator device on the Beast to keep track of it.

※ **FRED: "Didn't mean to snap."**
   CORDELIA: "I'm ready to crackle-pop, myself."
   Cordelia rounds out the names of the spokes-elves for Rice Krispies cereal.

※ **"Why go all Terminator on his own team?"**
   Gunn wonders why the Beast's behavior resembles that of the titular character from the Arnold Schwarzenegger film trilogy.

※ **"Or that Sherlock got his facts wrong."**
   Gunn sarcastically compares Wesley to Sir Arthur Conan Doyle's famed literary detective, Sherlock Holmes.

※ **"So what's it say about the Big Bad Wolf if it can just stride right in and suck the energy out of evil Red Riding Hood?"**
   Gunn compares their situation to the characters from the familiar folktale.

THE NAME GAME

"Habeas Corpses" is a pun based on the legal term "habeas corpus," referring to a writ that is issued to bring a person before a court. The phrase is Latin, meaning "you should have the body," which are the first words of the writ.

OUR HEROES

ROBERT HALL (SPECIAL EFFECTS MAKEUP ARTIST): "I think the Beast was one of the first times I can remember where everyone came to Almost Human [the special effects shop]. Most of the time we work via drawings and sometimes e-mails of some sculptures and progress. We must have done fifteen designs of that character. They wanted him old school. They didn't want to reinvent the wheel on him. They wanted . . . imposing. So they wound up hiring Vlad, who was already six-five/six-six, and we added another six inches to him. Then the horns and we've got a seven-foot-four Beast running around Los Angeles.

"The producers all came here while we were sculpting, which was really cool. I welcome that. I love that. The last thing I'd ever want to do is show up with something that someone didn't like or didn't expect. They knew he was such an important part of the arc that they wanted to be specific. They came by when we were sculpting, offered some notes, and they came by when I was painting the suits and offered some notes. They definitely wanted him to have that stature and old-world beast physicality, but not look like muscle. They wanted him to look like molten lava, which is kind of an interesting spin."

The head that the Beast holds as it walks through the halls of Wolfram & Hart is—naturally—fake, and designed in the image of Special Effects Makeup Artist Robert Hall.

"LONG DAY'S JOURNEY"

CASE № 4ADH09

ACTION TAKEN

The gang is still trying to research the mysterious Beast, but Angel's having trouble playing well with others, instead preferring to remain in his room alone. Lorne senses the vibes and

WRITTEN BY Mere Smith
DIRECTED BY Terrence O'Hara
SPECIAL GUEST STAR: Andy Hallett (Lorne)
GUEST STARS: Alexa Davalos (Gwen), Jack Kehler (Manny), Michael Chinyamurindi (Ashet), Vladimir Kulich (The Beast)

correctly infers that the mood has to do with Cordelia and Connor, but the vamp would rather brood than talk about it.

In a seemingly unrelated event, Gwen Raiden meets with a client to discuss obtaining a protective amulet. As the client, Ashet, tries to persuade her to help, the Beast attacks, punching its fist through the man's body and knocking Gwen aside with its free hand. A beam of light shoots out of Ashet and the Beast reaches into the body to retrieve something. Once Gwen regains her footing, the Beast is already gone.

Cordelia gets a flash of the Beast and leaves Connor to tell Angel about it. The gang continues their research, but Gunn wants to focus on the evil little girl's warning that "the answer is among you," believing the "answer" to be Connor. Wesley and Fred come up with at least a kind of answer when they learn that the little girl from Wolfram & Hart is an entity known as Mesektet.

> **WESLEY:** "Mesektet was one of five enormously powerful beings which are linked to an embodiment of the ancient god Ra."
>
> **FRED:** "Which makes them totems, right? Symbolic manifestations?"
>
> **WESLEY:** "Yes. Totems which together form an order called the Ra-Tet."

Lorne reports on the death of another member of the Ra-Tet at the hands of the Beast right before Gwen arrives with news of her meeting gone bad. They realize three members of the Ra-Tet have died, making a nice little pattern to follow. Angel then takes Gwen out to Death Valley to find the fourth totem.

Angel and Gwen arrive too late to either save or kill the totem since it's already dead. Conveniently the fifth totem, an immortal guy nicknamed Manny, is still alive and waiting. He reveals that he knows the Beast's plan is to turn off the sun. Angel takes Manny into protection in Gwen's swank high-security apartment that is built into a dilapidated old warehouse.

Manny is safely locked away in Gwen's panic room and the team splits into two watch groups. When Cordy takes over the watch with Angel, she tries to get him to talk about their romantic situation, but he shuts her down. The next thing either of them knows is that Gunn and Gwen are waking them—because someone had spiked their drinks. Manny is dead and something has been taken out of his body.

Clues point to its being an inside job, and Cordelia naturally suspects Gwen, especially when the burglar admits to not mentioning that she had seen the Beast take something out of the body of her client. Research reveals that the Beast took pieces of an object from each totem and that when the object is put together, the Beast can enact a ritual to turn off the sun. Gunn still thinks Connor is involved, but Angel only agrees that Connor should be brought up to speed on what's going on. When the team arrives, they are surprised to find Connor flying out of his window.

They have found where the Beast is conducting the ritual.

RESOLUTION

As Cordelia looks after a beaten Connor, the rest of the team tries to stop the Beast. It looks as though they meet with success, but the Beast is not stopped and the sun goes dark. The Beast then swallows the orb so the ritual cannot be reversed. Cordelia has another flash of the Beast at the same time it reveals that Connor is not his real concern.

"I told you once . . . . You need not be my enemy . . . . Join with me . . . Angelus."   —*The Beast*

As the Beast makes his exit, the team sees that the sun is gone. They regroup with Cordy and Connor and share what they've learned about the Beast's knowing Angelus. The problem is that Angel does not know the Beast. Wesley realizes that the only way to figure out what is going on is with the help of Angelus.

DOSSIERS

CLIENT The final member of the Ra-Tet, **Manjet** (or **Manny**), is placed under the team's custody.

SUSPECTS All the suspects in this episode are either members of the Angel Investigations team or have some kind of relationship with the team. **Gwen** is the most obvious suspect as far as Cordelia is concerned. Everyone but Cordelia and Angel feels that **Connor** is the most suspect. However, in the end it looks like Angel—or more accurately, **Angelus—is** the one at whom people should be pointing fingers.

CONTINUITY

Two days have passed since the events of "Habeas Corpses" and the team has learned little about the appearance of the Beast. Gwen Raiden, and her mysterious power over electricity, was introduced in "Ground State."

OFFICE ROMANCE

Lorne picked up on the Connor-Cordelia vibe and tries to get Angel to talk about it. The rest of the team is unaware of the situation. Cordelia apologizes to Angel for hurting him, but she tells him to get over it since there are bigger problems at the moment. Cordelia is instantly suspicious of Gwen, which likely has more to do with jealousy than anything else. She had been able to see everything that transpired between Angel and Gwen when she was a higher being. Angel picks up on the vibe and allows the flirting to continue. Gwen also flirts a lot with Gunn and tells him she noticed how Wesley and Fred acted with each other. This will play out in her next appearance, in "Players."

> This episode was dedicated "In Loving Memory of Glenn Quinn," who played Doyle. The actor died December 3, 2002.

QUOTE OF THE WEEK

"The Powers are sending us a wake-up call, people. Sure we've been . . . I don't want to say demolished . . . beaten. And, sure, it's . . . slightly demoralizing . . . But from here on out, we're on the offensive. We're gonna find out this thing's weakness, go in prepared, and fight smart. It's time to take down the Beast." — Angel rallies the troops.

THE DEVIL IS IN THE DETAILS

EXPENSES

Gas for the four-hour drive to Death Valley and back.

THE PLAN

It's a three-fold plan to keep the sun shining. Gunn and Angel are to distract the Beast so Gwen can use her powers to melt the metal wings of the device it has put together from the totems. At the same time, Fred and Wes call up a portal to another dimension to send the Beast through.

The plan fails.

DEMONS, ETC. . . .

Wesley's sources confirm that without the little girl, whomever is left at Wolfram & Hart is cut off from the Senior Partners. Their research explains that the entity presenting itself as the girl was **Mesektet**, a member of the **Ra-Tet**. The origins of the Ra-Tet have been shrouded in mystery since the dawn of time, with only the totems themselves knowing their true purpose. The second victim of the Beast is **Ashet**, a being composed entirely of light (though he took a human form). A metal box was taken out of his body. The third victim, a white magic shaman named **Ma'at**, had her heart ripped out of her chest. The fourth totem, **Semkhet**, is shown symbolically as a saber-toothed tiger. It lives in a cave in Death Valley. The final totem, **Manjet**, Sacred Guardian of the Shen, Keeper of the Orb of Ma-at, represents man. He was living in Belize, but the recent murders brought him to Los Angeles. He kept the orb object in his head.

THE PEN IS MIGHTIER

FINAL CUT

Wesley points out the brilliance of the Beast's plan in a line that was cut from the episode.

"So that every demon who fears the day, every vampire forced to flee the sun—they all rise up, unhindered, with nothing left to keep them at bay."

POP CULTURE

* **"Who else could Creepylocks've been talkin' about?"**
  Gunn compares the evil little girl from Wolfram & Hart to the Goldilocks character of children's story fame.
* **"Bad news, munchkins."**
  Lorne calls his friends a nickname based on the miniature characters from *The Wizard of Oz.*
* **"Rumor mill has Dr. Feelbad attached to another slice and dice yesterday."**
  Lorne does a riff on the song "Dr. Feelgood" by Mötley Crüe.
* **". . . evil right down to her Mary Janes."**
  Manny refers to a popular style of girls' shoes.
* **"Okay, then. I'll take Denzel."**
  Once again Gwen goes flirty by comparing Gunn to Oscar-winning actor Denzel Washington.
* **"Don't suppose this joint's got Skinemax?"**
  Manny refers to the nickname for the cable channel Cinemax, which is known for its more adult-themed after-hours programming.
* **"No way all that Stephen King came out of a normal guy."**
  Gwen uses the name of the famous horror writer as a synonym for blood and gore.
* **"Gosh, no—'cause you're Supertramp."**
  Cordelia does a little play on words with the name of the famous band.

THE NAME GAME

The title of this episode comes from the name of the Eugene O'Neill Pulitzer Prize–winning play, *Long Day's Journey into Night.*

OUR HEROES

ROBERT W. ANDERSEN (PROPERTY MASTER):
"The time that the Beast had to eat a black orb, they were talking about making it CGI. But with CGI you start at two grand and work your way up. We were hashing it out in the production meeting and I opened my big mouth and said that we could make a black Jell-O orb. He could suck down this black Jell-O orb and it wouldn't have to be CGI, which was great in theory . . . and it actually worked. I spent a few days searching, because no

one had a perfectly good orb mold for Jell-O. So we ended up greasing the inside of racquetballs, pouring the Jell-O in and then splitting the racquetballs once it was hardened—and we put extra gelatin in so it was nice and firm. I went to a good culinary store and got black food coloring and totally changed it out to black. It was great. Vlad just went straight into it, although he took the first one in so quick that I think it lodged in the back of his throat. He got it all, but was coughing it down. He probably did like four or five of them and I think the crew ate the rest. I think they were lime and strawberry."

"AWAKENING"

CASE Nº 4ADH10

ACTION TAKEN

The sun has set on Los Angeles and Angel Investigations is on the case trying to bring it back. Unfortunately they have nothing to go on until Wesley returns with a shaman who can do the unthinkable: remove Angel's soul and bring forth Angelus.

Both Angel and Cordelia are strongly opposed to the idea, until Cordelia accidentally talks the vampire into it. The team prepares for the reawakening of Angelus by constructing a cage in the basement to keep the demon vampire contained. Knowing what they are about to unleash, Angel takes Connor aside with a word of warning.

WRITTEN BY David Fury & Steven S. DeKnight
DIRECTED BY James A. Contner
SPECIAL GUEST STAR: Andy Hallett (Lorne)
GUEST STARS: Vladimir Kulich (The Beast), Roger Yuan (Wo-Pang)
COSTAR: Larry McCormick (News Anchor)

"Whatever Angelus says . . . Whatever he does . . . Remember, he's not your father. I am. And no matter what happens. Or . . . Happened . . . I . . . love you."
—Angel

On a darker note, Angel also tells his son that he may need to kill Angelus if anything goes wrong. It's a charge Connor quickly—and gladly—accepts.

Angel is strapped down inside the cage, and the shaman, Wo-Pang, begins his work. It doesn't take long for something to go wrong when the shaman attacks a defenseless Angel. The team rushes to the rescue, but Wo-Pang kills himself before he can tell them anything. His body, however, reveals much as it is tattooed with the story of a weapon that can take down the Beast. Cordelia has a vision of the weapon known as the Sword of Bosh M'ad. As they set to the task of locating the sword, Wesley apologizes to Angel for bringing the evil shaman as well as his past transgressions.

Cordelia, Angel, Wesley, and Connor follow Cordelia's vision underground to a dimensional hub that makes the sword location accessible from a hundred points around the world. The group completes a series of tasks and is forced to split into two groups to find the weapon. Once they do, Cordelia admits to Angel that she can finally move past his history and try to be with him. Angel forgives her for her recent past as well.

Connor witnesses their reunion and is not happy with the situation at all. He runs off to be alone while the remaining trio returns to the hotel . . . and the Beast soon follows. Angel must drive the sword through the Beast's head to kill it, but since doing so will release a tremendous amount of power, he insists that his friends leave. He then takes on the Beast, but is joined by Connor midway through the battle. Together, father and son destroy the Beast and have their long-awaited resolution.

RESOLUTION

Angel and Cordelia also have a long-awaited resolution—they finally can make love. But things are moving too fast, and Angel remembers what happened the last time he had been so happy, with Buffy. As Angel experiences another moment of perfect happiness he feels himself begin to change.

Suddenly the world shifts and Angel is back in the cage. It had all been a dream to allow Angel to experience the happiness that would remove his soul, which is then stored in a glass jar. The vampire turns his head and looks out at the people surrounding him, but he is no longer their friend, he is . . .

"Angelus."

—Cordelia

DOSSIERS

CLIENT From this point forward, the Angel Investigations team will mostly be focused on saving **the world,** hardly taking on any other clients.

CIVILIAN SUPPORT The shaman, **Wo-Pang**, is a dark mystic from the Order of the Kun-Sun-Dai.

CONTINUITY

The sky is still darkened from the previous episode, though the phenomenon has not yet spread beyond Los Angeles. Gwen did decide to take off on that vacation to Tahiti she had been talking about. Cordelia reminds everyone of Angel's Gypsy curse and how it is reversed when he experiences a moment of perfect happiness, which was seen in full effect in the *Buffy* episode "Innocence." Cordy's reluctance to let Angelus loose stems from her experiences when he was out and about in Sunnydale during the second season of *Buffy* as well as what she saw when she was a higher being.

OFFICE ROMANCE

In Angel's dream everything works out perfectly for him and Cordelia. He also makes amends with his son and Wesley.

QUOTE OF THE WEEK

"You've made a difference. Each of you. Not just to me, but to the world. We've been pushed to the edge so many times. Done things we're sure can never be forgiven. But we're always there for each other. We've never let the darkness win. And it's not because of The Powers That Be. Or the super strength. Or the magical weapons. It's because we believe in each other. Not just as friends, or as lovers. But as Champions. All of us. Together."

Angel makes an impassioned speech to his friends in the dream.

THE DEVIL IS IN THE DETAILS

EXPENSES

The team has to spend some cash to build a cage in their basement. Other than that, since the majority of the case takes place in a dream, it's fairly inexpensive.

THE PLAN

The idea of taking Angel's soul meets with no support from Angel in the beginning; however, Wesley is quick to point out that there is no Plan B.

AS SCENE IN L.A.

The news anchor is played by Larry McCormick, the actual anchorman for the WB news affiliate in Los Angeles.

THE PEN IS MIGHTIER

FINAL CUT

The script translates Wo-Pang's ritual to take Angel's soul as follows:
"I call upon the Five Powers . . . Kun, Zhen, Xun, Kan, Li . . . Grant me access to the being. The fire within. That it may be brought without . . . I call to the One who has awakened. His will be done . . ."

POP CULTURE

✳ "Although your choice of 'The Night the Lights Went Out in Georgia' mighta thrown me a wee. Personally, not huge with the Vicki Lawrence love."
Angel apparently chose a time-appropriate seventies song to sing for Lorne.

✳ "Wood. Why did it have to be wood?"
When seeing that the first underground task would result in the victim being speared with wooden stakes, Angel echoes one of Indiana Jones's most memorable lines from *Raiders of the Lost Ark* (though Indy was talking about snakes). This is fitting since the dream itself is somewhat reminiscent of the Indiana Jones movies.

✳ "Don't look at me. I'm not a Thomas Guide."
Cordelia refers to the map books produced by Thomas Bros. Maps.

✱ **"All I could Kolchak was a rumor of Bad Mojo Risin' down in the warehouse district."**
Lorne invokes the name of the Night Stalker and the song "Bad Moon Rising," by Creedence Clearwater Revival.

✱ **"Drop the Hallmark crap."**
Cordelia doesn't buy Angel's greeting card sentiments.

OUR HEROES

DAVID BOREANAZ: "I think that Angel's relationship with Wesley has always been one of information and getting Wesley's tick on who they're searching for, what the mission is, all that stuff. When Wes took his son away from him there was a lot of anger and resentment and Angel held it against him for a while. It took him a while to get over that, until he found out Wes was doing it for a greater purpose. It was touch and go, but I think where they are now in their relationship is a respect and I think they both look at each other with different eyes."

"SOULLESS"

CASE Nº 4ADH11

ACTION TAKEN

Los Angeles is still trapped in darkness and the native vamps and demons are getting restless—not to mention the influx of evil tourists visiting the land of perpetual night. The Angel Investigations team is focusing most of its energies on one newcomer in particular: Angelus. Wesley is the first to interrogate their caged visitor while the team watches over closed-circuit TV, but before he goes down to the basement, he gives an important warning.

WRITTEN BY Sarah Fain & Elizabeth Craft
DIRECTED BY Sean Astin
SPECIAL GUEST STAR: Andy Hallett (Lorne)
GUEST STAR: Vladimir Kulich (The Beast)

> "Watch the monitor when I go down. Pay attention to everything he does. Everything he says. He'll try to confuse you, to play on your emotions so you drop your guard. If he succeeds, even for an instant . . . we're all dead." —*Wesley*

Angelus is impressed by how much Wesley has read up on him, but the vampire knows a lot about the former Watcher too. As the team watches the video feed, Angelus brings up Wesley's feelings for Fred and relentlessly pushes all Gunn's buttons in the process. The vampire drops some hints that he knows the Beast, but he refuses to further enlighten Wes. He's much more interested in twisting the truth and revealing to everyone that Cordelia slept with Connor.

Wesley takes a break from the interrogation to get Angelus some blood and refocus their efforts. When Fred takes down a glass of blood, under Gunn's watchful eye (and crossbow), Angelus starts again with the innuendos and accusations. He then turns the tables, literally, on Fred and makes a grab for her. Gunn is forced to drop his weapon as he tries to pry his girl from Angelus's arms. Wesley comes to the rescue with tranquilizer darts, knocking the vampire out.

Back upstairs, Fred takes a moment to thank Wesley for saving her. Their conversation ends in a kiss that Gunn nearly walks in on. Although he doesn't see the actual kiss, Gunn knows something is going on between the pair and a heated argument ensues. The fight distracts them from noticing that Connor has snuck down to see Angelus on his own, carelessly crossing over the line of safety as he steps up to get some answers.

212

Angelus continues his mind games with Angel's son and just when it looks like the vampire is making his impression, Cordelia enters, telling Connor to leave. Once they're alone, Cordelia cuts through Angelus's games and makes an offer of herself for the information he has on the Beast.

Though the team is left out of the loop on the deal, they are excited to find that Angelus does have useful information on the Beast. He claims that they did meet in the past, but that Angelus refused the Beast's request to help it deal with a threat from a trio of Svea Priestesses that ultimately banished the Beast. A quick hit of research locates descendants of the Priestesses living only minutes away. However, their good luck takes a horrible turn when they get to the family home of the Priestesses and find a massacre has already taken place.

The entire family has been wiped out and the bodies have been there for days. All evidence points to the fact that the family had been working on a banishment spell when the Beast came to kill them. The revelation hit hard for all, but no one more so than Connor, who—in all his battles with demons and vamps—has never witnessed such a *human* tragedy.

RESOLUTION

The group returns home to report the situation to those left behind. Angelus tells Cordy that he's ready to enjoy her part of the bargain, but she declines, reminding him that the offer of herself was if he helped them save the world. Since the world is not saved, the deal is ended and Angel will be re-ensouled. However, there's a problem with that plan.

"Angel's soul. It's gone." —*Fred*

CONTINUITY

Angelus tells Wesley a little about Angel's dream from the previous episode, "Awakening." The vampire then brings up some of Wesley's failures, including letting Lilah suck out part of Lorne's brain in "Slouching Toward Bethlehem" and the trouble he had with Faith when he was her Watcher in the third season of *Buffy*. Angelus later uses events from the past to haunt Connor, by bringing up Darla's "suicide" in "Lullaby."

OFFICE ROMANCE

Angelus begins his mind games by using Wesley's feelings for Fred against some of them. It doesn't take long for that to start up an argument among all three members of the triangle. When the fight becomes physical, Fred gets caught in the middle as Gunn accidentally knocks her to the ground when he pulls back to punch Wesley.

QUOTE OF THE WEEK

"He distorts everything, he lies with the truth. That's what makes him dangerous."

> Cordelia gets to the heart of the threat of Angelus.

THE DEVIL IS IN THE DETAILS

EXPENSES

The team sets up an in-house TV monitoring system to watch Angelus and listen to anything he may have to say.

DEMONS, ETC. . . .

The **Svea Priestesses** are also known as the Svear. The mystical order is made up of descendants of a powerful Nordic priestess, Svea. They are known for banishing evil.

THE PEN IS MIGHTIER

FINAL CUT

In the scene where Wesley comes to Fred's defense with a tranq gun, the stage directions even provide sound effects.

> *Then, PPHHHHTT! A tranquilizer dart pierces Angelus's shoulder. A flash of annoyance passes across his face. Then, woozy, he STAGGERS back releasing Fred.*
>
> *REVEAL Wesley, halfway down the stairs, tranq gun still leveled as, PPHHHHTT! Wesley shoots another dart—this one into Angelus's neck. Angelus goes slack and hits the ground with a THUD.*

POP CULTURE

* "Here's one for you. What's the deal with Angel and *Raiders of the Lost Ark*?"

   Angelus reveals Angel's dream from the previous episode and its thematic similarities to the Indiana Jones film.

* "Othello and Desdemona. My favorite couple . . . Oh wait, Desdemona *wasn't* in love with the other guy."

   Angelus compares Gunn and Fred to the lead characters from Shakespeare's *Othello, The Moor of Venice*.

* "So much for stand-by-your-man."

   Angelus invokes the name of Tammy Wynette's hit song.

* "Doin' your mom, and tryin' to kill your dad . . . There should be a play."

   And there is. It's called *Oedipus Rex* and was written by Sophocles in 430 B.C.

* "Oh, for the love of Mike Tyson."

   Lorne brings up the infamous boxer when Gunn and Wesley start with the fisticuffs.

* "Why is Sid Vicious suddenly Mr. Show-and-Tell?"

   Gunn compares Angelus to the deceased bass player of the Sex Pistols (at least, in name).

SIX DEGREES OF . . .

This episode was directed by Sean Astin, an actor who is no stranger to mythic adventures as one of the stars of *The Lord of the Rings* trilogy and *The Goonies,* among many other films.

OUR HEROES

AMY ACKER: "In L.A. I hardly ever get recognized, but if I do it's always by the last person who I would ever expect to watch the show. There was a man at McDonald's the day after Wesley had kissed me and Gunn had walked in. He goes, 'Fred, how you gonna dog my man Gunn like that?' He was yelling at me in the middle of McDonald's. And I was like, 'It's not really me. I'm an actress. I didn't do it, really.' There are definitely die-hard fans."

"CALVARY"

CASE № 4ADH12

ACTION TAKEN

Wesley takes Cordelia and Connor back to question Wo-Pang about Angel's missing soul, but the shaman knows nothing about the strange turn of events. They aren't the only ones going visiting, however. Lilah sneaks into the hotel basement through the sewers so she can have her own Q & A session with Angelus. She's even brought along a crowbar and an offer to let him out of his cage.

Unaware of the secret meeting that's taking place below their feet, Gunn and Fred finally have the talk they've been putting off. Fred admits that she let Wesley kiss her, but they both know there were problems long before that, and they effectively end their relationship. As Wesley, Cordelia, and Connor return to the hotel, Gunn sees Lilah on the monitor and hurries to the basement, with the rest of the gang on his heels. Lilah flees through the tunnels and Wesley goes after her. As the others wonder if Lilah was the one who stole Angelus's soul, Wesley asks her straight out and she says no. She then admits that she's been living underground since the Beast killed everyone at Wolfram & Hart and gave her the wound that refuses to heal.

WRITTEN BY Jeffrey Bell & Steven S. DeKnight, Mere Smith
DIRECTED BY Bill Norton
SPECIAL GUEST STAR: Andy Hallett (Lorne)
GUEST STARS: Stephanie Romanov (Lilah), Vladimir Kulich (The Beast), Roger Yuan (Wo-Pang)

Lilah turns over a copy of a book Wesley had already used in his failed research of the Beast. However, this copy is from another dimension and does have a section of great interest. Meanwhile the rest of the team suspects that Lilah could be one of the Beast's minions, but Angelus has another idea.

> **ANGELUS:** "That big rock doesn't have minions. It *is* the minion."
> **FRED:** "No it's not. We've seen what it can do."
> **ANGELUS:** "You've just seen the warm-up act."
> **CORDELIA:** "What are you saying?"
> **ANGELUS:** "I'm saying there's something bigger. Something worse.
>   The Beast has a boss."

Wesley brings Lilah back to the hotel where the gang regroups and recaps. They suggest that whatever wiped the pages in this dimension of the text Lilah brought with her also wiped Angel's mind of the Beast. While the gang goes into research mode, Gunn goes down to the basement to watch Angelus and subjects himself to another round of dark debate over his failed romance. Upstairs, Lilah picks up on the vibe between Fred and Wesley and gets in whatever digs she can.

As the growing tension between Lilah and Cordelia hits breaking point, Cordy has a vision of how to re-ensoul Angel and sets the team about gathering objects for a ritual. Once the items are collected—including the skull of a not-entirely-dead Soul Eater—they gather in the basement to enact the dark magic to call back Angel's soul.

The ritual is a success. Angel comes back to his body and even though he passes Cordelia's and Lorne's tests, he refuses to leave his cage prematurely. Angel sets the team to a new list of tasks, but after they leave the basement Cordelia convinces him to leave his cage. It's just what he was waiting for and he reveals that his soul didn't come back; he's still Angelus.

RESOLUTION

Angelus knocks Cordelia cold before tricking his way past the others and out into the world. It doesn't take long for the team to stumble over Cordy and realize things went wrong. They hit the streets tracking Angelus, but Connor loses the scent and they realize that the vampire doubled back to the hotel, where Cordelia and Lilah had stayed.

Angelus attacks, sending an arrow through Cordy's leg and giving chase to Lilah through the hotel. Lilah manages to get the best of Angelus and it looks like she's in the clear until Cordelia reaches out and grabs her. Lilah reminds Cordelia that they don't have time to stall since Angelus will kill them. Cordelia then quite calmly slams a dagger into Lilah's neck and responds . . .

"Why do you think I let him out?"   —*Cordelia*

CONTINUITY

The shaman Wo-Pang is seen once again in an opening scene that mirrors his introduction in "Awakening." Lilah resurfaces after disappearing during the Beast's attack on Wolfram & Hart in "Habeas Corpses." She reveals that the Beast not only killed everyone in the building that day, but also has since taken out *everyone* including field ops, liaisons, and people who had been out sick. Angelus is able to piece together the fact that Gunn killed Fred's former professor in "Supersymmetry."

OFFICE ROMANCE

Gunn and Fred's relationship effectively comes to an end in this episode, going out with a whimper instead of a bang. Angelus reveals to Fred that Wesley had been sleeping with Lilah. The news does affect Fred's feelings for Wes.

QUOTE OF THE WEEK

ANGELUS: "You're gonna use black magic to restore my soul? People, this *never* goes well. Am I the only one paying attention?"

LILAH: "Ten to one the entire hotel gets sucked into a hell dimension."

DEMONS, ETC. . . .

Gunn and Connor are sent to collect the skull of a **Soul Eater** that was buried by the Chumash a couple hundred years ago. Although buried and decayed, the Soul Eater still has some fight left in it and can move at incredible speeds.

AS SCENE IN L.A.

The streets of L.A. burning around Angelus and the group following him are actually on the Paramount Pictures New York Street backlot.

THE PEN IS MIGHTIER

FINAL CUT

Presumably to keep the secret of Cordelia being the big bad from leaking, the episode revelation is written as follows in the script:

> *Lilah hightails it, rounds a corner, hurries down the long hallway, looks back over her shoulder when WHAM! She's GRABBED by someone in an open doorway (and very much O.S.). Lilah gasps, real fear on her face.*
>
> **LILAH:** "He's gonna kill us!"
>
> ***REVEAL it's ANGELUS***
>
> **ANGELUS:** "I know."
>
> *He spins Lilah around in one fluid motion—DRIVES the BEAST'S DAGGER into the side of Lilah's THROAT, destroying her only chance to scream.*

POP CULTURE

❋ "We've got Darth Vampire living in the basement."

Gunn compares the evil Angelus to the evil Darth Vader (among other Darths) from the Star Wars series.

* **"Cut the Fu-Manchu."**
  Gunn refers to the evil literary character known for his insidious plots.
* **"Nobody's heard bo peep about Angel's soul."**
  Lorne references the nursery rhyme heroine, Little Bo Peep.
* **"Suits by Liberace."**
  Lilah takes a look at Lorne's ensemble and compares it to those flamboyant outfits worn by the late pianist.
* **"I haven't forgotten how she poked my head open like a Capri Sun . . ."**
  Lorne waxes metaphorical about the juice that comes in a pouch and requires a piercing by plastic straw to get out.
* **". . . well then, braid my hair and call me Pollyanna."**
  Lilah refers to the titular perky heroine from the book and Disney movie.
* **"You might be their only hope, Obi-Wan."**
  Cordelia paraphrases one of the more notable phrases from the film *Star Wars: A New Hope*.

TRACKS

Angel sings a line of "Raindrops Keep Falling on My Head," prompting Lorne to invoke the name of the singer, B. J. Thomas.

OUR HEROES

DAVID BOREANAZ: "For me it's always been a matter of tapping into the wicked stuff and really having fun with Angelus; really heightening and exploring his personality, depending upon the type of scene he's going into and the circumstances surrounding him. I kind of look at the whole and make it as simple as I possibly can, but at the same time bring out that demon in him. It's pretty hard to say how I really prepare for it. There's a lot of things I do that I'd rather not discuss. But still, at the same time, one of the things that I do is just understand the character and where he's coming from by doing my homework as far as what the scene is all about, playing the scene, and then getting into him that way."

"SALVAGE"

CASE N° 4ADH13

ACTION TAKEN

The gang returns to the hotel and finds Cordelia with an arrow in her leg and Angelus snacking on an already dead Lilah. Angelus escapes and Connor wants to follow, but Wesley stops the boy, citing that they need to prepare before going after the vampire again. Since they all think Angelus killed Lilah they also believe there is a chance she may have been sired, so Wesley takes her down into the basement to destroy her.

Word spreads quickly that Angelus is back and he is welcomed with open arms at a demon bar. There he finds some vamps who can lead him to the awaiting Beast, who has the bloody rock dagger that Cordelia used to kill Lilah. In the meantime Lorne phones for some help from the Furies and places the hotel under another anti–demon violence spell.

Wesley has a difficult time destroying Lilah because his conscience keeps visiting him in the form of his former lover. He gets to talk out his feelings, realizing that he did care for her more than he thought, but failed to save her as he had hoped. Wes apologizes to the dead body and cuts off her head.

Meanwhile Connor keeps getting antsy about going to kill Angelus.

WRITTEN BY David Fury
DIRECTED BY Jefferson Kibbee
SPECIAL GUEST STARS: Andy Hallett (Lorne), Eliza Dushku (Faith)
GUEST STARS: Stephanie Romanov (Lilah), Vladimir Kulich (The Beast)
COSTARS: Joel David Moore (Karl), Billy Rieck (Paco), Addie Daddio (Rosaria), Brett Wagner (Bohg'Dar), Alonzo Boddin (Prison Guard), Spice Williams (Debbie), Kara Holden (Young Woman), Joshua Genrock (Demon)

"I've seen his true face. He's tasted blood. There's no going back now. He has to be destroyed . . . And I'm The Destroyer."
— *Connor*

Just as the boy is about to go out on his own, Cordelia stops him by fainting . . . twice. She is taken up to her room for some rest alone. Connor stays at the hotel while Angelus and the Beast have their reunion, where the vampire baits the Beast into a fight. Once Angelus leaves, Cordelia shows up to scold the Beast for the fighting, but gives him some sugar anyway.

When Wesley comes up from the basement, he announces that the plan has changed. He realizes that they need their Champion—Angel—to

defeat the Beast, so they must take Angelus alive. The only person he knows who could do that is Faith so he goes to meet her in jail. Just after an attack from another inmate, Faith is surprised to find Wesley has come to speak with her. As soon as he tells her Angelus is back, Faith decides to break out. The escape is quick and the two are back on their way to L.A.

Faith takes charge, doling out assignments, but Connor still insists they must kill Angelus. When he proves unstable on recon, Faith sends Connor back to the hotel, with Gunn to look over him. That leaves only Faith and Wesley to take on Angelus. But they lose the element of surprise because Angelus has already heard that she is in town.

RESOLUTION

Faith and Wesley split up. While Wes takes on some lesser vamps, Faith meets up with Angelus and the Beast. The fight is intense and Faith gets a brutal beating. As it looks like the Beast is about to go in for the kill, Angelus picks up the dagger made out of the Beast's rocky body and plunges it into the demon. It explodes in flame and shoots a beam up to the sun, bringing back the day.

Angelus is upset with the unintended sunny result, but he takes pleasure in the fact that he can finish off Faith himself. In a last-ditch effort, Faith swings a block and tackle rigging at the vampire, who steps out of the way, laughing at the weak assault. The rigging continues and smashes through the clouded glass window behind Angelus, letting in the burning sun. Angelus sees that Faith is safely bathed in warm light and leaves to kill another day.

Connor returns to the bathed-in-sun hotel and goes up to Cordelia's room to share the joy with her. But Cordelia's got another bundle of joy to share.

"We're having a baby."

—Cordelia

CONTINUITY

The story continues moments after "Calvary" left off, with Angel coming across Lilah's already dead body. Connor is the first to realize that Lilah must be destroyed, much like he had to decapitate Holtz in "Tomorrow." Lorne reapplies the sanctuary spell that he previously had on Caritas and the hotel. "Lilah"—or Wesley's conscience—reminds him that he has a signed dollar bill in his wallet, referring to their relationship bet in "Slouching Toward Bethlehem." The darkness enveloping L.A. has not yet spread north to the women's penitentiary in which Faith is being held. She previously appeared in "Five by Five" (which Wesley references with one of Faith's catchprases—"five by five"—after Faith breaks them out of jail) and "Sanctuary," when Angel helped her see the error of her ways. Then she made a cameo in "Judgement," when Angel needed someone to talk to. The attack she comes under in the yard has to do with the plot arc regarding the First Evil occupying the gang on the final season of *Buffy the Vampire Slayer*. The knife used in that attack is of the same design as the one used by the Bringers.

OFFICE ROMANCE

"Lilah" suggests that Wesley either hated himself for being with her or hated himself for *loving* her. Connor has a little schoolboy crush on Faith, evoking the comment from Cordelia that father and son apparently share a weakness for Slayers. After she reveals they are going to be parents, Cordelia notes that she and Connor will be connected forever.

QUOTE OF THE WEEK

"I don't give a flying sluk what Wesley says."
Connor rebels, invoking the name of the slug demons Angel Investigations battled in "The Price."

THE DEVIL IS IN THE DETAILS

EXPENSES

The gang manages to save some money by substituting herbs and other items they have on hand for the Furies' sanctuary spell.

WEAPONRY

Wesley uses the stake/sword rig attached to his arm that was introduced in "Spin the Bottle." Unfortunately it doesn't hold up in the field since one of the vamps stomps on it, snapping the sword in two. Angelus realizes that the only thing that can kill the Beast is a weapon forged from its own body.

THE PLAN

Faith makes the plan to grab Angelus plain and simple.
"In case anyone has any other ideas, this is a *salvage* mission, not a search and destroy."

AS SCENE IN L.A.

When Angelus is loose on the streets of the city and overhears that the Slayer is in town, he is once again on Paramount's New York Street backlot. If the camera had showed the other side of the street, the audience would have seen the exterior of the original building that housed Angel Investigations in Season One.

THE PEN IS MIGHTIER

FINAL CUT

The reintroduction of Faith appears as follows in the script:
CLOSE ON THE STEEL DOOR, sliding open, allowing in sunlight, hitting the slightly bowed head of a prisoner. As she looks up . . .

PUSH IN, POWER SHOT on the lovely face of
FAITH.

POP CULTURE

❋ **"The birth of a notion, kids . . ."**
Lorne does a riff on the title of the noted classic film *Birth of a Nation.*

❋ **"Angel has left the building."**
Angelus conscripts a popular phrase regarding Elvis Presley and makes it his own.

❋ **"Soon as FTD's delivering in the city again, expect a big 'Thanks a Bunch' bouquet from me, girls."**
Lorne refers to the popular network of flower deliverers.

❋ **"Come on, Rocky, If that's all ya got, you better throw in the towel and call it a night."**
Angelus compares the Beast to the pugilist character played by Sylvester Stallone in the movie series of the same name.

❋ **"When the Beast Master's ready to peek out from behind your skirt . . ."**
Angelus references the classic B movie *The Beastmaster* from 1982.

❋ **"See, I just wanted Beastie Boy to soften you up."**
Angel makes a little play on words with the famous rap group.

❋ **"Well, ding dong the Beast is dead."**
Lorne plays on one of the more popular lines/songs from *The Wizard of Oz.*"

SIX DEGREES OF . . .

Brett Wagner, who plays Bohg'Dar, is no stranger to the Buffy/Angel universe. He previously played the Nahdrah Prince in "Provider" and the trucker in the *Buffy* episode "Grave."

OUR HEROES

SHAWNA TRPCIC (COSTUMER): "For Faith I went to Melrose Avenue. I wanted her tough and sassy. I saw what had been done with her character before, but I wanted to take it up a notch. So I found this place on Melrose that sells these heavy metal pants that are skintight that have leather insets into them, and they made them in doubles and triples, which is what I needed. I was able to use black on her, whereas I don't use black on any other character except for Angel. So that's what we did with hers. I just went and found the toughest, coolest, hippest pants. And she felt so sexy and so hot in those pants that her whole character was like, 'Yeah!' She really worked with me on that."

"RELEASE"

CASE Nº 4ADH14

ACTION TAKEN

Faith enters Wesley's apartment with her body beaten and her spirit broken. As she cleans up, Faith takes her frustration out on the defenseless tile wall in the shower. Refreshed, she exits the bathroom seemingly ready for round two.

Angelus revels in his victory against Faith, bragging to his demon brethren in a bar when the voice of the Beast's Master

WRITTEN BY Steven S. DeKnight & Elizabeth Craft & Sarah Fain
DIRECTED BY James A. Contner
GUEST STARS: Christopher Neiman (Frotor Demon), Eliza Dushku (Faith)
COSTARS: Catalina Larranaga (Vamp Waitress), Darren Laverty (Lackey Vampire #1), Sam Stefanski (Lackey Vampire #2), Peter Renaday (Master's Voice), Becka Linder (Drugged Girl), Chris Huse (Drugged Vampire #2), Ian Anthony Dale (Drugged Vampire #3), Paul Tigue (Reg), Andrew McGinnes (Mullet Head)

enters his head. Angelus tells the Master that he's not one for playing well with others, but the Master is persistent—that is, until she is interrupted. Across town Cordelia holds a glowing orb in her hand that projects her altered voice into Angelus's head. But when Connor enters her room, she has to cut the conversation short. Connor is concerned for her well-being, and for the health of their secret unborn child.

Fred is in research mode when Angelus makes a surprise visit carrying an amulet that makes him invulnerable to the sanctuary spell. He terrorizes Fred for a few moments until she realizes the amulet is a fake. But it's too late to stop him from stealing the book Lilah had brought as well as the information Wolfram & Hart had sucked out of Lorne's head. Connor tries to fight off Angelus, but the sanctuary spell that keeps the place from demon violence works against Connor as well.

As Angelus exits the hotel he runs right into Faith and Wesley and takes Wes hostage. Faith freezes as Angelus threatens her former Watcher's life.

"It's all about choices, Faith. The ones we make, the ones we don't. Oh, and the consequences. Those are always fun . . . Don't worry about good ol' Wes. What's one more dead body to us? Come on! Where's my girl?"

—Angelus

As Faith wonders what to do, Gunn enters the fray, surprising Angelus but not enough so that he can't escape. Connor goes to check on Cordelia, and she realizes that he's confused by the fact that an anti–demon violence spell works on him. She manages to calm the boy, though he still has many questions.

Wesley prepares for the next round against Angelus, taking heavier weaponry because he knows they have to step it up a notch. The only fear is that Faith is not ready to take the battle to that level for fear of losing the control she had worked so hard to achieve.

Wesley and Faith follow Angelus's trail to the demon bar where they find a collection of human and vampire junkies in the back room. Apparently the new fad is to get a human high on drugs so the vampire can drain it with the person's blood. Wes tortures one of the human druggies to get information on Angel, much to Faith's discomfort.

Lorne awakens after having been accidentally tranqued during Angelus's visit. He recognizes the fake amulet and his tip leads Wesley and Faith to the guy who makes the cheap knockoffs. Instead of finding more clues, they find a waiting Angelus.

RESOLUTION

Faith fires on Angelus, but the vamp dives out of the way. Once again he gets his hands on Wesley, sending him through scaffolding and out of the fight. Angelus then puts the smackdown on Faith, who is still unwilling to tap into the anger that made her such a dangerous Slayer before.

"Come on, Faith! You're not even trying! Or is that why you really came back? Not enough to punish yourself in prison? Is that it? Still looking for someone to help beat the bad out of you? Know what the funny part is, darlin'? I could beat you to death and it wouldn't make a difference. Nothing'll ever change who you are, Faith. You're a murderer. An animal. And you enjoy it. Just like me."   —*Angelus*

Those words are just the thing Faith needs to hear as she reenters the battle full of animal rage. It does not seem to be enough, however, when Angelus gets hold of her and bites down on her neck with the promise of making her like him.

DOSSIERS

CIVILIAN SUPPORT

A **Frotor demon** and a **drugged girl** both provide useful information to Wes and Faith, after some requisite beating and torture, respectively.

225

CONTINUITY

The episode opens as Faith licks her wounds from her battle against Angelus and the Beast in "Salvage." When Fred mistakenly aims her gun at Connor, he remarks that she's more of a Taser girl, referring to the time she got him good with that particular weapon in "Deep Down." Both Wesley and Angelus remind Faith of her past behavior, particularly her heartless actions in "Five by Five."

OFFICE ROMANCE

Fred attempts reconciliation with Gunn, apologizing for her kiss with Wesley as well as the stuff that went down before that. The two share a kiss, but it's not really a rekindling when Gunn backs away and makes an excuse to leave. Cordelia (as the Master) uses a glamour to show Angelus that she is the one with his missing soul.

QUOTE OF THE WEEK

"Hey, you're preaching to the guy who ate the choir."   Angelus knows how to turn a phrase.

DEMONS, ETC. . . .

A **Strom Demon** can be shot in the face and the face will grow back . . . eventually.

THE PEN IS MIGHTIER

FINAL CUT

Connor spends some teen time in front of the mirror, as laid out in the script.

CLOSE ON CONNOR as he bares his teeth, feeling for fangs. He relaxes into a normal face. Then—

A SERIES OF RAPID SHOTS: cut together a bit jarringly, as we watch Connor wrinkle his brow; push his forehead in with his fingers, then his palms; as he looks under his eyelids to check for yellow; examine his teeth for new pointyness again.

POP CULTURE

✳ "Now that I've killed your pet rock, how 'bout a little face-to-face . . ."
Angelus refers to the fad from the seventies of keeping stones as low-maintenance pets.

✳ ". . . all to maneuver the Brady Bunch into releasing Angel's inner me."
Angelus compares the Angel Investigations team to the wholesome family from the seventies TV show.

✳ "Good night, not so sweet Prince."
Lorne paraphrases a little of Shakespeare's *Hamlet.*

✳ ". . . he tries dancing in here and pulling a Dark Shadows again . . ."
Gunn refers to the otherworldly soap opera that ran in the sixties and early seventies.

✳ "Vampire Moriarty strolls in waving the anti-mojo mojo . . ."
Gunn compares Angelus to the highly intelligent villain from the Sherlock Holmes mysteries.

✳ "Save the head trip, GQ."
Faith refers to the men's magazine known for its stylish models.

OUR HEROES

ANDY HALLETT: "I grew into the part. It just happened. I know that I thought that it was going to be a couple of times at best. When Joss told me the whole concept I thought it was great and I thought it was a wonderful idea; however, I didn't put that much thought into it right away. I was too excited about just going in. I just thought, 'How many times can you go back to the karaoke bar without the audience getting tired of it?' I think it's safe to say it worked the opposite. Then I

ended up doing seventeen shows the first year, which was shocking because they kept calling. They just would call each week. I remember then there were a couple of shows where they didn't call and I was like, 'What do you mean they didn't call?'

"Then the next season I went back as a guest cast and then the next one. Then it was the middle of season four and there was this total surprise phone call from Joss Whedon. He said, 'We'd like for you to join us as a regular part of the team for the back nine. We're all hoping we come back next season, but you never know. So if we do not get picked up for season five, I want you to have the opportunity to say that you were a regular.' That was the best part. It really holds a lot more weight when you have the ability to put on your résumé that you were a regular. He was just out for all of our best interests and he had enough consideration to count me in."

"ORPHEUS"

CASE Nº 4ADH15

ACTION TAKEN

Angelus continues to chomp down on poor Faith, when he suddenly throws himself off her body. A flash of confusion crosses his face and he staggers back and realizes that Faith has poisoned her own blood and it's now in his system.

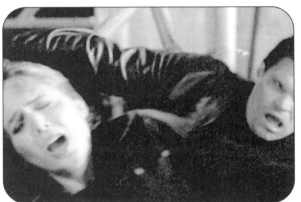

WRITTEN BY Mere Smith
DIRECTED BY Terrence O'Hara
SPECIAL GUEST STARS:
Alyson Hannigan (Willow),
Eliza Dushku (Faith)
COSTARS: Peter Renaday
(Master's Voice), E. J. Callahan
(Old Man), Adrienne Wilkinson
(Flapper), Nate Dushku
(Gunman), Jeremy Gushkin
(Cashier)

The silence of morning is shattered in the hotel when Gunn comes in with a bound Angelus. Having answered Wesley's call he now starts shouting orders as everyone springs into action to get the vampire back in his cage. Moments later Wesley comes in with Faith, who hovers near death. As Faith is put in Angel's room to rest, Lorne pieces together what happened when he sees the hypo mark on her arm.

The green guy knows all about the mystical drug called Orpheus that Faith had pumped into her system, and he's livid that Wes would allow her

to do something so dangerous. Connor reports the latest news to Cordelia, who is suffering some evil mood swings as her plan unravels. They are all unaware that while unconscious, Faith and Angelus are sharing a flashback of Angel's life.

The mental history begins in 1902 when Angel first came to America on a ship while crouched in the filth of animals to avoid human temptation. Their ride then flashes to the twenties when Angelus is ashamed to relive Angel's saving of a cute little puppy from becoming roadkill.

"We're reliving Angel's good deeds! You are in Hell! Wicked!"   *—Faith*

Back in the real world, Wesley reveals that the new focus is to bring Angel's soul back. Fred is already two steps ahead, having called for reinforcements in the form of an incredibly powerful witch by the name of Willow Rosenberg. Introductions are made and Willow goes up to see Cordelia, unaware that her old friend has a knife hidden under the sheets. A slipup by Cordy leads Willow to the answer to their problem of finding Angel's missing soul; instead of searching for the jar containing it, she can magically break the glass and free the soul into the ether. Willow quickly bolts from the room, unaware that Cordelia almost knifed her to death.

Faith and Angelus trip to the seventies to witness another good deed. However, instead of seeing him rush to the rescue during a diner theft, they watch as Angel pitifully gives in to his needs to drink from the blood of the murder victim.

Willow calls up a spell known as Delothrian's Arrow to smash the jar holding Angel's soul. A magical marble goes flying through the hotel and is about to hit its mark when Cordelia magically stops it and throws some magic of her own back at Willow. It's a magical showdown between Willow and the unknown force, but it comes to an abrupt end when Connor bangs on Cordy's door, distracting her long enough for Angel's soul to be free.

RESOLUTION

Faith is fading fast when Angel joins his alter ego in the mindwalk. The two faces of Angel wage battle as he tries to convince the Slayer not to let herself die. Meanwhile Willow and the team work to channel Angel's soul into the Orb of Thessulah and then back into his body. Cordelia conspires against them, convincing Connor to kill Angelus before it's too late.

Connor knocks Gunn unconscious and goes in for the kill when he is stopped by a very-much-alive Faith. Angel managed to convince her that life was worth living and she got up and hurried to his rescue just in time for his soul to be restored. The day saved, Willow takes Faith with her to Sunnydale where there's another fight awaiting them. As Angel begins to address his friends, Cordelia comes downstairs for the first time since she fainted.

"Sorry, Angel, but if this is the speech about how the worst is behind us . . . ya may wanna save it for later."   *—Cordelia*

As she hits the bottom step, Cordelia turns to the side and it's suddenly clear that somehow she's already *very* pregnant.

DOSSIERS

CIVILIAN SUPPORT Willow takes a break from battling evil in Sunnydale to make a guest appearance since she was the one to re-ensoul Angel the first time. It was, in fact, the witch's first big spell.

CONTINUITY

Once again we pick up right where we left off in the previous episode, although we learn that Faith spiked her blood with the drug being used in the back of the demon bar. Both Cordelia and Willow recall that Faith has been in a coma before. In Angel's flashbacks he's seen in 1996, just before he met Whistler, the man who charged him to look after Buffy, as seen in the *Buffy* episode "Becoming, Part 1." Once again, Willow relies on an Orb of Thessulah to retrieve Angel's soul, as she did in "Becoming, Part 2." Willow and Faith leave Los Angeles and *Angel,* and return to Sunnydale in the *Buffy* episode "Dirty Girls" to take on the First Evil.

OFFICE ROMANCE

Cordelia plays the jealous lover card when Connor seems to be smitten with Faith. There's also some sparkage between Willow and Fred, at least on the witch's side, which results in Willow blurting out that she's already seeing someone when Fred's natural exuberance begins to overwhelm.

QUOTE OF THE WEEK

"Yes! Hi. You must be Angel's . . . handsome . . . yet androgynous son."

Willow meets Connor for the first time.

DEMONS, ETC. . . .

Orpheus is an enchanted drug that, in combination with the vampire biting, leads to some serious psychic psychedelics.

THE PEN IS MIGHTIER

FINAL CUT

The spell Fred and Willow use to retrieve Angel's soul is translated as follows in the script:

FRED: "What was lost, shall now be found."

WILLOW: "Not dead, nor not of the living . . . Spirits of the interregnum I call . . . I call on you, Gods, do not ignore this supplication! Let the orb be the vessel to carry his soul to him. . . . It is written, this power is my people's right to wield. . . . Let it be so! Now!"

POP CULTURE

✳ **"So what is this? Puff the Magic Dragon City?"**

Angelus compares his drug-induced state to the children's song by Peter, Paul & Mary that some claim has a more mature theme than most kids know.

* "Me, I'm guessin' this is 'Angelus, This Is Your Life' . . ."
  Faith refers to the classic TV show in which people took a stroll down memory lane with friends and family from their past.
* "Why do you get to be Marley's ghost?"
  Angelus wonders why Faith is the equivalent of the former friend of Ebenezer Scrooge from Charles Dickens's *A Christmas Carol*.
* "Then I'm . . . whatever. Dust in the wind, candle in the wind . . . there'll be a general wind theme."
  Faith brings up the songs by Kansas and Elton John, respectively.
* "'Mandy,' huh? Must kill you he's got a jones for the power ballads." —Faith
* "Worst were the concerts . . ." —Angelus
  Faith and Angelus discuss one of Angel's dirty little secrets—his love for Barry Manilow when he's feeling down.
* "Does kind of seem like you've given in to the grumpy side of the Force."
  Willow refers to the all-powerful force from the Star Wars series.
* "You wanna go, Glinda? We'll go."
  Cordelia calls Willow by the name of the Good Witch of the North from *The Wizard of Oz*.
* "And now for a poem: 'Faith Goes Gently Into That Good Night.'"
  Angelus revises the title of Dylan Thomas's poem "Do Not Go Gentle into That Good Night."
* "You're the one behind this whole True Hollywood sob story."
  Angelus brings up the behind-the-scenes series from the E! Entertainment network.

THE NAME GAME

"Orpheus" is a character from Greek mythology who traveled to the underworld to appeal to the god Hades to let him take his love, Eurydice, home with him. Hades agreed, but as with most myths it did not end well, and Eurydice wound up having to stay behind. This makes Wesley's line about the drug quite appropriate when he says:

"It leads you down to Hell . . . and leaves you there."

SIX DEGREES OF . . .

The gunman is played by **Nate Dushku,** the brother of **Eliza Dushku.** And speaking of acting families, it's fitting that Willow and Wesley share a scene together as **Alexis Denisof** and **Alyson Hannigan** were engaged at the time the episode was filmed and have since married.

TRACKS

In the flashback, Angel plays Barry Manilow's "Mandy" on the jukebox. It's the same song he sang on his first trip to Caritas in "Judgement."

OUR HEROES

STUART BLATT (PRODUCTION DESIGNER): "We did a scene where Angel arrived at Ellis Island, and we kept saying, 'How are we going to do this?' Well, we took all of stage five, which is our largest

stage, and we created what the crew called The Walltanic. It was one really long wall of a ship that was full height so you couldn't ever see off it. We had portals, gangplanks, and about a hundred extras in period costume along with horses and carts and rigged cargo nets coming down. It, to me, was one of the best things we had ever done because it was so much fun. Not only was it bizarrely simple, but it was the kind of thing where we were not making reality. If the camera strayed ten feet to the left or ten feet to the right you would have seen a stage and crew members, which is true everywhere, but this really was one long wall. You had two directions to shoot and it created a scene far better than I think anybody ever thought it would. It was really great.

"We had little pans of water to reflect back onto the side of the boat as if it was sitting in dock. And oddly enough we had to figure a way to have about 120 feet of reflective water, without being able to build a long trough, so we ended up putting down water pans. Our special effects crew came up with an ingenious way of moving the water without having guys everywhere paddling it along. They got little wind-up frogs from Chinatown and set them in the pans so the frogs just moved around and made the water move."

SHAWNA TRPCIC (COSTUMER) ON JOINING THE SHOW MID—FOURTH SEASON: "With Cordelia's pregnancy, that was a really fun time to walk into the series because I got to do what I wanted to do. I didn't have to mind what had been done in the past. We played a lot with fabrics, with the draping and the flowing to show that she was pregnant without making her look big. We ended up with that black-and-white-striped chiffon that just flowed and looked gorgeous, but it also had sort of an evil, mysterious tone to it. We played around with black beading to give it that sparkle and elegance that she could tap into. We had a lot of fun with that and it just draped gorgeously on her because she was full and beautiful at the time. With her I really tried to use the wardrobe to reflect where the character's going internally to kind of hint on the outside where they're going."

In the script, Lorne's original reaction to seeing Faith read: "SHE'S ALIVE! IT'S A MIRACLE! CALL ABC!" This is likely a reference to the short-lived, though critically acclaimed series, Miracles, which Angel series cocreator David Greenwalt was working on at the time.

MICHAEL GASPAR (SPECIAL EFFECTS COORDINATOR): "They wanted the jar with Angel's soul to explode. They had already shot the aftermath so they said, 'Now we want to break it, but we've already established what it looks like broken.' Now, you can't get the thing to break the same way that somebody hammered it to a certain way. I was like, 'Okay. Let me see the video tape . . . okay, great . . . let's just try this.' One of my assistants and I were going to shoot this thing out with capsule guns with marbles so you wouldn't be able to see the marble hit this thing. It was just supposed to explode. So we're both sitting onstage with a gun. They said, 'Action' and on three we pulled the trigger at the same time and we shot two holes in it. The thing didn't even break.

"So, we did it again, I said, 'Just let me shoot this thing.' And I shot it and it broke. The director said, 'Yeah, but we need the top to come straight down, because the top had come off at an angle and rolled off. So I said, 'Okay.' The assistant director said, 'Mike, what are you going to do?' I said, 'Nothing. I'm just going to shoot it the same way I did last time.' The director asks, 'Are you going to get the top to come down?' over the set wall. And I yell back, 'Yeah. It'll come straight down.' They're all going, 'What, are you crazy?' And I sat there and I shot it and the top went straight down. I handed them the gun and said, 'I gotta go.'"

"PLAYERS"

CASE № 4ADH16

ACTION TAKEN

The team is shocked by Cordelia's pregnancy revelation, and their reactions do not go unnoticed by Connor. He already

WRITTEN BY Jeffrey Bell & Sarah Fain & Elizabeth Craft
DIRECTED BY Michael Grossman
GUEST STAR: Alexa Davalos (Gwen)
COSTARS: David Monahan (Garrett), Michael Patrick McGill (Guard), Dana Lee (Takeshi Morimoto), Hope Shin (Japanese Girl), Wendy Haines (Over-Jeweled Woman), John Fremont (Security Guy)

believes that they don't like him and expects they will feel the same way about his child, but Cordelia tells everyone that there is nothing to worry about.

"I know it's hard to understand. None of you have ever had a living being growing inside you. And this . . . my sweet baby . . . we're connected. I feel what it feels . . . I can't explain it, but I can sense its goodness, its love . . . You'll see. My baby will be here soon . . . and then you'll all see."
—*Cordelia*

She then goes off to console Connor, telling him that they will be fine as long as they stick together and he does what she tells him.

The rest of the team continues to worry about what this strange pregnancy means, particularly since Cordelia's belly is growing at an alarming rate. Angel adds this strange event to his thoughts about the other weirdness of the past few weeks. He takes a moment to clarify that Angelus did not kill Lilah, bringing at least some kind of closure for Wesley. As they go into research mode to look into the coming child, they get a surprise visit from Gwen Raiden, freshly back from her vacation in Tahiti.

Gwen asks to borrow one of the team, and all are surprised when the request is for Gunn and not Angel. Gunn was feeling somewhat useless since they didn't need any muscle at the moment, so he goes along willingly on a mission to rescue a young girl being held by a businessman named Takeshi Morimoto. Gwen and Gunn go the direct approach and use the front door while Morimoto hosts a fancy party. When a glitch in the system has security about to throw the well-dressed guests out, Gunn's quick thinking gets them into the soiree.

Cordelia pops in on Angel, trying to redirect his focus from the task of figuring out the identity of the Beast's Master for obvious reasons. She hits a major setback, however, when she learns that Lorne has found a ritual to fix his apparently broken empathic abilities since his readings have been so wonky lately. The ritual requires him to go off on his own to perform, but he should be able to read Cordelia by morning.

Gunn manages to fight off Morimoto's men, but when he finds the girl he's been sent to retrieve, he discovers that she is the businessman's daughter and realizes it's a setup. He then finds Gwen breaking into a safe trying to retrieve a device that can regulate body chemistry. Another run-in with Morimoto and his muscle leads Gunn to the correct assumption that Gwen is in this for herself, hoping the device can fix her electrical problems. Although it's not the altruistic reason that had brought him along, Gunn still helps her take the item.

RESOLUTION

Gunn goes back to Gwen's place where he opens up a bit about feeling like he's little more than the muscle of Angel Investigations. Gwen, in her own way, tells him that he's much more than what he thinks of himself. Gunn offers to help enact the device, and straps it onto her bare back after he gets a little shock from touching her exposed skin. When Gunn realizes Gwen has never felt the touch of a man he moves the already sensual moment to the next stage. When Gwen warns that she doesn't know how safe they can be with the untested device, his response is simple.

"You already killed me once. Happens again, you know where my battery is."   —*Gunn*

Lorne goes off to perform his solitary ritual, seemingly unaware that he is not alone. Cordelia has followed and is armed with a dagger to take out the empath. As she gets closer, the lights come up and she finds herself surrounded by Angel, Wesley, and Fred.

DOSSIERS

CLIENT   Gwen Raiden comes back for some help under the guise of planning to rescue a girl named **Lisa.** As it turns out, L.I.S.A. is a military acronym for Localized Ionic Sensory Activity.

SUSPECTS   Gwen tells Gunn that their suspect is **Takeshi Morimoto,** a Japanese businessman known for his charitable efforts, but secretly the equivalent of public enemy number one.

CONTINUITY

Cordelia is still in the process of her stunning revelation when the episode opens. Wesley recalls that this is not her first mystical pregnancy, citing the blessed event that came to term in one day in "Expecting." Gwen returns form the vacation she said she was taking in "Long Day's Journey. " She previously said she had been hit by lighting fourteen times, and gets another jolt from a bolt when meeting with her informant. Wesley and Fred pull up the files on everything they learned about Darla's mystical pregnancy to help research this new one.

OFFICE ROMANCE

Wesley admits to Fred that even though Connor and Cordelia's being a couple is a hard concept to grasp, he understands at least some of the reasons behind it based on his unlikely relationship with Lilah.

QUOTE OF THE WEEK

When Angel tries to re-create what he remembers from the text of the book Lilah had brought, his memory isn't one hundred percent accurate. As Wesley translates:

"Yes, I recognize the text. It's an early Fallorian code system. Let's see . . . 'The green . . . cart-like vehicle . . . eats I-am-not-a-buckethead.'"

THE DEVIL IS IN THE DETAILS

EXPENSES

Gunn gets a nice, new, *free* suit out of the deal.

DEMONS, ETC. . . .

The spikes of a **Gatbar demon** grow to full size while it is still in the womb.

POP CULTURE

✳ **"Everything's been so *Clash of the Titans* around here."**

Cordelia brings up the mythological film from 1981, starring Harry Hamlin.

✳ **"Let me give you a tip, Sugar Bear."**

Gwen uses the name of the mascot for the Post Sugar Crisp cereal.

✳ **". . . and quick as you can say Easy-Bake Oven, there's a gigantic bun in hers."**

Gunn brings up the children's baking toy made by Hasbro.

✳ **"That why you retreated to the Fortress of Solitude?"**

Cordelia refers to Superman's nearly impenetrable "private home" when she finds Connor sitting all alone in an empty hotel room.

* **"It's like being stuck in a really bad movie with those *Clockwork Orange* clampy things on my eyeballs."**
  Fred refers to the (hopefully) fictional devices that force one to keep one's eyes open to witness what is being displayed.
* **"Please, do you think this Dungeons and Dragons cloak is a fashion statement?"**
  Lorne refers to the popular mystical role-playing game.
* **"Just me and my shadow, secluded in a dark, dusty nowhere."**
  Lorne mentions the song written by Al Jolson and Dave Dryer.

OUR HEROES

J. AUGUST RICHARDS: "The relationship between Gunn and Fred did kind of end a few times. In some ways it seemed like it was over and then we were going to give it another try, then it was over. I feel like Gunn's super objective is constantly to protect the people that he loves. I think in that instance he didn't protect himself in terms of his relationship to Fred because he left himself sort of wide open to be hurt because of the whole Wesley scenario. I think my character had to ultimately decide to give up on somebody that he loves. I think that was a big moment for my character. That's not like him. He doesn't give up on anybody. He's always the most resistant to anyone new coming into the group. I'm always the last one to give in because I know that when I like somebody or that I let them in, then I have to go to the extreme for them. That's kind of how I see my character."

In the real world, Charisma Carpenter gave birth two days before this episode aired.

"INSIDE OUT"

CASE № 4ADH17

ACTION TAKEN

Angel faces off with a very evil Cordelia as Fred, Wes, and Lorne watch with weapons raised. A simple slip of the tongue on Cordelia's part had awakened Angel's suspicions, and her attempted attack on Lorne is the proof that she was the Master. Before Angel can get the real answers he's looking for, Connor bursts in and rescues Cordelia, misunderstanding the situation. The team returns to the hotel and updates Gunn on the situation before hitting the books for some serious research.

WRITTEN & DIRECTED BY
Steven S. DeKnight
GUEST STARS Gina Torres (The Woman), David Denman (Skip), Stephi Lineburg (Anna)
SPECIAL GUEST STAR:
Julie Benz (Darla)

While Cordelia sways Connor to her side by distorting the truth, the good side of the team hypothesizes some ugly truths of their own. The first conclusion they reach is that they woke whatever was either inside of Cordelia or had taken her place when they brought back her memory. From there, they figure the evil being twisted events in her favor from that point forward.

As Cordelia has Connor gather a few things to prepare for the birth, Angel goes in search of more answers by contacting Cordy's spirit guide, Skip. The demon reveals that he doesn't really work for the

Powers That Be, but has no intention of saying more, preferring to talk with his fists. The armored demon gives Angel a severe beating, but the vampire is able to fight back and tear off one of Skip's horns before knocking the demon cold and bringing him back to the hotel.

Connor gathers the items on Cordelia's list, including an innocent young girl for sacrifice, but his conscience is starting to get the best of him. He is even more confused when he gets a visit from his mother, Darla, imploring him to stop what he's doing.

The Angel Investigations team holds Skip in a column of energy and threatens the demon with torture to get him to talk. He reveals that they are, indeed, dealing with their friend Cordelia, but she's got a cosmic hitchhiker in her body with an unspeakable name synonymous with unspeakable horror. This bit of info leads the team to realize that Cordelia's ascension to a higher plane was all part of the evil being's plan and that the being probably maneuvered Cordelia to receive her visions in the first place.

> **ANGEL:** "It wasn't just her ascension. Everything that's happened to Cordy these last few years . . . All of it was planned."

> **SKIP:** "You think it stops with her, amigo? You have any concept of how many lines had to intersect for this to play out? How many events had to be nudged in just the right direction? (to Lorne) Leaving Pylea . . . (to Gunn) Your sister . . . (to Fred) Opening the wrong book . . . (to Wes) Sleeping with the enemy . . . Gosh. I love a story with scope."

As the team struggles to deal with the idea that their fates aren't their own, they come to a much larger revelation: that the evil being arranged everything so that the big nasty inside Cordelia can give birth to itself.

RESOLUTION

Skip reveals a little info that helps with locating Cordelia, and the team prepares for battle. However, Angel informs them that he's going alone. Since the only way to stop the evil is by killing Cordelia, he does not want his friends to have to live with that.

Darla begins to make some headway with Connor as the poor innocent girl watches through tears. But Cordelia interrupts, senses Darla, and twists the truth again to allow Connor to believe that Angel is behind the vision of the boy's mother. Filled with hatred once again, Connor takes the girl to Cordelia, who kills the innocent. Connor then uses the girl's blood in the ritual for Cordelia to give birth. As the birthing begins the world trembles.

The earthquake frees Skip from his invisible prison, and the heavily armored demon goes on the attack. With the odds stacked against them, Wes sees a chink in the armor where Angel had ripped out Skip's horn, and he shoots the demon dead.

Angel arrives to kill Cordelia, but Connor fights his father, trying to stop him. It all proves too late as a shining light bursts forth from Cordelia and a demon that turns into a fully grown woman appears before them. Angel falls to his knees in worship.

"Oh my god. . . . You're beautiful."   —*Angel*

CONTINUITY

The episode opens in the final scene of the previous episode and has numerous mentions and flashbacks to previous episodes, including Cordelia's slip by using the same words as the Master ("Players"), Lorne's memory spell ("Spin the Bottle"), the blood spiking and Manny murder ("Long Day's Journey"), murdering the Svea Priestesses ("Soulless"), taking Angel's soul (presumably also in "Soulless"), the failed spell to re-ensoul him ("Calvary"), the key used to find Skip ("Billy"), Skip's other visits ("Birthday" and "Tomorrow"), the death of Gunn's sister ("War Zone"), Fred being transported to Pylea (revealed in "Belonging"), Wes hooking up with Lilah ("Tomorrow"), and two vampires coupling and giving birth ("Reprise" and "Lullaby").

Gunn comes back into things wearing the suit Gwen had given him for their heist. Skip mentions that no one comes back from paradise, well, except for a Slayer once, referring to Buffy's resurrection at the beginning of *Buffy the Vampire Slayer,* Season Six.

OFFICE ROMANCE

Cordelia convinces Connor that Angel hates him for being with her. Fred is instantly jealous when she sees Gunn return from Gwen's in a nice new suit, but the two share a nice moment when Gunn calms her over the whole "our fates are already sealed" issue.

QUOTE OF THE WEEK

"Kid Vicious did the heavy lifting. Cordy just mwah-ha-ha-ed at us."

Lorne gives Gunn a quick recap of events.

THE DEVIL IS IN THE DETAILS

EXPENSES

Once again the hotel suffers some earthquake damage.

THE PEN IS MIGHTIER

FINAL CUT

Darla tries to make a connection with Connor in a line cut due to length.

> **"I know what it's like. Being drawn into the darkness. Not knowing which path to take. Or if there even is one."**

POP CULTURE

❋ **"That's it? I get away with bringing the world down around you and two eensy words tingle your spider sense?"**

Cordelia compares Angel's instincts to the supernatural ones possessed by Spider-Man.

* **"Lizzy Borden. It wasn't wearing any."**
  Wes figures that Cordelia killed Manny in the buff just as the famed ax murderess did when she killed her parents to make sure there was no blood on her clothes.
* **"What are you, Tarzan?"**
  Skip compares a swinging Angel to the character created by Edgar Rice Burroughs.
* **"It could be when you're duking it out with the Legion of Doom . . ."**
  Gunn invokes the name of the evil team that fought against the Superfriends.

SIX DEGREES OF . . .

Gina Torres, who plays the woman who will come to be known as Jasmine, also starred on Joss Whedon's short-lived series *Firefly*. Her costar Nathan Fillion joined the *Buffy* cast as the evil preacher, Caleb, for the show's final episodes.

OUR HEROES

SANDY STRUTH (SET DECORATOR): "We dress a lot of warehouses and the challenge is always to make it different. What crates do you use versus what shelves? Sometimes you go back and see how the other ones were shot and sometimes it's just the architecture of the building allows you to bring the same things in and place them differently. It's the same with the alleys. The alleys are pretty much down to, 'Okay, here's our dumpster.' There's only so much you can do and there's usually a stunt there so you want to try and make it work."

"SHINY HAPPY PEOPLE"

CASE N° 4ADH18

ACTION TAKEN

Angel continues to bow in supplication to the Woman to whom Cordelia gave birth. The Woman forgives Angel for coming there to kill her, then disappears.

WRITTEN BY Elizabeth Craft & Sarah Fain
DIRECTED BY Marita Grabiak
GUEST STAR: Gina Torres (The Woman)
COSTARS: David Figlioli (Vamp Leader), Suzette Craft (Teacherly Woman), Steven Bean (Middle-Aged Man), Annie Wersching (Awed Woman), Sam Witwer (Young Man), Lynette Romero (News Anchor), Chane't Johnson (Martha Jane), Jackie Tohn (Woman #1), Lyle Kanouse (Counter Guy), Tawny Rene Hamilton (Anchorwoman)

Back at the hotel Fred is fretting when Connor comes in. Fred prepares to go on the attack, but Angel stops her. They have brought Cordelia home, no longer pregnant, but in a coma. Angel and Connor are behaving strangely and not the least bit concerned over Cordelia's evil offspring.

"We don't want to kill her. We just want to find her so we can worship her. That's all."   —*Angel*

The team is confused by Angel and Connor's behavior, but everything becomes much clearer when the Woman enters the hotel. Each of the members of Angel Investigations falls to his or her knees in worship.

The Woman explains to her newly devoted followers that she is effectively a Power That Was, and has come back to Earth to help restore the balance that has been missing since her people first walked on the planet before the time of Man. She directs the team on a new battle against evil to change the world.

The team attacks a bowling alley overrun by vampires while the Woman and Fred look on, though Fred suggests they should be at a safer distance. A vampire gets past Angel and claws the Woman, drawing blood. Angel chases the vamp out of the alley and through an outdoor restaurant, when the vampire falls on a patron before turning to dust. When the Woman arrives, the restaurant-goers all join the worship upon first sight of her, except for the patron on whom the vamp fell. He tries to kill her.

Angel beats the man into submission, until the Woman tells him to stop. The team returns to the hotel and sets about finding a name for her. Fred is upset over the fact that she let the Woman get hurt and vows to clean her shirt of the blood from the vampire. The Woman works to put Angel's mind at ease over his newfound happiness as they talk amid the night-blooming jasmine in the hotel garden.

The team continues their battle against evil and makes great strides in lessening the crime rate in the city. After much scrubbing of blood, Fred finally gives up and buys the Woman a new shirt to replace the battle-ruined one. When Fred goes to present the shirt, however, she does not see a beautiful god. Instead she sees a horribly disfigured and rotting face. She stumbles out of the room in shock and no longer feeling the love of The Woman.

Fred visits the restaurant patron in the hospital and is shocked to find him locked in the mental ward and disfigured from where the Woman touched him. She confirms that they have seen the same thing in the alleged goddess, and the man insists that Fred has been called to take action. Never having received a calling before, Fred is overwhelmed, and she returns to a crowded hotel full of worshippers and confides in Wesley about what she's learned. He goes right to the Woman with the information.

RESOLUTION

Fearing for her life, Fred holds Lorne hostage and tries to kill the Woman. Angel and Connor come to the Woman's defense, but Fred manages to escape. She makes her way through the city alone and afraid, wondering what she can do to stop the Woman. Over breakfast in a diner, Fred sees a local morning program on the TV that tells her she is about to be much more alone.

"Welcome back. Chef Arnold Michske will join us later. But right now, we've got the most amazing surprise. Please join me in welcoming a very special visitor . . . Jasmine!"

—*Anchorwoman*

Fred watches in horror as the Woman appears on-screen and begins to spread her message to the city. Patrons of the diner, and out on the street, all fall to their knees as they listen to Jasmine's words.

CONTINUITY

The opening scene continues from the end of "Inside Out." Following the birth of the Woman, Cordelia falls into a coma that will last for quite a while. Jasmine claims that Angel did not fail the tests he went through for Darla in "Judgement." Instead, that was the day that earned Darla a second chance at life by giving birth to Connor. Jasmine finally gives Connor the answers he's been looking for concerning his unlikely birth. She calls him the "unique soul" she had been looking for to provide for her own birth.

OFFICE ROMANCE

Jasmine uses her influence to convince Gunn and Wesley that their shared love for Fred should bring them together as friends, not tear them apart.

QUOTE OF THE WEEK

FRED: "There's been an awful lot of dismembering going on in that basement lately, if you ask me."
LORNE: "It's been a busy month."

THE DEVIL IS IN THE DETAILS

EXPENSES

Wes and Gunn both have purchased coveralls and a buzz saw to use while dismembering Skip. Fred buys a new shirt for the Woman.

DEMONS, ETC. . . .

According to Jasmine, her history is as follows:

JASMINE: "In the beginning, before the time of Man, Great Beings walked the Earth. Untold power emanated from all quarters—the seeds of what would come to be known as 'good' and 'evil.' But the shadows stretched and became darkness, and the malevolent among us grew stronger. The Earth became a demon realm. Those of us who had the will to resist left this place. But remained ever watchful."

GUNN: "You're a Power That . . . Was?"

JASMINE: "But then something new emerged from deep inside the Earth, neither demon nor god . . ."

WESLEY: "Man."

JASMINE: "It seemed for a time that through this new race a balance might be restored."

FRED: "Guess we let you down."

JASMINE: "But you didn't. It was *we* who failed *you*. We became little more than observers. I could bear no longer to just watch . . ."

AS SCENE IN L.A.

The news anchor reporting on the drop in southland crime is played by Lynette Romero, who is the news anchor on the local Los Angeles news for the WB affiliate.

Once again, Paramount's New York Street backlot doubles for Los Angeles when Fred escapes the diner at the end of the episode. This time a glimpse of Angel's first-season office building can be seen as Fred goes down the street.

THE PEN IS MIGHTIER

FINAL CUT

Fred's consultation with a comatose Cordelia was a bit longer in the original script.

"I'm sorry we just left you here all alone. It's just, everything's been so . . . well, great. I thought . . . I wanted to *believe* we were gonna be all rah-rah good guys and . . . win. 'Cause there's this person . . . your daughter actually. You and Connor had a girl. She's like six-two. And black. And apparently a god. Anyway, I'm really miserable about being so happy and all when I'm . . . not. Does that make sense?"

POP CULTURE

✳ "Dismember mama?"

Lorne has some fun with the movie title *I Remember Mama*.

✳ "And here comes the sun."

Lorne makes with the Beatles references.

✳ "It was like 'A Hard Day's Night.' Everybody followed her back."

THE NAME GAME

"Shiny Happy People" is the title of an R.E.M. song from their CD "Out of Time."

SIX DEGREES OF . . .

Lyle Kanouse, who plays the counter guy at the diner, also appeared in Joss Whedon's other series *Firefly*, as a salesman in the episode "Out of Gas."

OUR HEROES

SHAWNA TRPCIC (COSTUMER), WHO, LIKE GINA TORRES, CAME OVER TO *ANGEL* AFTER PRODUCTION WRAPPED ON *FIREFLY*: "With Jasmine it was great because I already knew her body. So I started doing sketches immediately. We made just about all of her stuff, because she has sort of a figure model's body; you can't just go shopping and throw something on her. She's very thin and very narrow and just has a perfect body.

"Jeff Bell said 'Oprah Winfrey.' What he meant by that was someone who all of America would relate to and would love. So we were kind of going Oprah Winfrey in a very elegant, very fashion-model way. The fabrics were flowing and natural colors and natural tones, just sort of not abrasive— somebody that you can approach easily. We did get some stuff at Saks that were these natural turquoise colors and then I mixed it with linens that were just all natural fabrics just to give her a very approachable, soft look."

"THE MAGIC BULLET"

CASE Nº 4ADH19

ACTION TAKEN

Fred runs through the streets of L.A., chased by the two men who once loved her more than anything. She manages to elude her pursuers, leaving Wesley and Gunn to return to the hotel, which is now overflowing with Jasmine's followers. Her words have spread across the city, bringing peace and love while pretty much removing everyone's ability for free thought.

Fred makes a trip to a local occult/conspiracy theorist store called the Magic Bullet, hoping to find more reference on mass hypnosis. The clerk recognizes Fred from her visit three days earlier, and reveals that he is now under Jasmine's thrall. He seems to know what Fred is up to, which worries her when she sees he keeps a gun in the store. But it's a false alarm as his mind is so full with thoughts of Jasmine that he doesn't think anything ill of Fred.

WRITTEN & DIRECTED BY
Jeffrey Bell
GUEST STARS: Gina Torres (Jasmine), Danny Woodburn (Creature), Patrick Fischler (Ted)
COSTARS: Mia Kelly (Woman), Andre Hotchko (Man in Lobby), Steve Forbess (Mexican Man), Ajgie Kirkland (Black Man), Michael McElroy (Young Boy), Chad Williams (Rock Dude), Terrylene (Deaf Woman), Phyllis Flax (Very Old Woman), Amy Raymond (Weeping Woman)

Jasmine is in the process of expanding her mental powers and joins with Angel and the team to locate Fred by using her many followers across the city to be her eyes. Fred narrowly escapes the acolytes when Jasmine's powers unexpectedly backfire on her.

While fleeing additional pursuit later, Fred falls into a cavern occupied by a demon squatter. The creature tries to lull Fred into a sense of security, but she doesn't buy it, especially when she sees he has stockpiled some human body parts. The creature attacks and bloodies Fred's sleeve before she manages to take a hatchet to his head. After she pushes the body off her, Fred looks at the sleeve and is struck with inspiration.

Fred goes back to the Magic Bullet and reveals herself to Jasmine's followers. The clerk alerts her to the fact that Jasmine is on her way, and Fred gets herself into position. When Jasmine arrives, Fred grabs the clerk's gun and shoots the self-proclaimed god. The bullet tears through Jasmine, entering and exiting her body before hitting Angel behind her.

As Connor protects Jasmine, Angel springs into action. He holds Fred down, but when she gets him to look at Jasmine, he sees the same rotting flesh that Fred had seen previously. The bullet carried some of Jasmine's blood into Angel's body, and he was affected just as Fred had been by that same blood when she cleaned Jasmine's shirt days earlier.

Jasmine takes Connor back to the hotel after she realizes why she lost Fred and Angel, but she tells her closest followers a slightly different tale.

"My kindness turned him. By being too loving to Fred, I opened the door to her hate. By trying to save Fred, I lost Angel. That won't happen again. We must eradicate their hate."   —*Jasmine*

RESOLUTION

Together, Fred and Angel combine what they know and realize that Cordelia's blood might have the same mind-altering affect as Jasmine's since their friend did give birth to the god. They sneak into the hotel and are in the process of draining some of Cordelia's blood when Lorne comes in. Angel subdues the green guy and gives him a dose of Cordy blood, ripping him from the Jasmine-induced Utopia. Lorne then lures Wes and Gunn into the same trap and sets them free as well.

As the team comes down from their blissful high Jasmine has another collection of followers brought to her room. Connor stands guard at the door while a brilliant light peeks out the cracks and a glowing Jasmine steps into the hall alone.

> **JASMINE:** "My sweet boy."
> **CONNOR:** "Where are those people?"
> **JASMINE:** "I ate them."
> **CONNOR:** "Cool."

Wesley lures Connor away from Jasmine and the team traps the boy. As Angel holds him, Wesley slices Connor's chest and allows Cordelia's blood to mix with his. The mixture seems to have an effect, until Connor hurries out into the hall shouting that Jasmine's enemies are there.

CONTINUITY

The hotel is now full of Jasmaniacs (as the creature Fred meets calls them) since it has been several days since she spread her message over local television. Jasmine explains that she has not sent her words beyond L.A. because the world is not yet ready for it, which explains why Sunnydale residents weren't feeling the love on *Buffy*. Fred's sudden realization of Jasmine's true image in "Shiny Happy People" is explained when she makes the blood connection in this episode.

OFFICE ROMANCE

Both Gunn and Wesley have turned their love to hate when talking about Fred in this episode.

QUOTE OF THE WEEK

LORNE: "I can't believe little ol' Fred managed to sway Angel back to the dark side."

GUNN: "Evil. Not evil. Evil again. I wish he'd make up his mind."

WESLEY: "I guess the good news is it doesn't matter anymore. Jasmine says Angel has to die. He dies."

THE DEVIL IS IN THE DETAILS

EXPENSES

Fred has some out-of-pocket costs for reference materials, a motel room, and other living expenses.

WEAPONRY

Short on cash and resources, Fred makes good with some found items, including a hatchet and a gun.

DEMONS, ETC. . . .

As has been previously established, Lorne's people have their hearts in their butts.

THE PEN IS MIGHTIER

FINAL CUT

In the original script Jasmine's powers were slightly exaggerated, as explained by one of the faithful on open mike night:

> "I've been legally blind for the past twelve years. I heard Jasmine on the radio last night and when I woke up this morning . . . I could see—I could see . . ."

POP CULTURE

* **"Don't be shy, Slim Jim."**

   Lorne refers to the meat stick snacks often found at 7-Elevens.

* **"This close and she pulled a Houdini."**

   Gunn compares Fred's disappearance to that of the legendary escape artist.

* **"Nothing really good on since Art Bell retired."**
  Ted, the clerk at the Magic Bullet, refers to the radio talk show host who specialized in the subject of the unexplained. Since this episode aired, the host has come out of retirement.
* **JASMINE: "I sound like the prologue to one of those movies about magical dwarves."**
  GUNN: "Hobbits?"
  Of course, they refer to the films in The Lord of the Rings trilogy (or at least the first two, since the third was not out yet at the time this episode aired).
* **". . . why you don't sashay into a TV studio, say, 'Scoot over Regis,' and sweet talk your love to the whole wide world."**
  Gunn refers to talk show (and former game show) host Regis Philbin.
* **LORNE: "Well, you know what they say about people who need people?"**
  CONNOR: "They're the luckiest people in the world."
  Now that their minds are linked by Jasmine, Connor's got a better understanding of the works of Barbra Streisand.
* **"Any monkey business and I'll chop you down like a cherry tree."**
  A hatchet-wielding Fred refers to one of the more colorful stories about George Washington.
* **"Mind if I quest for fire?"**
  The creature makes reference to the French film from 1981.
* **"That's some gift you got, Kreskin."**
  Gunn brings up the noted "mentalist."
* **"Tonight, the role of Judas Iscariot will be played by Krevlornswath of the Deathwok Clan."**
  Lorne compares himself to the most famous betrayer of all time as he is about to awaken Gunn and Wes to the reality of Jasmine.

THE NAME GAME

"**The Magic Bullet**" is a phrase used by conspiracy theorists when referring to the Warren Commission's report that a single bullet killed John F. Kennedy, then exited his body and struck Governor Connally, much in the same way a "magic bullet" passes through Jasmine to hit Angel.

TRACKS

The episode opens with the happy sounds of The Beach Boys' hit "Wouldn't It Be Nice?" Angel and Connor share an open mike night duet to one of the vampire's favorite songs, "Mandy," with the words changed in honor of Jasmine.

OUR HEROES

ROBERT HALL (SPECIAL EFFECTS MAKEUP ARTIST) ON THE DEVOLUTION OF A GODDESS: "Jasmine was a big surprise. We weren't really sure what was going on with that. She wound up being subtle, with a couple different stages of appliance makeup, then she reached the final stage puppet with the maggots and blood oozing out of it. That's really all we did for it and then wound up taking that back and making a couple of appliances to put on Gina that started to resemble the puppet.

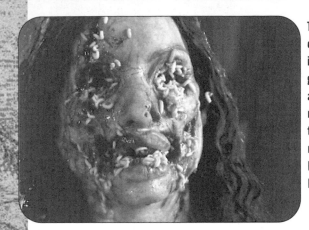

Then, sometimes, CGI would comp the puppet head onto her. That was really the extent of her. She was in her beautiful form for the most part. Then Vincent got to smash his fist through her head. Vincent had a great time doing that, by the way. There was a multitude of stuff that went along with Jasmine— the grossest one being the maggoty puppet head. I mean, come on, a bunch of maggots on a rotted head, there's not much grosser than that. I can't believe we even got away with that."

"SACRIFICE"

CASE Nº 4ADH20

ACTION TAKEN

Angel tries to convince his son to join him and the team in their new fight against Jasmine, but Connor refuses, calling even louder for help. As Jasmine's followers rush to them, Angel slams the door shut and tells the others to leave via the fire escape while he delays the growing army alone.

"Someone who knows the truth has to live through this . . ."
—*Angel*

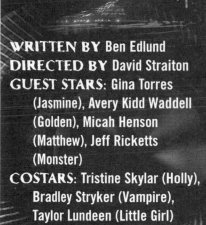

WRITTEN BY Ben Edlund
DIRECTED BY David Straiton
GUEST STARS: Gina Torres
(Jasmine), Avery Kidd Waddell
(Golden), Micah Henson
(Matthew), Jeff Ricketts
(Monster)
COSTARS: Tristine Skylar (Holly),
Bradley Stryker (Vampire),
Taylor Lundeen (Little Girl)

The gang reluctantly flees to the car while Angel takes on Connor and the horde of Jasminites. As the escapees wonder what to do next, Connor's unconscious body comes flying down onto the hood of the car, followed by Angel. The vampire leaves his lost son behind, telling Wes to drive.

It's Angel Investigations against the entire city of Los Angeles as Jasmine searches for the heroes through the eyes of her followers while Connor heals from his physical and emotional wounds. The gang is forced to stop for gas and fight off innocent victims with a new little toy surprise inside; Jasmine can not only see through their eyes, but now her voice comes out of their mouths. With the entire police force after them, the team literally heads underground to the sewers trying to figure out their next move, unaware of more looming danger.

Jasmine joins Connor in watching over Cordelia and plants more of her seeds of evil by convincing the boy that his father's hate led him to cut Cordelia and draw her blood. Of course, she leaves out the part where she realizes that same blood is a danger to her. Jasmine asks for some time alone with her mother and uses the distraction to have Cordelia moved to a secret location.

Back in the sewers, the gang runs into a booby trap set by a group of scared kids who had fled

251

underground themselves back when L.A. was trapped in the dark. They are unaware of the new world order and more concerned with the evil demon hunting them through the sewers. At first they don't warm to the gang, until the young leader recognizes his late brother's old friend Gunn.

Angel and team take up weapons to help the kids against the demons, but when they come under attack, Wesley is taken and Angel's vampire self is revealed to the young fighters. They hadn't been happy working with the demon Lorne, but finding a vampire in the mix doesn't sit too well at all, and the youngest member of the group flees topside. Gunn and Fred go after the boy, while Lorne keeps the teens occupied and Angel goes in search of Wes, fearing the worst.

Wesley is still alive and conversing with a rather cryptic-speaking monster who claims, "We loved her first." Wesley suspects that the monster means Jasmine, although the creature goes on a tangent about the human penchant for naming things. The creature continues to work on a macabre wall of "blood magic," trying to lure the goddess back to his people and their dimension. Through the creature's ramblings, Wesley comes to realize that the monster has revealed that Jasmine's weakness is her real name.

RESOLUTION

Fred and Gunn find the young boy above ground, and bring him back, presumably before he'd been infected by Jasmine's love. However, they were wrong in that assumption, and the boy spreads Jasmine's love to his friends, putting Gunn, Fred, and Lorne on the run once again. As they flee through the tunnels they run into Connor, leading a heavily armed strike force.

Angel finds Wesley and manages to take out the creature. They reunite with the others, slamming the door to the monster's secret room behind them. As Jasmine's followers try to break in, Wesley stands over the monster's glowing orb, which is a key to the portal leading to the demon's world. Wes realizes that his own blood is just the magic he needs to open the portal.

Angel tells everyone to flee into the dimension, but Wesley stops them, knowing they won't be able to breathe in the atmosphere. Only Angel, who does not need to breathe, can go. Angel is reluctant to leave his friends, but Wesley uses the vampire's own words to convince him.

"Someone who knows the truth has to live through this . . . Angel. That's *you.*" —*Wesley*

Angel grabs the key and enters the portal in search of the High Priest who knows Jasmine's real name, while his friends stay behind to do battle against overwhelming odds. But Angel's odds aren't that much better when he arrives in the demon dimension to find himself surrounded by a horde of evil creatures.

CONTINUITY

The action starts where it left off in "The Magic Bullet." The team wonders why Jasmine could not name herself in "Shiny Happy People," and Wes eventually comes to the realization that her true name had prevented her from choosing another one. Her power is beginning to spread through the state and she has the governor under control. One of the lost kids is the brother of a former member of Gunn's demon-fighting gang.

QUOTE OF THE WEEK

"And that's why when we use words like 'ugly-ass' and 'beastie,' we can sometimes do more damage than we intend to. It ain't about the sticks and stones, my young friends. That's all. Little life lesson, one to grow on . . ."   Lorne preaches a message of tolerance to the sewer kids.

THE DEVIL IS IN THE DETAILS

EXPENSES

Everyone's clothes pretty much go through the ringer and will likely need to be replaced once the world goes back to normal.

WEAPONRY

The team follows Fred's previously established lead of making due with found items by borrowing the sewer-dwelling kids' weapons, including a pipe, bat, hockey stick, homemade spear, and machete.

THE PLAN

Once again the team finds itself lacking a serious plan, as noted in this exchange as they enter the sewers.

ANGEL: "Should buy us some time . . ."
GUNN: "Time to do what? Get all stanky and starve to death?"
ANGEL: "You know what, I don't know what we're going to do, Gunn! I don't have a plan! Now I guess this whole Jasmine World Order thing kinda took me by surprise!"
GUNN: "Well, I ain't eatin' no rats!"
ANGEL: "Good! Neither am I!"
GUNN: "All right then, plan's comin' together!"
ANGEL: "Glad you're on board!"

THE PEN IS MIGHTIER

FINAL CUT

The demon dimension is described as follows in the script.
EXT. THE 'WE LOVED HER FIRST' DIMENSION—NIGHT
ON THE OTHER SIDE OF THE PORTAL, swirling, all but filling screen, veils of AMMONIA VAPOR waft past us. Angel steps out, GLOWING ORB in hand, stumbling forward into a CU.

Then he hears it: first one, then another, until the air is shredded by MONSTROUS WAILS OF ALARM.
CGI CAMERA PULLS BACK—revealing Angel, standing at the brink of a PRECIPICE in a hostile ALIEN WORLD.
CAMERA KEEPS PULLING BACK—a bridge stands before him, and beyond it, the stepped form of a MOUNTAINOUS ZIGGURAT—over it, like ants on a cast away bit of hard candy— MONSTERS (like the one we just killed) turn to Angel, WAILING . . .

POP CULTURE

❋ **"Anyone else feel like the last feisty wife in Stepford?"**
Lorne compares their situation to the one in the Ira Levin book turned movie *The Stepford Wives.*

❋ **"Hate to say it, Dr. Pep, but I've been lost for two hours."**
Lorne comes up with another apropos nickname, based on the soda Dr Pepper.

❋ **"Uh-uh, Dracula."**
Golden compares Angel to the most famous vamp of all time (who, coincidentally, has friends in common with Angel since his appearance in the *Buffy* episode, "Buffy vs. Dracula").

❋ **"*Knowing* . . . Knowing is half the . . ."**
Lorne starts to use the tagline that was seen in public service announcements that ran after the *G.I. Joe* cartoon series in the eighties, in which the audience learned that "Knowing is half the battle."

SIX DEGREES OF . . .

Ben Edlund, creator of the comic book and TV series *The Tick,* joins the *Angel* writing staff on this episode, following his work on Joss Whedon's science fiction series *Firefly.*

Jeff Ricketts, who plays the monster, has made several appearances on Joss Whedon's shows, first as Weatherby in the *Buffy* episodes "This Year's Girl" and "Who Are You?" and the *Angel* episode "Sanctuary." He also appeared as Blue Glove #1 in the *Firefly* episodes "The Train Job" and "Ariel."

OUR HEROES

ROBERT HALL (SPECIAL EFFECTS MAKEUP ARTIST): "The most difficult had to be the—I don't know what we're even calling him—the spider/flea creature from 'Sacrifice,' Ben Edlund's episode. That one was probably the worst. Jeff [Ricketts] had been on *Star Trek* a lot. He had worn a lot of prosthetics and stuff—I love Jeff too—great actor, great guy, personally. I don't know if he knew what he was getting into with this. He got a little claustrophobic in the suit. To his credit, it was a lot to take care of. He wasn't just wearing a rubber suit. He was

wearing a rubber suit, a silicon face appliance, upper and lower dentures, contact lenses, silicon hand pincers, a lower body harness that held all the back legs that were puppeteered by someone else . . . a whole thing this guy had to do. Luckily, he made it through and did a great job with the episode. That one, just by sheer nature of being such a big job, made it really hard to put together."

LONI PERISTERE (VISUAL EFFECTS SUPERVISOR): "We often collaborate with Rob Hall. He'll create creatures that are so elaborate that they are not only inhuman in look, but they're also inhuman in action. So they'll be unable to actually move the way they should move in real life and we'll need to work with Rob to create a digital facsimile of his creatures, not unlike the tick creature.

"On the makeup fitting day, the actor has to come to the shop and get fitted with their gear. When they dress him up that one time, we'll take him over to the scanning facility and the scanning people will scan the character and we'll get a 3-D facsimile of that character, which will then be brought here to Zoic where the team will then fix the model, rig it to be moved, and texture it and prepare it for animation. Then Rob's actual design will take the close shots where it's fighting Angel directly and then we'll take the wider shots where it crawls up a wall or drops off a thirty-foot ceiling and animate that with CGI."

ROCCO PASSIORINO (DIGITAL EFFECTS SUPERVISOR): "That particular episode with the whole tick creature and everything was so much fun because of the fact that Ben Edlund had basically written the episode. He, of course, was the creator of The Tick, so it was kind of funny to have a character on the show we all called the tick. When he conceived of the designs for what this other world was going to be like he actually broke out a pen and paper and just started drawing stuff, which is just so funny to see a comic book artist that you've always seen his work in books and so forth and so on, to actually have him sit down with a pen and paper and start drawing out this other world right in front of you. It's so great to have the resources of the actual writer on the show able to give you imagery himself as opposed to just writing words on paper and saying, 'I wrote it and it's supposed to look like this. Now you guys need to translate it into something that is a visual medium.' So that was really helpful in that particular episode."

"PEACE OUT"

CASE № 4ADH21

ACTION TAKEN

Both Angel and his friends face overwhelming odds in the demon dimension and on Earth. Luckily, when Angel holds up the key that transported him there, the horde of monsters steps away in fright. Meanwhile Wesley, Gunn, Lorne, and Fred aren't as lucky when Jasmine's followers capture them. Just as Connor is about to make with the massacring, Jasmine's voice stops him. She has seen the dead monster through her followers' eyes and tells Connor to bring the prisoners to her.

WRITTEN BY David Fury
DIRECTED BY Jefferson Kibbee
GUEST STARS: Gina Torres (Jasmine), Stephanie Romanov (Lilah)
COSTARS: Bonita Friedericy (Patience), Robert Towers (High Priest), Eliza Pryor Nagel (Susan), Bob Pescovitz (News Producer), Gerry Katzman (Technician), Audrey Kearns (Young Woman), Kristin Richardson (Female Reporter), Kyle Ingleman (Jeremy), Jeff Scott Bass (Brent), Kimble Jemison (Cop #1), Blair Hickey (Male News Reporter), Angelica Castro (Telemundo Reporter), Brian Bradley (Grizzled Reporter)

Jasmine tries to get information on Angel's whereabouts, but the team refuses to answer. She admits that she recognized the creature in the sewer as one of her followers from her last, failed attempt at creating paradise. Fred tries to reason with Connor to get him to see what they see, unaware of the fact that he already does.

Angel climbs up to the temple for the goddess known in his dimension as Jasmine and finds the High Priest who is Guardian of the Word. The Priest has the power of foresight and knows what Angel has come for. But getting her true name is not as easy as he thought it would be, since the hulking Keeper of the Name has its mouth sewn shut and is ready for a fight.

"The Keeper will not be forthcoming. Only with its last breath will it divulge the true name of the blessed Devourer."
—High Priest

Connor locks his former "friends" in the cage built for Angelus. They try to convince him of Jasmine's true face, but Connor reveals that he's known all along. Wesley is able to piece together the fact that Jasmine is consuming many of her followers based on the fact that the now-dead creature he met had referred to her as "The Devourer." They then raise Connor's suspicion about Cordelia's well-being enough that he asks Jasmine about it.

The goddess is not quite forthcoming as she prepares to address the entire world and put everyone under her spell. While she is at her largest feeding yet, Connor takes that distraction to beat some followers into admitting where they took Cordelia. He finds her lying on the altar of a church and confesses his mixed feelings to her while she sleeps. Connor is confused over why Angel keeps fighting the utopian world and admits that he's so tired of fighting and torn up even more than he had been before.

RESOLUTION

Jasmine begins her address to a world audience when Angel appears via portal in the center of the lobby. He holds off the followers by holding up the head of the Keeper of the Name. Angel then cuts the mouth open, releasing Jasmine's true name. The response is instantaneous as the world sees Jasmine for what she truly is. The residents of Los Angeles all suffer the extreme pain of the loss and go rioting through the streets.

Angel follows Jasmine, trying to convince her that her plan has failed. But Jasmine has a new plan. Instead of saving mankind, she will destroy it one body at a time, starting with Angel. Using the strength of a goddess, Jasmine manages to pummel Angel fairly badly, until Connor arrives, answering her call. At first she thinks he is there to help her, but Connor punches his fist right through her head, putting an end to her reign. Angel tries to talk to his son, but Connor just backs away.

Gunn manages to break the team out of the cage in time to find the hotel empty. As they start out to find Angel, an unexpected visitor stops them. Later, when Angel returns, they try to update him on the latest surprise, but the vampire's mind is still on his son.

> **ANGEL:** "I've never seen him like . . . He wasn't hurt. Or angry. He just killed her and his face, it was . . . just blank. Like he had nothing left."
>
> **WESLEY:** "Angel, you really—"
>
> **ANGEL:** "I've got a bad feeling. He's just . . . given up. I think he's gonna do something. He might—"
>
> **LILAH:** "End world peace?"

Angel looks up in shock to find the recently departed Lilah standing before him.

CONTINUITY

The episode begins within the moments seen at the end of "Sacrifice." The team is locked in the cage they built for Angelus in "Awakening." Jasmine indicates that Angel is fulfilling his piece of the

Shanshu prophecy by bringing about the apocalypse. He will later learn that the prophecy had nothing to do with this particular apocalypse. Lilah makes a surprise return appearance, following her death and dismemberment in "Calvary" and "Salvage."

QUOTE OF THE WEEK

HIGH PRIEST: "Her true name is known only by the Keeper of the Name."

ANGEL: "Right. That's you."

HIGH PRIEST: "No. I am the Guardian of the Word."

ANGEL: "You said the Word *is* the Name."

HIGH PRIEST: "Yes. And I guard the Keeper of it."

ANGEL: "So you're the Keeper's . . . keeper?"

HIGH PRIEST: "I am the Guardian of the Word."

ANGEL: "Yeah, yeah. Okay. So where's this Keeper of the Name?"

THE DEVIL IS IN THE DETAILS

WEAPONRY

Angel uses Jasmine's real name against her. In turn, Jasmine tries to throw a car at him.

DEMONS, ETC. . . .

Jasmine had a "trial run" of her peace plan in the demon dimension that Angel visits. According to her, a few millennia ago that world was similar to Earth in its fear, hatred, and warring. Although the inhabitants weren't as evolved as humans, she managed to kick up their evolution a bit. Long after she left, most of her followers eventually gave up hope that she would return, except for a few, including the High Priest. Wesley believes that Cordelia's connection to Jasmine may make their comatose friend a threat. Later Connor proves that the parental connection is what Jasmine feared since only Connor has the power to destroy her.

THE PEN IS MIGHTIER

FINAL CUT

A "grizzled reporter" indicates just how much the world has changed with his first question at Jasmine's press conference, which had to be cut.

"Yeah, I got a question all right . . . One I think the world demands an answer to . . . Exactly how do you get your hair so shiny and bouncy like that? What is that, like, a special conditioner or . . ."

POP CULTURE

✳ **"It's 'To Serve Man' all over again."**
Gunn refers to the classic episode of *The Twilight Zone* in which an alien race befriends humanity, planning to cook them up with recipes from their aptly titled cookbook.

✳ **"Then what, Kato?"**
As Gunn tries to kick his way out of the cage, Lorne compares him to the sidekick character played by Bruce Lee in the *Green Hornet* TV series.

✳ **"Never give up, never surrender."**
Gunn uses a rallying cry from the film *Galaxy Quest*.

✳ **"Only in a post-apocalyptic 'Night of the Comet' kinda way."**
Lorne refers to the 1984 film set following a comet strike that wipes out most of the Earth's population.

OUR HEROES

MICHAEL GASPAR (SPECIAL EFFECTS COORDINATOR): "We took a car and gutted it and then we suspended it over a bridge on a crane by three cables. Two cables that were on one side of the car were just looped around a couple of hooks. Then there was one cable going through the center of the car. We literally just pyrotechnically cut that cable and when that cable broke, the car leaned and then the other two cables held onto it for a second and then it just rolled off those two cables. When it came down we had fake power lines stretched across with sparks on it. So when that went, it hit the power lines and sparked, then fell on top of another car and exploded.

"That was an interesting night. We don't get much time and there were probably two days total to prep that gag. We couldn't test that. In a feature, we'd test that for two weeks over and over and over again with three or four cars and test and test and test. The time on features is huge, but for TV there isn't much of that. We were betting on how it would come down. 'Do you think it will do one revolution? Will it do half of a revolution? Will it fall down on its top? Will it just go down on the side?' We all made a bet on what it would do. All we knew was it was going to fall down."

The sign outside the church holding Cordelia reads: "God is Nowhere. Jasmine is the Way." The first part of that edict is a tip of the hat to series cocreator David Greenwalt's other series, <u>Miracles,</u> in which "God is Nowhere" (or "God is Now Here") was a recurring theme.

"HOME"

CASE Nº 4ADH22

ACTION TAKEN

Lilah explains that the Wolfram & Hart Senior Partners have sent her as a messenger from Hell, because her contract with them extended beyond her death. The message she brings is an offer: As thanks for ending the utopian bliss Jasmine brought about, the Senior Partners want to hand over the reins of their L.A. office to Angel Investigations.

WRITTEN & DIRECTED BY
Tim Minear
GUEST STARS: Stephanie Romanov (Lilah), Jim Abele (Connor's Dad)
COSTARS: Jason Padgett (Suicidal Cop), Jason Winer (Preston), Michael Halsey (Sirk), Merle Dandridge (Lacey), Jonathan M. Woodward (Knox), James Calvert (Surgery Patient), Lynette Romero (Newscaster), Anthony Diaz-Perez (Hostage Father), Stacy Solodkin (Connor's Aunt), Adrienne Brett Evans (Connor's Mother), Emma Hunton (Connor's Kid Sister)

After a considerable amount of speechlessness, the team is immediately suspicious of the unexpected offer, particularly since the building—and entire staff—was recently destroyed by the Beast. Lilah assures them the law firm is back in business and, even though it's an arm of ultimate evil, the resources that will be available to Angel Inc. would be considerable to say the least.

Lilah leaves them with the promise that a limousine will be back to pick them up before sunrise if they're interested in learning more. The team tries to put Lilah's offer on the backburner while they put together a plan to find Connor and Cordelia. Gunn, however, can't get it off his mind and reveals to Wesley that it sounds a little tempting. Angel, however, is not tempted in the least and leaves to find his son. The others also divide up for bed, each considering what Lilah had said.

Connor wanders the still burning streets of L.A., crossing paths with a suicidal cop. He manages to talk the man out of taking his own life, but when Connor learns that the cop was going to leave a family behind, he rages against the man.

Fred silently sneaks out of the hotel to find the Wolfram & Hart limo waiting. She stands on the sidewalk, debating whether or not to get in, when Wesley surprises her, admitting that he's been standing doing the same thing. They are soon joined by Gunn and Angel, and the team reluctantly decides to at least look into what Wolfram & Hart is offering. As Angel opens the limo door, they're all surprised to see Lorne already inside enjoying the perks.

Lilah meets up with the team at Wolfram & Hart and assigns each their own tour guide. While Lorne is off in the entertainment division, Fred is taken to the science wing and shown the part of the company that she will head. Wesley tours the magical archive system with a former Watcher, but knocks his guide out and sneaks off. Gunn is taken up to the White Room where he meets with the new conduit to the Senior Partners and receives a tempting secret offer. But it's Angel who gets to see all the fun perks of the job, and Lilah puts the offer into terms he can understand.

"Think of what you could do with the resources of Wolfram and Hart at your fingertips. The difference that would make. Nothing in this world is the way you think it oughta be. It's harsh and it's cruel—that's why there's you, Angel You live as though the world were as it should be. With all of this you can make it that way. People don't need an unyielding Champion. They need a man who knows the value of compromise . . . and how to beat the system from the inside . . . the belly of the beast."

—Lilah

Angel is about to reject the offer when Lilah calls his attention to the TV screen in what would be his new office. Breaking news shows Connor as the madman behind a hostage situation.

As Angel races off to his son, Lilah goes down to the file room and finds Wesley. It comes as no surprise to her that he'd want to get into the law firm's restricted files, but his true motivation for being there is unexpected. Wesley tries to destroy her contract to set her soul free, but fails when the legal form proves to be a little too binding.

Angel manages to get into the sporting goods store where Connor is keeping his hostages rigged with explosives. The vampire tries to talk his son out of what he intends to do, but Connor refuses to listen. He is tired of questioning who he is and feeling nothing inside. He rages against his father and reveals that his hostages include a still-comatose Cordelia, also rigged with explosives. Angel rushes his son and—seeing no other choice—is forced to live out the formerly false prophecy that "the father will kill the son."

RESOLUTION

The team reconvenes in the lobby of Wolfram & Hart. Lorne and Gunn seem quite keen on accepting the offer, though Fred and Wesley are excited but still unsure. Angel ends the uncertainty when he announces that he made an executive decision and accepted the offer. As the rest of the team comes to terms with their new deal, Angel insists that Lilah make one more compromise. Lilah reluctantly agrees to have the limo take Angel to Connor. As the vampire leaves, his friends watch in confusion.

"Who's Connor?" —*Fred*

The limousine winds through wooded hills as Angel is taken to a quaint little house. He peeks inside to see Connor celebrating his high school graduation with his new family. The boy is blissfully unaware of the hellish life he had led, and Angel is the only one who remembers that he had a son.

CONTINUITY

For the last time this season, the action picks up where the previous episode, "Peace Out," left off. Lilah makes it clear that, even though Angelus drank from her dead body in "Salvage," she is not a vampire. The scarf hiding the mark on her neck where Wesley chopped off her head is also a reminder that her being turned was impossible. The little girl who was formerly conduit to the Senior Partners has been replaced by a being in the form of a jaguar. While in the archive room, Wesley acknowledges that he knows the Watchers Council has been destroyed, as was seen in the *Buffy* episode "Never Leave Me." As part of the agreement to take over the firm, Lilah gives Angel some important information and a powerful amulet that he will give to Buffy in the series finale of *Buffy the Vampire Slayer,* "Chosen." The amulet will lead to the undoing of the First Evil but will kill Spike in the process. However, that same amulet will be returned to Wolfram & Hart in Season Five, along with Spike when James Marsters joins the cast. The team will formally take over the law firm in the first episode of Season Five, "Conviction," and will learn of the secret deal Gunn struck, in which his brain is infused with an unparalleled knowledge of the law, among other things. Cordelia remains in her coma, and will until the episode "You're Welcome" in Season Five.

OFFICE ROMANCE

Gunn notes that Wesley must feel weird about seeing Lilah, considering their past, and the two men bond over Wes's pain. Lilah is visibly moved by Wesley's attempt to free her from her contract.

QUOTE OF THE WEEK
WESLEY: "It's a lie."
LILAH: "—lah. 'It's a Lilah.'"

THE DEVIL IS IN THE DETAILS

EXPENSES
The team gets a sudden windfall since the offer to take over the firm includes all the research materials they could ever hope for, a fully stocked science department, hundreds of employees, a penthouse apartment for Angel, and a fleet of cars.

WEAPONRY
Wesley has a device strapped to his arm that shoots out a grappling hook. It is unclear if this is the same stake/sword device, but if it isn't it was probably made by the same arms dealer.

DEMONS, ETC. . . .

Lilah's contract with Wolfram & Hart had a standard perpetuity clause that keeps her working for the firm after her death.

THE VAMPIRE RULES

The new Wolfram & Hart has windows made of necro-tempered glass so Angel can bask in the rays of the sun without that pesky side effect of bursting into flames.

AS SCENE IN L.A.

Once again the riots on the Los Angeles streets were actually filmed on Paramount's New York Street backlot. Also, the scene in the sporting goods store was filmed in the lobby of Paramount's on-lot theater that hosts many movie premieres and special events.

THE PEN IS MIGHTIER

FINAL CUT

The long, silent scene as the team first considers Lilah's offer is written as follows in the script.

> *A moment has passed. Everyone's standing more or less frozen, staring at Lilah. Our endless opening credits over this. No one speaks. This is weird and un-TV like. But it's covered. Wide shots, two shots, close-ups. It goes on for a long time. All the way up to the "directed by" credit, 'cause that would be funny. Just a'cuttin' back and forth. Until finally, the last credit, then . . .*

Knox refers to Fred's buddy Matt Partney when he hacks into her cell phone address book. Matt Partney is actually the name of producer Kelly A. Manners's assistant, who was invaluable in arranging the interviews for this book.

POP CULTURE

* **"Come on Charlie. Let me show you the chocolate factory."**
  Lilah compares the Wolfram & Hart tour to that of the confectionary dream experienced in Roald Dahl's book *Charlie and the Chocolate Factory*, which was adapted into the film *Willy Wonka and the Chocolate Factory*.
* **"I'm strictly R&D. Although, occasionally some D&D."**
  Knox makes an attempt at a joke, centering on the Dungeons & Dragons role-playing game.
* **"So you're like the MacGyver of Wolfram & Hart."**
  Fred compares Knox to the titular character from the eighties series about a very resourceful scientist.
* **". . . to play Let's Make an Evil Deal."**
  Angel refers to the popular game show hosted by Monty Hall.
* **"*Die Hard* your way up here?"**
  Lilah compares Wesley's maneuvers to get into the file room to those seen in the Bruce Willis film.

SIX DEGREES OF . . .

Jonathan Woodward, who portrays Knox, also played the vampire psych major in the *Buffy* episode "Conversations with Dead People."

OUR HEROES

SHAWNA TRPCIC (COSTUMER) ON THE OUTFIT IN CONNOR'S FAMILY SCENE: "That was really fun for us. I love research. I love images to go off of, so I was in *Leave it to Beaver* kind of images. I really wanted that wholesome family look. Normally with Connor I would shop really textured T-shirt materials and make extra-long sleeves and sort of decadence and that grunge with all the shirts. This time we went to the Gap to get that all-American, middle-class midwestern character. I got photos of midwestern families to see  where I wanted to go with him because it was that innocence. If you think of somebody from Nebraska with freckles you think of this innocence and purity. So I just really wanted that to reflect in the last scene that we see him in."

STUART BLATT (SET DECORATOR): "It was very, very sad when the hotel set came down. I shed a quick tear. It's always sad to see your big sets come down and that set, it was just a beautiful set. And it was a real special set for me for some reason, I don't know why. When it came down, it was hard at first. Then it came tumbling down in a matter of a couple days. We only saved a hallway and one room, just to use—not as a hotel, but we do enough hallways and rooms in apartment buildings and tenements or other who knows what. So it's nice swing material to have."

LOOK HOMEWARD,

ANGEL

TEASER

As "Home" would indicate, Season Five of *Angel* will bring new changes to the series as the team takes over the firm of their enemy when they are placed in charge of Wolfram & Hart. Not only does the shift in locale bring a new set of story possibilities, but also it has helped to reinvigorate the production team's approach to the series. "They've really reinvented the whole show," says David Boreanaz. "And they've taken it to such a great level."

"This is a total reinvention," agrees J. August Richards. "Because it's more of an episodic structure as opposed to the soap opera structure that we kind of had before." The show returns to the origins of the series, taking on individual cases and episodes as opposed to season-long story arcs. Of course, any Joss Whedon series is going to have multilayered storytelling that will carry across the season.

"How do you take these people that are fighting the system and put them in charge of it?" asks Alexis Denisof rhetorically. "That's the ambiguity that's being explored in this season along with the new relationships, the arrival of Spike and the addition of some other people, and the loss of Cordelia. So it's changed the chemistry that had been in place for quite a few seasons."

The change in the group dynamic comes in various forms, from returning favorites to new additions and surprising guests. Spike is, naturally, the most anticipated of the new arrivals. Following his death in the series finale of *Buffy,* Spike is resurrected at the start of the new season in a rather incorporeal form. His return is not only significant due to what the character—and James Marsters—brings to the series, but also because of the ramifications of Spike's mere existence. Now the series has a pair of vampires with souls to deal with. The battle to decide which of the two could be the player in the Shanshu prophecy will carry over the season.

One person who could possibly have that answer is the newest member of the recurring stable of characters: Eve. She's a riddle wrapped in an enigma, even to the actress playing her, Sarah Thompson. "I'm just going with the information I have," Sarah explains, when faced with the question of whether Eve is good or evil, "which is that she's the liaison between the Senior Partners and Angel and she's

trying to help out. She likes to play with people and likes to have fun, but she's here to help. That's the premise that I'm operating off. I'm as anxious as everybody else to find where this character's going because there's definitely some mystery to her."

That mystery was one she had very little time to prepare for when she originally accepted the role. The audition process went down to the wire and she had her final callback on the Thursday before the Monday her character was set to shoot. "Then Friday, they called me—I was at the car wash of all places and my manager was like, 'So, you booked *Angel*.' And I started work on Monday. But since there was a weekend in between I had no time for a wardrobe fitting. So I got here Monday morning and they threw me into some clothes, some of which fit, some of which didn't because they had to guess. I told my manager my sizes, who told someone else, who told the wardrobe department. So we had a mad wardrobe fitting an hour before I went on camera."

It was a daunting task to be thrown into the mix so quickly, but Sarah was ready for the challenge. She spent the weekend digging into her script and on the phone with Joss Whedon getting into some of the finer points of her character. Joss assured her that even though things were down to the wire, the production would do everything in its power to make sure she was comfortable when the cameras started to roll.

"I was really nervous the night before I started work," Sarah explains. "I could barely sleep because I felt like it was the first day of school—because the show had been on the air for four years and everyone knows each other. I hoped that I would feel comfortable. But the minute I stepped on the stage, everyone was so wonderful and warm and welcoming. I immediately felt comfortable. And now I feel like I've been here forever. It's quite an amazing group of people."

But that amazing group was still growing.

Considering all the sturm and drang normally associated with the battle of good versus evil, the firm needed a little levity in the day. For that little spark of humor, the production went back to an old friend. Reenter Mercedes McNab as Harmony Kendall. "I'm like old school," says Mercedes. "I auditioned for the part of Buffy, didn't get it. Then they called me in and asked me to do Harmony for the pilot. It was a couple lines in a couple scenes; no big deal. We shot it and I thought that was it. But, needless to say, they brought me back and they continued to do so for so long, and here I am in season five of *Angel.*"

Harmony will continue to provide fun and frustration for Angel and team throughout the season. Though she's not a regular cast member, she is a permanent recurring character, which is a bit of a switch for the actress who previously never knew when she was going to be called in or how long she was going to stay around. "For me it was really exciting because when I used to read the scripts I always checked the very back to make sure I didn't die," Mercedes explains. "So at least now I know I don't have to do that. I'll be around for a while. Now I actually read the whole thing without skipping to the end, so that's pretty good."

Along with the new characters, our returning favorites will also see some interesting changes in their lives. Angel goes from the dark, brooding leader of a small band of rebels to being the dark, brooding leader of a small band of rebels in charge of a huge organization that still wants to hold on to its evil ways. For the first time in his long life, he will finally step out of the shadows and into a very public position, which will be rather uncomfortable for the character.

The team member most comfortable with the new attitude is also the one with the most significant change in personality. Due to a deal with the Senior Partners, Gunn goes from being the group's self-proclaimed "muscle" to the legal brains of the operation. J. August Richards explains why the transition was so natural: "I think my character struggles with this sense of feeling powerless, like he's constantly fighting the monsters. So I think wanting to join Wolfram and Hart was an easy decision for him because he wanted to finally have a sense of power."

With the new attitude comes a new look, more appropriate for the office. "I love the new look," he continues. "This is more me, anyway. I don't wear suits and ties every day, but I'm more of a dressy person. It's funny, because now that I've been dressing like this here at work, I'm dressing very athletic in my real life. It's got to give somewhere."

Fred, like Angel, is a little less comfortable with the change as it goes against her character to suddenly be in charge and telling a staff what to do. "I was really glad that they had the line at the beginning of the year when I say like, 'I'm not really much for running things. I'm more running away from things,'" Amy Acker explains. "It sort of made everyone realize that she wasn't totally comfortable with this whole thing. But I think just being a smart girl, and even back in high school, I would imagine if there was a group project that she would be the one who was in charge to make sure it got done the way she wanted it to. I think that as soon as she'd realized the responsibility and stuff started happening, it's become easier for her to be in charge of this."

Another member of the team making a (mostly) easy transition is the new head of the entertainment division, Lorne. Although he is emotionally prepared for the position, Andy Hallett reveals that there are some more physical concerns. "Before with the bar we could get away with being green because it was underground . . . literally. When we were coming into Wolfram and Hart it was a whole other story, because there are a lot of times when I go out. Like in the first show I was sitting in the back of the courtroom. I was sort of incognito, with my little hat in the back. So clearly I can't go out in every public setting, so I was worried about that in Wolfram and Hart. I was wondering how the hell are we gonna do that and make it work. Of course, now seeing some of our clients and the people we represent . . ." Needless to say, the problem is of little concern.

Finally, rounding out this band of players is Wesley Wyndam-Pryce. It is easy to see that the largest change in his character has already occurred over the previous seasons. Though he now has the challenges of overseeing a formerly evil department, his growth this season appears to be less due to the external factors of running the firm and more in line with other surprises that will come up along the way. It is both of those things that so excite Alexis Denisof, as he echoes what everyone on the production team has said about the changes. "I think it's given a real breath of fresh air to the show," he says. "I think the change of location, the new set, the new cast members, and some of the story lines that I know are coming up for season five are fantastic."

A TOUR OF
THE WOLFRAM
& HART SETS

THE CHANGING FACE

OF EVIL

WITH
PRODUCTION
DESIGNER
STUART BLATT
AND
SET DECORATOR
SANDY STRUTH

STUART BLATT: "The big push this year was to move Angel and his gang out from their sort of odd cloistered life in the hotel into this much bigger public life. They're in a public space in front of a bunch of people every day that they work with.

"The first season, Angel had a really teeny, tiny office. It was great looking, but it became very frustrating to shoot in. The second, third, and fourth seasons we had the hotel, which became much more spacious, but it ended up all their meetings took place around the reception desk. So all of a sudden in this large hotel it became one area to meet. Once in a while they'd go to Angel's little office or his hotel room, but mostly it took place in the center of the lobby or the reception desk. So this year Joss said, 'No, I want different areas for them to move around.'

"We knew we had already set up Wolfram and Hart as somewhat a visual that the audience knows about. Mostly what they know is Lilah's office. We had Lilah's office, which earlier had been Lindsey's office, which previously had been Holland's office. It was the same office; we just changed name tags. We've gone on location a lot for some of the larger work in the lobbies and some of the bigger hallway scenes. Last year we built a large labyrinth of Wolfram and Hart hallways for the episode with the big bad Beast ["Habeas Corpses"]. So we knew we had already come up with a look that we somewhat liked and we didn't want to stray far from that look. This couldn't look so different, because it is another arm of Wolfram and Hart. It wasn't just built for the Angel gang. They had to take this over. So it does still fit into that corporate feel. Not that it would have mattered that much. The audience is somewhat forgiving, especially if they like what they see.

"What Joss had asked for in our initial meeting was a space that was huge [so that] our guys really seem out of place and they could walk from room to room and up and down stairwells. He wanted to be able to use a steadicam and not have to cut a shot to be able to wander from Angel's office to Wesley's office to Gunn's office to Harmony's desk to up the stairs to down

273

the hallway to Fred's lab. And within reason we were able to give them as much of that as we could and it's been really successful so far.

"Jeff Bell had chimed in, and he wanted a place that looked very presentational. It was very much about a modern, designed office space that you would find at a high-end law firm or an advertising agency. The idea is that the sinister aspects of Wolfram and Hart are behind doors. It wasn't that you'd walk in and say, 'Wow, this place is giving me a creepy feeling.' So in the design sense we didn't try to tip our hand in any way what goes on here except for the fact that this is just a big major law firm."

SANDY STRUTH: "The biggest thing about Wolfram and Hart is it's just gotta be this really high-end place. So no matter where you go you want to feel like this place has an unending supply of money."

STUART: "We got books on office spaces and we took them out. We got photographs of large advertising agencies or law firms, or other presentational companies, and we presented it to them. And they said, 'Well, we like this, we like this, we don't like that.' Then we went back and did some more drawings and we built a small scale model. Our first pass at it had balconies all the way around and we saw that we couldn't afford balconies all around. The second pass had a real giant conference room raised on a level on the end opposite Angel's office. Everybody liked that, but they said, 'Well, we really want Wesley and Gunn to have their offices on the same floor as Angel's.' So we had to downsize the set and put the conference room as part of Angel's office. We ended up building Angel a giant office with whole floor-to-ceiling views of the city throughout the entire office."

SANDY: "With Angel's office I keep the sense of history and a certain sense of weaponry and artifacts. I think the artifacts represent the time and the history with him. I also think there's a spirituality to them. In this particular year, I think we've really tried to bring some of that spirituality in because Angel's rooted now. He's getting a little out of the funk and he's able to bring things around that make him feel—I don't know if  *good* is the word—but they represent everything to him. We've got a warrior mask in there but I think that's okay because that's part of him. We picked several different icons for his wall, a few of them that are symbolic. The Irish sword that's hanging on the wall has been there since the beginning and one of the samurai swords he's had from episode two. The other icons are just lovely, semi-symbolic pieces."

STUART: "The Wolfram and Hart sign behind Harmony's desk has some history. We hadn't planned on having signs there from the beginning, but Joss had asked us, 'Let's remind people of where we are and to let them know it is an office space. It is a public space.' This sign, in particular—these letters—have been around probably since season one. They've been used in different Wolfram and Hart signs all over the place. We've done a lot of establishing shots outside office buildings. We dragged our sign out and shot outside the Sony building and shot outside the Unical building, and shot outside of this building and that building. Then we've taken those letters and set them up inside abandoned buildings and shot the interior as a floor of Wolfram and Hart."

SANDY: "When you move into Gunn's and Wesley's offices, you want to have them all different. You don't want to put poor Wesley in the same kind of office he's had before, but you still want to show the learned quality. You want to have some of the English influence, which is why we have the tea set and a few pictures of England or the English countryside. We have a few more classic English antiques in there.

"Gunn's we made a little more modern. We bring in a little color in his room, which is nice because the one thing about everything is it's a little somber. There's a lot of wonderful color to start with in the building and then I have to bring in the other colors. It's interesting with the basic furniture, the tuxedo sofas and chairs, they really look better and more classic if

they're darker. But then you want to bring something in and I was able to bring in a beautiful burnt orange chair for Gunn, which is really nice because there's a little bit of color in there.

STUART: "Joss had asked for one thing specific with Fred's lab. He wanted Fred to have a lab that she was able to overlook from her office, surveying down her workplace. We don't get to do levels that often because it becomes very expensive. We originally built just a small por-

tion of this lab for an episode a couple years ago in season two when there was a physicist who wanted to stop time ["Happy Anniversary"]. So we built part of her office for that, and the curved walls, and we saved those, knowing that they'd come in handy someday for something.

"When the germ of the idea came up—that it has to be a lab with an overlooking office—I looked at my art director and he looked at me and said, 'We still have that time-stopping lab.' So we pulled it out of storage, then we pulled out the blueprint and drew up and elaborated on it. The idea for this is that there are a lot of lab shows on the air right now with *CSI* and *CSI: Miami* and all these other shows and we wanted to do our version on a much smaller budget because it isn't our one big set. They enjoy shooting in here because it affords them area to move around in and interesting story lines."

SANDY: "Fred's has been nice because she's near the lab and we really haven't done any real details for Fred since she's come to the show. In the hotel you really didn't get to put much character. It was a few little things. I'm having fun with the fact that they brought the Dixie Chicks poster in. That came from props, but that kind of thing tells me a lot about her. It tells me about her independence, it tells me about her spunkiness, it tells me that she's more contemporary than you might think. One little icon or one little object can tell me a lot about the rest of the character. It's fun when that happens. That little thing and I knew where to go with her. I can mix a lot of fun things. And she's from Texas so we have an armadillo. We're still pulling stuff into hers.

"Lorne's office has been a lot of fun too. I'm hoping that we can continue Lorne's because it's the first time we've really been able to spend time with him. We've had two great sets of his in the past, but this one is a textural one that has the personalities of Lorne. It has that Vegas feel, that retro-fifties feel, mixed with some of the contemporary elements. We've been able to clear Dean Martin so we have a wonderful picture of Dean Martin there. A great thing that's happening now is Nancy Sinatra has approved a picture and she's going to write 'To Lorne, Love Nancy.' So those are just so fun to have in there. And it's fun when you contact those people and they go along with it."

STUART: "The idea behind Angel's penthouse is that Angel lives upstairs from his office and the only way to get there is a private elevator. The private elevator has five buttons: *PH* for Penthouse, *OF* for Office, *L* for Lobby, *PK* for his private parking garage, and *SW* for Sewer. Angel has his own access to his own private sewer entry to the world. This is the only in and out of Angel's penthouse. The idea of the penthouse is that he's still a fish out of water. These are places that were given to them; who knows if it was built for a CEO before Angel or if it was specially redesigned for Angel. He has a new public persona and now he has living quarters that befit a CEO.

"It's got a gorgeous view of the city; it's got a spacious bedroom and bathroom. The whole idea for the offices this year was that we kind of took a nod of being Japanese modern. We kind of have a nod to the idea of shoji screens, but with beautiful birch wood and frosted Plexiglas. We worked in as many wood and stone elements as possible, which are very earthy design styles that we liked a lot in the art department."

SANDY: "Angel's penthouse is my favorite of the new sets this season, because it's the one that I got to spend time with and work on and really pick each piece. It is Asian inspired and we want a sense of history, because Angel always has history. He's been around for a long time so if he does contemporary, it still has something rooted in something deeper.

"I picked a lot of the art as textural because, I can't even explain why that is, but that has a feel to me with him. There's an industrial, yet there's also a classic, artistic element. I think it's part of him going back into history and reaching for those textures because art today can be very flat. I've had a lot of fun with his art. It's the kind of thing that he didn't pick, but Wolfram and Hart set it up with him and he's okay with that for a while because the colors are earth tones and I think they're comforting. Color can be soothing, because you need it when you don't get out in the sun.

"There's a really special element for me in that set, which is, next to his bed there's a painting of the Golden Gate Bridge. It's a collage on steel and it's got this beautiful blue sky and I have it right next to the bed, above the bedside table, right next to the window. It's very symbolic to me because he can't go outside in the sun, but it's this beautiful, bright day. And it's the Golden Gate Bridge, only because that's what that artist had done. Had there been an icon of L.A. I would have put that there. But he's traveled around the world so I don't have a problem with that."

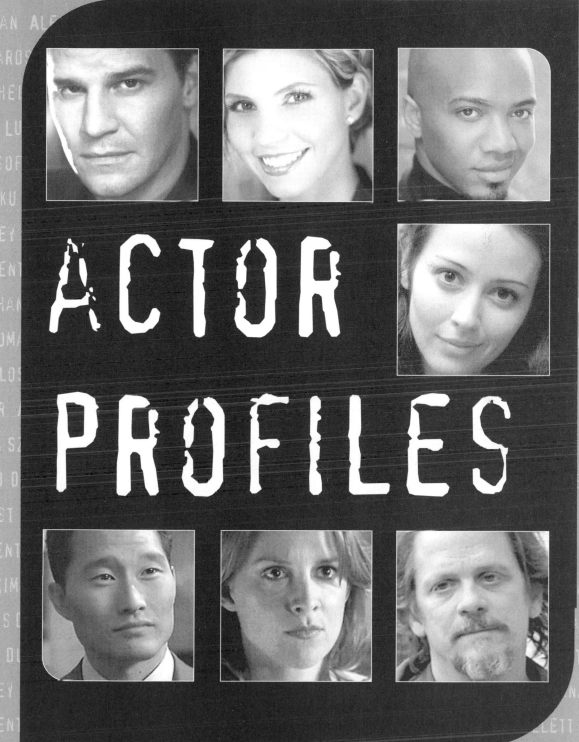

ACTOR PROFILES

JULIE BENZ   ANDY HALLETT   AMY ACKER   J. AUGUST RICHARDS   VINCENT KARTHEISER
DAVID BOREANAZ   CHARISMA CARPENTER   ELIZA DUSHKU   LAUREL HOLLOMAN   GINA TO
ENMAN   ALEXA DAVALOS   DAVID BOREANAZ   CHARISMA CARPENTER   ALEXIS DENISOF   J.
ICHARDS   AMY ACKER   ANDY HALLETT   JULIE BENZ   STEPHANIE ROMANOV   ELIZA DUSHKU
ARTHEISER   KEITH SZARABAJKA   LAUREL HOLLOMAN   GINA TORRES   JACK CONLEY   DANIEL
ARK LUTZ   DAVID DENMAN   ALEXA DAVALOS   DAVID BOREANAZ   CHARISMA CARPENTER
ENISOF   J. AUGUST RICHARDS   AMY ACKER   ANDY HALLETT   JULIE BENZ   STEPHANIE ROMANO
USHKU   VINCENT KARTHEISER   KEITH SZARABAJKA   LAUREL HOLLOMAN   GINA TORRE
ONLEY   DANIEL DAE KIM   MARK LUTZ   DAVID DENMAN   ALEXA DAVALOS   DAVID BOREANAZ   C
ARPENTER   ALEXIS DENISOF   J. AUGUST RICHARDS   AMY ACKER   ANDY HALLETT   JUL
TEPHANIE ROMANOV   ELIZA DUSHKU   VINCENT KARTHEISER   KEITH SZARABAJKA
OLLOMAN   GINA TORRES   JACK CONLEY   DANIEL DAE KIM   MARK LUTZ   DAVID DENMAN
AVALOS   DAVID BOREANAZ   CHARISMA CARPENTER   ALEXIS DENISOF   J. AUGUST RICHA
CKER   ANDY HALLETT   JULIE BENZ   STEPHANIE ROMANOV   ELIZA DUSHKU   VINCENT KAR
EITH SZARABAJKA   LAUREL HOLLOMAN   GINA TORRES   JACK CONLEY   DANIEL DAE KIM   MA
AVID DENMAN   ALEXA DAVALOS   DAVID BOREANAZ   CHARISMA CARPENTER   ALEXIS DE
UGUST RICHARDS   AMY ACKER   ANDY HALLETT   JULIE BENZ   STEPHANIE ROMANOV   ELIZA
INCENT KARTHEISER   KEITH SZARABAJKA   LAUREL HOLLOMAN   GINA TORRES   JACK CONLE
AE KIM   MARK LUTZ   DAVID DENMAN   ALEXA DAVALOS   DAVID BOREANAZ   CHARISMA CA
LEXIS DENISOF   J. AUGUST RICHARDS   AMY ACKER   ANDY HALLETT   JULIE BENZ   STEPHANIE
LIZA DUSHKU   VINCENT KARTHEISER   KEITH SZARABAJKA   LAUREL HOLLOMAN   GINA TORR
ONLEY   DANIEL DAE KIM   MARK LUTZ   DAVID DENMAN   ALEXA DAVALOS   DAVID BOREANAZ   C
ARPENTER   ALEXIS DENISOF   J. AUGUST RICHARDS   AMY ACKER   ANDY HALLETT
TEPHANIE ROMANOV   ELIZA DUSHKU   VINCENT KARTHEISER   KEITH SZARABAJKA
OLLOMAN   GINA TORRES   JACK CONLEY   DANIEL DAE KIM   MARK LUTZ   DAVID DENMAN

DAVID BOREANAZ: "Angel/Angelus"

Born in Buffalo, New York, David Boreanaz is the son of David Roberts, longtime weatherman at WPVI-TV in Philadelphia, Pennsylvania. Inspired to become an actor at an early age and encouraged by his parents, he graduated from the Ithaca College Department of Communications in 1992 and moved to Los Angeles. He got off to a slow start, working at various odd jobs with uncredited appearances in a beer commercial, *Aspen Extreme,* and *Best Of The Best II.* His first credited roles were Frank in an episode of *Married . . . with Children* (1993) and the Vampire's Victim in *Macabre Pair of Shorts* (1996). David attracted the attention of an industry notable while walking his dog and was soon cast as Angel in *Buffy the Vampire Slayer* (1997).

David's portrayal of the dark, brooding vampire was an instant hit with fans, and the role has endured far beyond the one-shot stint as originally planned. Just as Angel reflected the actor's intensity and focus, the character also developed his wise guy sense of humor. After three seasons on *Buffy,* David went on to star in the spin-off series, *Angel.* As a result of this success, his career expanded to include

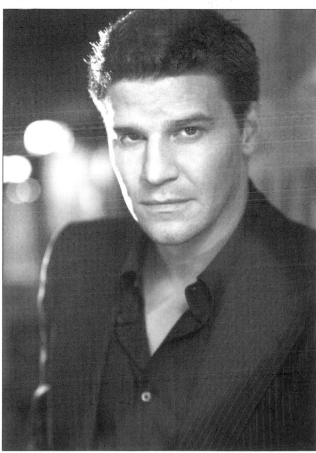

major films, beginning with a starring role in *Valentine* (2001). He was the voice of Leon in the Kingdom Hearts video game (2002) and played Luke in the romantic comedy *I'm with Lucy* (2002), which was not released in the States. David portrays the lead antagonist, Luke (or Luc) Crash, in *Crow: The Wicked Prayer,* which is scheduled for release in 2004.

Married to Jamie Bergman and the proud father of one son, David has a patient, confident, go-with-the-flow attitude toward life. Chosen as one of *People Magazine*'s 50 Most Beautiful People (1999), he has used his celebrity to promote the Make-A-Wish Foundation. He genuinely respects the cast and crew of *Angel* and appreciates the chemistry of real camaraderie that has contributed so much to the success of the show. He is particularly fond of Sarah Michelle Gellar *(Buffy the Vampire Slayer),* whom he never fails to thank for the boost to his career. The fifth season shift that put Angel and company in charge of the evil law firm Wolfram & Hart gave David a chance to explore other facets of the Angel character and to make his directing debut.

> **"One of the benefits of playing a character like this and being on a show that was created by Joss and blessed with great writers is that they are able to take [Angel] on so many different levels. I feel like every episode I'm playing a different character with him, depending upon the story. For me that has been a very refreshing course and one that has kept me very much in tune with the show for this period of time."**
>
> **—DAVID BOREANAZ**

CHARISMA CARPENTER: "Cordelia Chase"

Las Vegas born and raised, Charisma Carpenter was named after a perfume and always had trouble convincing people that Charisma was her real name. A student of classical ballet from age five, her career as an entertainer began with beauty pageants and performing in local lounges. She moved to Mexico with her family when she was fifteen, then to San Diego where she attended three high schools, including the Chula Vista School of Creative and Performing Arts. Between graduation in 1988 and moving to Los Angeles in 1992, she went to Europe, went to college, worked at assorted jobs, and was a cheerleader for the San Diego Chargers. She was waiting tables, intending to go back to school to become an English teacher, when she was discovered by a commercial agent.

Twenty commercials and several theater roles later Charisma landed a 1994 guest spot on *Baywatch*. After playing Ashley Green on *Malibu Shores,* a short-lived NBC daytime drama in 1996, she was called to audition for *Buffy* and asked to read for Cordelia Chase. Despite being late for her screen test, Charisma got the part and parlayed what was intended to be a temporary character on *Buffy the Vampire Slayer* into a series regular with a lead role in the spin-off series, *Angel.*

Although Cordelia Chase was in a coma at the close of the fourth season, Charisma will reprise the role in the 100th episode of *Angel* during Season Five. Since leaving the show, she has appeared in the TV drama *Miss Match* and starred in the made-for-TV movie *See Jane Date* (2003). Athletic, with interests in rock climbing, hiking, and skydiving, Charisma mostly enjoys spending her free time with her husband, her new son, her friends, and her dogs.

ULIE BENZ ANDY HALLETT AMY ACKER J. AUGUST RICHARDS VINCENT KARTHEISER

AVID BOREANAZ CHARISMA CARPENTER ELIZA DUSHKU LAUREL HOLLOMAN GINA T

ENMAN

ICHARD

ARTHEI

ARK LU

ENISOF

USHKU

ONLEY

ARPENT

TEPHAN

OLLOMA

AVALOS

CKER A

EITH SZ

AVID DE

UGUST R

INCENT

AE KIM

LEXIS D

LIZA DU

ONLEY

ARPENT

ALEXIS DENISOF: "Wesley Wyndam-Pryce"

Born in Salisbury, Maryland; raised in Seattle, Washington; and schooled in New Hampshire, Alexis Denisof received his professional training at the London Academy of Music and Dramatic Arts and the Royal Shakespeare Company. He spent fourteen years in Britain before returning to the U.S. His first acting appearance was in the music video for George Harrison's "Got My Mind Set on You." His pre-*Buffy* credits include multiple TV and film appearances, including *Highlander, First Knight,* HBO's *Hostile Waters,* and *The Misadventures of Margaret.*

Alexis entered the world of *Buffy the Vampire Slayer* in Season Three. The annoying Wesley Wyndam-Pryce was written to be killed off after two episodes, but the amusing, bumbling character Alexis presented was too endearing to lose. Phased out when Buffy rejected having a Watcher, Alexis appeared in the movies *Noah's Ark* and *Rogue Trader.* When asked to reprise Wesley in the new series, *Angel,* he eagerly joined the spin-off cast.

Alexis's new bride, Alyson Hannigan, appeared as Willow Rosenberg in the fourth-season episode "Orpheus." They also appear together in the film *Beyond the City Limits* (2001). Alexis is the voice of Nigel Taylor in the animated *Tarzan & Jane* (2002). An accomplished swordsman, Alexis enjoys scuba diving, horseback riding, and skiing.

"The degree of separation from everything that was home, which was Angel Investigations and Gunn and Fred, Cordelia, Angel—that was his compass. You have to track that all the way back. Or at least the way I treated it was that you had to look at the person that left England as a Watcher to go to Sunnydale, and the investment that had been made throughout his life in becoming a Watcher, and then becoming assigned to Buffy and Faith and all of the events that transpired in Sunnydale, and the eventual loss of everything that

was defining about the character, which we meet when he arrives in L.A. in the first episode. He's been fired and rolling around on a motorcycle, trying to figure out who he is and what he can do. And so, in those first three seasons, he's really marking out a new person and making conscious and unconscious choices about who he is and what his life is so that by the time we get to the phase of him kidnapping the child and the subsequent slitting of the throat, that becomes the loss of everything for him. In attempting to do something right, which was preventing the fulfillment of this prophecy, it meant the loss of everything, which was the sacrifice he was willing to make."

— ALEXIS DENISOF ON WESLEY
BEING CUT OFF FROM THE GROUP

J. AUGUST RICHARDS: "Charles Gunn"

A native of Washington, D.C., J. August Richards appeared in several plays while attending a performing arts high school and won scholarships and grants to study theater at the University of Southern California. Although his mother wanted him to be a priest or a lawyer, he began his acting career with a guest appearance on *The Cosby Show* in 1984 followed by a spot on *Family Matters* in 1989. His impressive television credits since then include *Diagnosis Murder, Space: Above and Beyond, JAG, Sliders, The Practice,* and *West Wing.* He has also appeared in numerous TV and feature films, such as *Op Center, Why Do Fools Fall In Love, Running Mates,* and most recently, *Critical Assembly.*

The character of Charles Gunn, vampire fighter, was introduced in the first season of *Angel,* with the possibility of the role becoming permanent. Richards was added as a regular in Season Two. Versatile and dynamic, he has portrayed Gunn's growth as a person with seamless believability. Professionally, he sets realistic goals he can control and aspires to play James Bond. Off camera, he enjoys art, music, and travel. His most memorable journey was to Panama, where his family originated.

"When I first started playing this character, I was patterning it after a dear friend of mine who I play chess with a lot, who's very intense. He never says anything that's not true and that he doesn't mean. Those are things that I took with me when I was working with the character. I think that's where a lot of his sense of humor comes from, just stating the most obvious thing, which is mostly referred to as dry humor.

"The hours are long and it's very grueling, but the coolest thing about working on this job is that I'm always asked to do something I've never done before. In every season I feel like I definitely get to grow as an actor, and that's the most important thing for me in any job is that I'm constantly growing. I feel like I'm growing on this job."

—J. AUGUST RICHARDS

AMY ACKER: "Winifred 'Fred' Burkle"

Born and raised in Dallas, Texas, Amy Acker was a student of dance for thirteen years before she discovered a love of acting at Southern Methodist University. Her numerous stage credits include *The Tempest* and *Much Ado About Nothing.* She appeared as various characters on the TV series *Wishbone* between 1995 and 1997 and made her way to Los Angeles via Wisconsin and New York. Her film credits include *The Accident* (2001), *Groom Lake* and *Catch Me If You Can* (2002), and *Return To The Batcave: The Misadventures of Adam and Burt* (2003).

Amy first appeared in *Angel* as the displaced physics student Fred during the climactic closing episodes of Season Two. Landing the recurring role two months after moving to Los Angeles, she joined the cast as a regular in Season Three. Quiet, calm, and a good listener, she practices yoga, reads, skis, rides horses, and travels in her free time. Amy recently took up golf to be with her friends, but admits that she hasn't quite mastered the game or the wardrobe requirements.

"I think I've been really lucky with my character. I know Joss does this with everyone, but when I was putting a tape together it looked like I'd been on five different shows.
My character has changed so much, especially in the third season where I started out almost in love with Angel because he'd rescued me and brought me back. Then he was gone and I was sort of left alone to make this cave in the hotel like the one in Pylea.
Then I started to grow and explore, to get out of my bedroom and stop writing on walls, at least for a couple episodes. I think we were trying to carry over the character I was in Pylea, but without the dirt on my face and potato sack and try to fit that into these characters who were real or seemed to be more realistic and just more grounded, even though one of them was a vampire and the other one had visions."

—AMY ACKER

ANDY HALLETT: "The Host/Lorne"

Raised in the Cape Cod township of Barnstable, Andy Hallett attended Assumption College in Worchester after graduating high school. Shy until Patti LaBelle invited him onstage to sing during a concert, Andy rediscovered a natural talent and love of singing and moved to Los Angeles to pursue acting. He was employed as a talent agency runner and property manager before being hired as a lounge singer.

Andy often took his friend Joss Whedon to karaoke bars. After seeing Andy sing the blues in a review, Joss Whedon developed the Lorne character and asked Andy to audition. Although he was not promised the role he had inspired, Andy was cast and appeared as a guest star in fifty-one episodes of *Angel* before Joss made him a regular cast member halfway through Season Four.

Playing the Host on *Angel* was Andy's first acting role. Since then he has appeared with James Marsters in the TV miniseries *The Enforcers,* and in *Chance,* an independent film written by and starring Amber Benson (*Buffy*'s Tara). A CD may also be in Andy's future.

"Every time I read the script now I'm wondering what's going to happen. I crack up. I get asked quite often by the viewers at events who say, 'Aren't you frustrated with or sick of getting tied up or beaten up or whatever.' I say, 'No. I love it!' It always cracks me up because my character's getting this certain type of reputation. Clearly he's not a fighter, *thank God,* because I'm not. I couldn't handle a fight scene. I was looking back the other day and someone had made me this little scrapbook of screen captures from each episode that I've been, like, held hostage in or whatever. I hadn't even realized how many there are. It all started with my head getting cut off. And then after that I've been pulled and prodded and beaten and . . . drilled. I had my head drilled. The horns knocked off . . . I've been unconscious so many times."

—ANDY HALLETT

287

JULIE BENZ: "Darla"

The daughter of a doctor and an ice skater, Julie Benz was born and raised in Pennsylvania. She began skating at age three, taking after her mother rather than following her surgeon father into a career in medicine, and was competitive in ice dancing until an injury forced her to retire at age fourteen. She began acting in local theater, enrolled and graduated from New York University, and moved to Los Angeles where she landed small roles in several TV productions.

Although Julie's vampire character, Darla, was staked early in the first season of *Buffy the Vampire Slayer,* the character was reprised in flashbacks on *Buffy* and then as the revived Darla in *Angel.* Her numerous TV and film credits include episodes of *Fame L.A., Sliders, Roswell, Taken,* and *Peacemakers.* She played the receptionist in *As Good As It Gets* and stars as Ursula in the film *George of the Jungle 2.*

STEPHANIE ROMANOV: "Lilah Morgan"

Stephanie Romanov was born in Las Vegas and her modeling career began at age fifteen. Working in Europe and New York, she appeared in various magazines, including *Elle, Bazaar, Vanity Fair,* and *Vogue.* Her first acting job was on *Models Inc.* in 1994. Since then she has had roles in numerous TV and feature films, including *Spy Hard, Cadillac, Thirteen Days* as Jacqueline Kennedy, and most recently an independent film, *Tricks.*

Stephanie's recurring role as Lilah Morgan on *Angel* began in the premiere episode and continued through Season Four. She plays Jennifer in an upcoming movie, *The Final Cut,* starring Robin Williams.

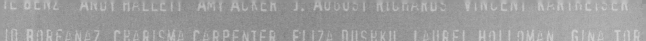

ELIZA DUSHKU: "Faith"

Eliza Dushku began her acting career at age ten in Boston. She appeared in several feature films, including *That Night, This Boy's Life, True Lies,* and *Race The Sun,* then spent the last two years of high school being a full-time student until she graduated in 1998. She immediately joined the cast of *Buffy the Vampire Slayer* as Faith. In addition to playing her recurring Slayer character in both *Buffy* and *Angel,* Eliza has recently appeared in the films *City By The Sea, Wrong Turn, Bring It On,* and *The Kiss.* She currently stars in her own new series, *Tru Calling.*

VINCENT KARTHEISER: "Connor"

One of six children, Vincent Kartheiser was born in Minnesota and was named for Vincent Van Gogh. At the age of six he was in a production of *A Christmas Carol* at the Guthrie Theater in Minneapolis. With interests ranging from reading to rock climbing, he majored in history at UCLA. His first role was as the orphan boy in the movie *Untamed Heart* (1993). Vincent moved from supporting parts to starring roles beginning with *Alaska* (1996) and including *Masterminds* with Patrick Stewart (1997), the acclaimed *Another Day in Paradise* (1998), and *Luckytown* (2000). More recently, he appeared in the movies *Falling Off the Verge* (2003) and *Dandelion* (2004).

Vincent was not aware that he was auditioning for the role of Angel's son when he read for the part. He was thrilled to be cast as Connor, a role he played in the third and fourth seasons of *Angel.* In addition to taking fencing lessons, he studied martial arts for the physically demanding role.

Though the characters he chooses to play are daring and fearless, Vincent describes himself as being reclusive and shy. He relaxes watching videos and televised sporting events, playing an Internet game, or reading classic literature. He looks forward to an opportunity to reprise his role as Connor.

KEITH SZARABAJKA: "Captain Daniel Holtz"

A native of Oak Park, Illinois, Keith Szarabajka has appeared in a variety of TV episodes and movies since playing Josh in *Simon* (1980). His movie credits include *Protocol* (1984), *Walker* (1987), *Under Cover of Darkness* (1992), *Andre* (1994), and *We Were Soldiers* (2002).

In addition to his appearances as Daniel Holtz in *Angel* (2001–2003), Keith had recurring roles as Mickey Kostmayer in *The Equalizer* (1986–1989), as Neil Gorton in *Law & Order* (1997), and as Reverend Goodacre in *Thanks* (1999). He has had guest spots in shows too numerous to mention, but including *Babylon 5* (1994), *Timecop* (1998), *Star Trek: Voyager* (2000), *X-Files* (2000), *Roswell* (2001), and *Charmed* (2003). His voice-over credits include animated projects such as *The Wild Thornberrys Movie* (2002) and several video games.

LAUREL HOLLOMAN: "Justine Cooper"

Born in Chapel Hill, North Carolina, Laurel Holloman began her career on the stage in Chicago, Los Angeles, and New York. She studied at the British American Dramatic Academy in London and New York University. Appearing in more than two dozen movies since starring in *The Incredibly True Adventures of Two Girls in Love* (1995), she has also appeared in TV episodes of *Cracker* (1997), *That's Life* (2001), and *Touched by an Angel* (2002). She is a regular on Showtime's *The L Word*. Her role as Justine Cooper in *Angel* spanned Seasons Three and Four.

GINA TORRES: "Jasmine"

The youngest of three children, Gina Torres was born and raised in New York City and attended New York City's High School of Music and Art. A mezzo-soprano, she was trained in opera and jazz and has performed in a gospel choir. Beginning with an appearance on *Law & Order* in 1992, Gina has had several recurring TV roles: Nebula in *Hercules, The Legendary Journeys* (1998–1999), Anna Espinosa in *Alias* (2001), on season three of *24,* and as Jasmine on *Angel* (2003). She was a series regular in *Cleopatra 2525* (2000) and *Firefly* (2002). She appeared in the movies *The Matrix Reloaded* (2003) and *The Matrix Revolutions* (2003), and a reprisal of her role as Zoe Warren is scheduled for the upcoming *Firefly* movie.

JACK CONLEY: "Sahjhan"

Jack Conley has appeared in numerous movies, including *Apollo 13* (1995), *Mercury Rising* (1998), *Payback* (1999), *Traffic* (2000), and *Collateral Damage* (2002). His television credits include roles in *NYPD Blue* (1995 and 2001), *JAG* (1996 and 1999), *Crossing Jordan* (2003), *She Spies* (2003), and as Sahjhan on *Angel* during the third season.

DANIEL DAE KIM: "Gavin Park"

Born in Pusan, Korea, Daniel Dae Kim holds an MFA degree from the Graduate Acting program at New York University. He has appeared in a wide variety of TV episodes, including *Law & Order* (1994), *Beverly Hills, 90210* (1997), *Star Trek: Voyager* (2000), *Charmed* (2001), and *Enterprise* (2003). He was a regular on *Babylon 5: Crusade* and had recurring roles on the second season of *24* as Agent Tom Baker and *Angel* as Gavin Park. His movie credits include *The Jackal* (1997), *For Love of the Game* (1999), and *Hulk* (2003).

MARK LUTZ: "The Groosalugg"

Born in Montreal, Quebec, Mark Lutz spent four of his teenage years living in Hong Kong before moving back to Canada, where he graduated from the University of Guelph with a degree in political science. A competitive swimmer who participated in the World Cup and Olympic Trials, his acting career began with a guest spot on the TV series *Side Effects* in 1994. In addition to his recurring role on *Angel,* Mark has appeared in *The Hardy Boys* (1995), *Relic Hunter* (1999), *Earth: Final Conflict* (1999), *Mutant X* (2001), *ER* (2002), and *Friends* (2002). He also appeared in *Specimen* (1996) and several TV movies, including *A Saintly Switch* (1999), *Harry's Case* (2000), and *The Facts of Life Reunion* (2001) among others.

Mark is a neighbor and good friend of Andy Hallettt (Lorne). Andy credits Mark with teaching him how to trust his instincts and improvise on the set.

DAVID DENMAN: "Skip"

Since appearing on *ER* in 1997, David Denman has had television roles in *The Pretender* (1998), *The X-Files* (1999), *C.S.I.: Miami* (2002), and *Crossing Jordan* (2002). His character, Skip, appeared in multiple third- and fourth-season episodes of *Angel*. His movie credits include *The Replacements* (2000), *Out Cold* (2001), and *Big Fish* (2003).

ALEXA DAVALOS: "Gwen Raiden"

A former model, Alexa Davalos has appeared in the movies *The Ghost of F. Scott Fitzgerald* (2002), *And Starring Pancho Villa as Himself* (2003), and *The Chronicles of Riddick* (2004), as well as three fourth-season episodes of *Angel*.

DIANA G. GALLAGHER lives in Florida with her husband, Marty Burke, five dogs, five cats, and a cranky parrot. Before becoming a full-time writer, she made her living in a variety of occupations, including hunter seat equitation instructor, folk musician, and fantasy artist. Best known for her hand-colored prints depicting the doglike activities of *Woof: The House Dragon,* she won a Hugo for Best Fan Artist in 1988.

After her first science fiction novel, *The Alien Dark* (TSR, 1990), was published, she was on deck when Pocket Books decided to publish YA Star Trek novels. In addition to DS9 *Arcade, Starfleet Academy Voyager: The Chance Factor,* and DS9 *Honor Bound,* Diana has written fifty intermediate reader, young adult, and adult novels in several series, including Buffy the Vampire Slayer; Charmed; Smallville; The Secret World of Alex Mack; Are You Afraid of the Dark? and Sabrina, The Teenage Witch.

PAUL RUDITIS has written and contributed to various books based on such notable TV shows as *Buffy the Vampire Slayer; Roswell; Charmed; Sabrina, The Teenage Witch; The West Wing; Star Trek: Voyager;* and *Enterprise.* He lives in Burbank, California.

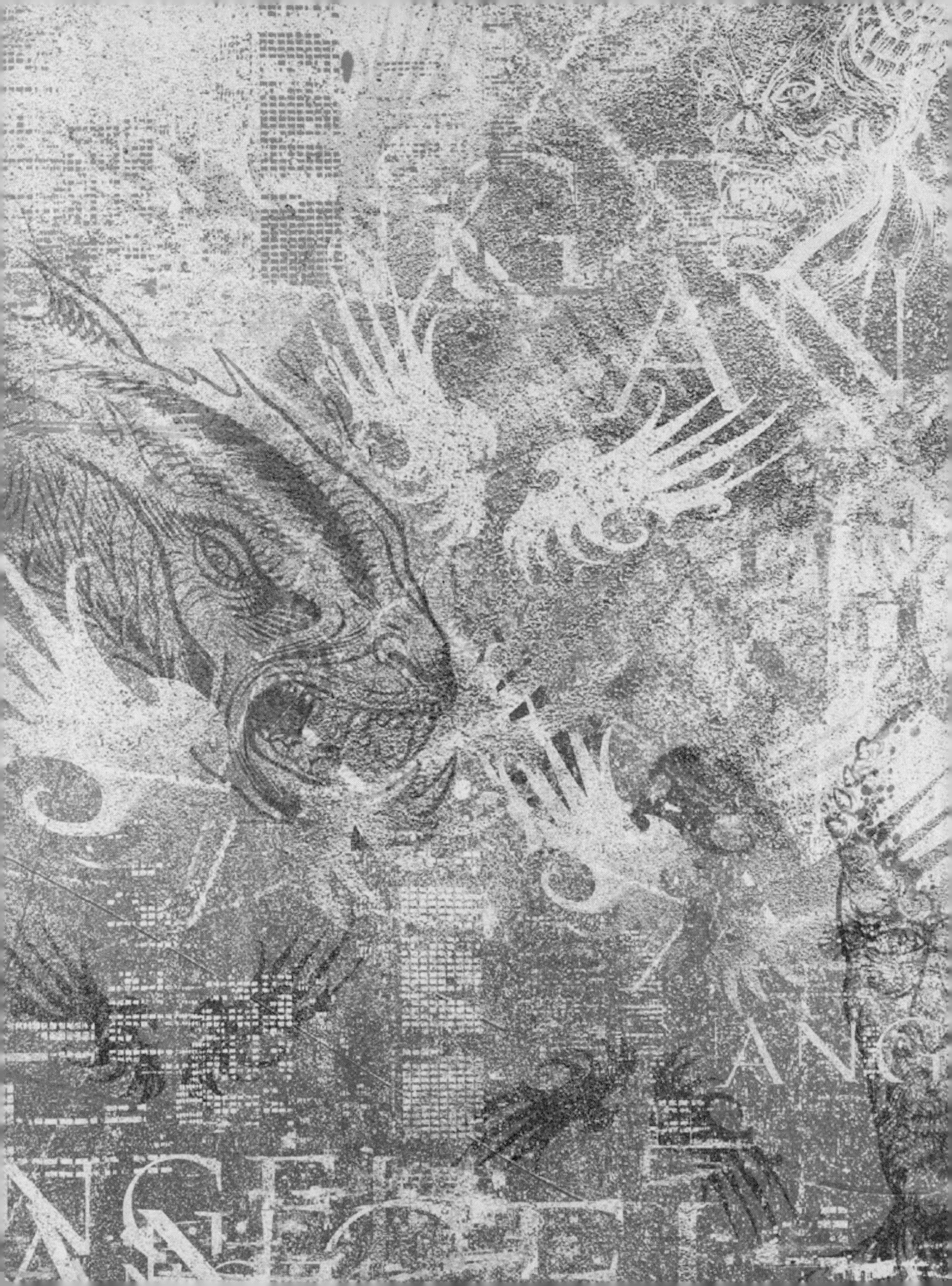